Praise for *The Myth of Popular Culture*

"Perry Meisel's study of popular culture is a surprising enhancement of received opinion and common wisdom on that vexed subject.

Moving from Shakespeare through Freud on to Bobby Dylan would seem something of a descent, yet Meisel provides a perspective that has its own descriptive justice.

Even if I am not wholly persuaded that Dylan's ultimate importance is as sublime as Meisel ventures it to be, I am given much here to intrigue me."
Harold Bloom

"Perry Meisel has written a boundary-smashing critique of the myth that popular culture is distinct from and inferior to the fine arts ... Many critics have traced the demotic roots of American musical, literary, and visual style, but not with the freewheeling familiarity that Meisel brings to the task. His broad range of knowledge enables him to move fluently from form to form, and to dig beneath the self-conscious democratic ideology of American literary rhetoric. Few critics fully comprehend the implications of this shift in the way we experience culture. Meisel does – and *The Myth of Popular Culture* is as contemporary as it is contentious. It is part of what it describes."
Richard Goldstein, Hunter College of the City University of New York

"*The Myth of Popular Culture* is simply brilliant. Turning Adorno's criticism of pop as non-dialectical against itself by showing that pop is indeed dialectical has never been done before and is in itself a major accomplishment. But Meisel has gone further in writing a book that is stunning in its originality, breadth, erudition, and in its understanding of the transatlantic evolution of popular culture."
Josephine G. Hendin, New York University

Blackwell Manifestos

In this new series major critics make timely interventions to address important concepts and subjects, including topics as diverse as, for example: Culture, Race, Religion, History, Society, Geography, Literature, Literary Theory, Shakespeare, Cinema, and Modernism. Written accessibly and with verve and spirit, these books follow no uniform prescription but set out to engage and challenge the broadest range of readers, from undergraduates to postgraduates, university teachers and general readers – all those, in short, interested in ongoing debates and controversies in the humanities and social sciences.

Already Published

The Myth of Popular Culture
from Dante to Dylan

Perry Meisel

A John Wiley & Sons, Ltd., Publication

Blackwell Publishing was acquired by John Wiley & Sons in February 2007. Blackwell's publishing program has been merged with Wiley's global Scientific, Technical, and Medical business to form Wiley-Blackwell.

Registered Office
John Wiley & Sons Ltd, The Atrium, Southern Gate, Chichester, West Sussex, PO19 8SQ, United Kingdom

Editorial Offices
350 Main Street, Malden, MA 02148-5020, USA
9600 Garsington Road, Oxford, OX4 2DQ, UK
The Atrium, Southern Gate, Chichester, West Sussex, PO19 8SQ, UK

For details of our global editorial offices, for customer services, and for information about how to apply for permission to reuse the copyright material in this book please see our website at www. wiley.com/wiley-blackwell.

Library of Congress Cataloging-in-Publication Data

The myth of popular culture from Dante to Dylan / by Perry Meisel.
     p.   cm. – (Blackwell manifestos)
  Includes bibliographical references and index.
  ISBN 978-1-4051-9933-9 (hardcover : alk. paper) – ISBN 978-1-4051-9934-6 (pbk. : alk. paper)
1. Popular culture. 2. Arts, Modern. I. Meisel, Perry.
  NX449.5.M88 2009
  306–dc22
                                    2009020181

A catalogue record for this book is available from the British Library.

1   2010

Contents

v

Contents

Preface: The Resistance to Pop

The Myth of Popular Culture is a history of popular culture, a theory of popular culture, and a critical account of three popular traditions – the American novel, Hollywood, and British and American rock music. It concludes with a historical and critical account of Bob Dylan, the figure who best summarizes "popular culture" and who, in the process, vividly erases the distinction between "high" and "low." America's historical anxieties about British influence provide this book with its context, and the history that rock music resolves. An anxiety about British culture motivates American culture as a whole and underwrites the historical creation of American pop from the canons of British art. When the British Invasion reverses this process in the early 1960s by canonizing American pop, particularly the blues and rock and roll, this history comes full circle. It completes a dialectic more than 500 years in the making, from Dante to Dylan.

Part I, "'The Battle of the Brows,'" is a history of high and low from Dante to Theodor Adorno. It rebuts the durable belief that, in Adorno's words (1962), "high" culture is "dialectical" and "pop" is not by show-ing that "pop" is also "dialectical." It is Adorno who most readily exemplifies the resistance to pop, and who serves as its historical center more clearly than does any other thinker. He gives us the reasons for it. The difference between high and low art, says Adorno, is the differ-ence between a dialectical art in conversation with its past – this is "high" culture – and a non-dialectical or formulaic artisanship – this is "pop." Adorno's contention and its mazy error are this book's own dialectical source. *The Myth of Popular Culture* proposes to replace

Adorno's position with a more responsible history, theory, and critical account of the "popular." Adorno challenges us to hold popular culture to the standard of dialectic. It is a more useful challenge than holding it to the standard of a worker's art, as do other Western Marxist critics, chief among them Stuart Hall. For all of his sensitivity to later changes in Marxist method, particularly the taking of ideology more seriously (1980), Hall's position never really changes, particularly the distinction between "folk" and "popular" art (Hall and Whannel, 1964). Hall devalues pop unless it is regarded as a form of insurgency on the part of a suppressed proletariat. Pop is neither dialectical nor non-dialectical. To the extent that it is good, it is a guerilla art; to the extent that it is not, it is neither here nor there. Adorno, even negatively, is more helpful in constructing a positive history of pop.

The myth of pop culture – Adorno's myth – is that it is not dialectical. The truth is that it is. Like high art, pop, too – *contra* Adorno – has a conversation both with its sources, which it revises and transforms, and with cultural authority as a whole, which it also revises and transforms. In Part II, "Dialectics of Pop," I enlist three representative pop traditions to prove this contention: the American novel, from its popular origins in James Fenimore Cooper and Mark Twain to its popular zenith in the capacious humility of Raymond Chandler; the history of Hollywood; and the history of jazz and rock music. Each tradition has a conversation with a different set of sources, and a different way of addressing cultural authority. American fiction converses with cultural authority through its conversation with the literary past, particularly the history of English poetry and politics. Hollywood converses with cultural authority through its conversation with the history of the image, particularly the photographic image and the history of silent film. Rock and roll converses with cultural authority through its conversation with the history of music, particularly jazz, which does the same through its conversation with classical music. My history of the American novel shows how plainly American fiction thematizes this transformation and the anxieties that accompany it. My history of Hollywood includes a history of stars as a way of gauging dialectic even more plainly than an auteurist approach can do, particularly because Hollywood's stars are a surrogate aristocracy for an America still nervous about its relation to British precedent. In pop music, the dialectical dynamic is the call-and-response of generations of musicians over time, in jazz, urban blues, folk music, and rock and roll, as each new wave sweeps away the one before it. How wrong Adorno is. Within the real cosmogony of jazz, be-bop dialectically overturns swing, and rhythm and blues does the same to bop. Urban blues misreads swing in a different way – by electrifying it to frustrate our assumptions about what is "natural" and what is not. The scrim here is the mythology of authentic black rural or "folk" culture against which the shrewd Muddy Waters trades upon his arrival in Chicago from the Delta. This moment constitutes the epistemological break that rock and roll is in cultural history. With electric guitar, it completes the philosophical work that begins with Dante.

Part III, "The World of Bob Dylan," focuses on the figure who, more than any other, shows what it means to synthesize and revise all traditions – music, poetry, iconography – and transform them completely. No single cultural figure since Shakespeare, except perhaps for Freud, is as "dialectical" a figure as Dylan. Dylan is all dialectic. I examine Dylan's reception over the years in "Dylan and the Critics" (Chapter 7), and show the relation between Dylan's music and his lyrics in Chapter 8, "Words and Music." "Dylan Himself" (Chapter 9) takes up the question of identity. Dylan is both the cause and the effect of the histories to be traced in these pages. His career begins in 1961, before, or just as, our widespread appreciation of pop begins, and is among the chief reasons for it. Still in process, the influence of Dylan's work continues to be felt today.

If one adds Dylan's iconography to the mix, Dylan's synthesis of pop history is complete. My concern with Dylan and iconography leads to a final chapter, "The Three Icons," which presents Dylan, Elvis Presley, and Frank Sinatra as the grand dialectical trio of pop at the crossroads. Dylan's revision of his great precursors erases not only the difference between high and low, power and the people, spectacle and spectator. It also erases the difference between the sexes. Dylan reinvents masculinity by abolishing it, too. Sinatra's masculinism and Presley's femininity combine to produce Dylan's androgyny. For Dylan, and for pop as a whole, dialectic remakes the world.

Accompanying this topical narrative is a historical one. Pop dialectic resolves not only the problem of high and low. It also resolves a specific transatlantic cultural history. American pop circulates within a wider British context, and does so from the start. As early as James Fenimore Cooper, American popular culture reveals what official American culture is too high-minded to reveal: America's anxiety about its cultural and political sources in British culture and political history. American culture is, by definition, post-colonial, and not happy about it. This uneasiness about Britain lies deep in the American grain. A century after Cooper's death, as I will show, a defensive Anglophilia actively structures the shaping of American intellectual opinion about American fiction and the films of Hollywood by the doyens of *Partisan Review*. Norman Mailer topples this defensiveness by co-founding the "hipster" *Village Voice* in 1955. Britain responds to its own post-colonial anxieties in like pop measure. As the Angry Young Men give way to the Teddy Boys, British culture's principal energies give way to the rock and roll of the British Invasion and the ska and reggae of the British Caribbean. British culture also reinvents itself by doing what American culture can only do through rock and roll – embrace the music of slavery. What Paul Gilroy calls "the black Atlantic" (1993) provides the transatlantic dialectic required by both cultural settings.

Each section of the book subsequent to Part I culminates with this transatlantic refrain. The history of American fiction, which begins with Cooper's anxieties about British aristocracy, concludes with Raymond Chandler's sublimation of them. Raised in England and writing as a young aesthete in London before settling in California after World War I, Chandler is the transatlantic pop novelist *par excellence*. The Hollywood star system resolves these anxieties about Britain by functioning as a surrogate and *faux* American version of aristocracy, leading to today's runaway cult of fame on both sides of the Atlantic. The music of the British Invasion, as I have noted, is the means by which Britain enters the pop conversation that America begins. Buddy Holly's tour of England in 1959 is the trigger for the British Invasion (Leigh, 2009), and for a good reason. Like Elvis Presley, Holly invents rock and roll by joining rhythm and blues with country music, whose own distinct source is British and Celtic hymn and jig. The British Invasion apprehends the "popularity" of American music at its source – not only its African American origins in the blues, but its British origins in gospel, which even the blues is forced to read, after the fact of empire. Holly resolves American anxieties about Britain by resolving British anxieties about America. The blues reading of gospel is how the transatlantic peace is made. This transatlantic conversation is wholly resolved by Bob Dylan, whose lyrics, as Christopher Ricks has shown (2003), bring the weight of English poetry to bear upon the history of American blues and folk tradition.

By "dialectical," I mean what Adorno means by the term – an exchange of differences that results in an outcome qualitatively different from them both, and that produces new differences from itself. Here is the vivid description Adorno provides in the *Introduction to the Sociology of Music* (1962), one to which I will recur in Part I when my history of high and low reaches Adorno's moment in it: "Dialectic," he says, "catches fire" on "historical form," "melts" it "down," "makes" it "vanish, and return in vanishing" (1962, 26). Here is Adorno's more technical description of dialectic in *Negative Dialectics* (1966):

> As a sense of nonidentity through identity, dialectics is not only an advancing process but a retrograde one at the same time. ... The concept's unfoldment is also a reaching back, and synthesis is the definition of the difference that perished, "vanished," in the concept. ... Only in the accomplished synthesis, in the union of contradictory moments, will their difference be manifested. (1966, 157)

What is new presents, not a unity or totality, but a difference both from the past and from itself. Every cultural product is entirely specific, never the emanation of an "ahistorical" paradigm because it is a dialectical product. This makes cultural production inevitably historical and inevitably specific, every thing the thing that it is and no other. The worry that if any theory works too well it must be "totalizing" is itself "totalizing" because it is polemical and tendentious.

Adorno's "negative dialectics," with its emphasis on "nonidentity," has its best counterparts, as I will note throughout, in deconstructive *différance* (Derrida, 1967b) and in Freud's *Nachträglichkeit*, or deferred action (1918). They share the same dynamic structure. Negative dialectics is a diacritics, based, like deconstructive difference, on what Adorno calls "unconscious remembrance" (1966, 54), or what Derrida calls "the trace" (1967b). It is an exchange of background for foreground, as in those scenes of emerging knowledge that Freud describes as instances of deferred action. The Freudian accent supplies the temporal mechanism that Marxist notions of dialectic, for all their historicism, too often lack. This is true of both group and individual *praxis* or "agency." In "Pop Culture in the Spectator" (Chapter 2), I will propose a mechanism for "agency," and show how it is bound to temporality through deferred action. Agency's condition is both reactive and sensory. Time is the medium in which its effects occur. No sufficient theoretical model exists to describe the mechanism of historical agency. To provide one is one of this book's key theoretical labors. Agency, particularly the dialectical way in which the high becomes the pop, is defined in Chapter 2 as a "trickle-down effect." This phrase, trickling down to us from Reaganomics, originates with William Jennings Bryan's "Cross of Gold" speech in 1896, and is the name I give to the way "high" dialectically converts to "low" historically. This series of assumptions about dialectic guides my assessment of both Adorno himself, and of dialectic as a notion. Mine is a descriptive account, not a philosophical one. I will hold Adorno at his word in the face of the empirical evidence of a variety of "pop" traditions to see whether or not they, too, are dialectical, like the "high" culture to which Adorno customarily opposes them.

By "culture," I mean what Terry Eagleton (2000) means by the word – its early etymological sense as "husbandry," or a reciprocal relation between species and environment. Eagleton draws on Raymond Williams to plot this history (1958, 1976), which is a traditional one. The word is used to mean husbandry by Bacon (1626), Dryden (1697), and even by Emerson (1856). Thomas Beddoes (1793) and Wordsworth (1805) use the word "culture" in a sense midway between the cultivation of the environment and the cultivation of the mind, forecasting how the word culture will grow also to mean, as it does most memorably in Matthew Arnold, "the intellectual side," as the *Oxford English Dictionary* puts it, of "civilization." Arnold's *Culture and Anarchy* (1869), as I will point out, solidifies the new usage, distinguishing "culture" from an "anarchy" of taste which it is the job of culture to correct. This notion of culture has a prehistory that begins, as I will show in "A History of High and Low" (Chapter 1), at the start of the nineteenth century. Beginning late in the nineteenth century, "cultural" anthropologists, in a long tradition from Edward Tylor and James Frazer to Franz Boas and Clifford Geertz, gradually restore the wider meaning of "culture" in Eagleton's traditional environmental sense. Culture viewed as a holistic enterprise ensures that one grants a systematic regularity to the workings of all its parts, high and low. This sense of culture is what initially cleared space for the study of "pop" in the 1980s. Andrew Ross's *No Respect* (1989) is both a good example and a good reaction. The anthropological justification for the study of pop is also why fully historical and aesthetic accounts of pop are hard to come by, despite the widespread assumption that taking pop seriously goes without saying.

This is a simple and schematic book. It is not only a topical study; it is also a historical one. Like the wider history of high and low with which it begins, each history within it is introduced by a reception history that begins with a classical account of the medium in question. These histories of interpretation have eroded because their paradigms have. It is time to rewrite them both.

Acknowledgments

A shorter version of "The Blues Misreading of Gospel" first appeared in *A Concise Companion to Postwar American Literature and Culture*, ed. Josephine G. Hendin (Oxford: Blackwell, 2004). A shorter version of "The World of Bob Dylan" first appeared in *Raritan* (Winter 2007).

Part I

"The Battle of the Brows"

1

A History of High and Low

"Highbrow," "Lowbrow," "Middlebrow"

The terms "highbrow" and "lowbrow" come from phrenology, the nineteenth-century science of regarding the shape of the skull as a key to intelligence. A "high" forehead meant intelligence; a "low" one meant stupidity. Phrenology thrived as a popular science in the late nineteenth century and led eventually to the racial theories of the Nazis, for whom the Jewish cranium and pale, sunken face were clear indications of Jewish racial inferiority. But in its origins, phrenology was actually the beginning of serious brain science. If one of its destinies was Nazism, the other is today's neuroscience. By 1820, phrenology, despite its notorious future as a cult practice and locus of popular assumption about intelligence, had emerged as the first attempt to map the brain. Its background was the discovery in 1781 of "animal electricity" by Luigi Galvani and the notion that the crackle of mental activity could be broken down into component parts and quantitatively studied. The anatomy of the soul had replaced its salvation. Erasmus Darwin, in *Zoonomia* (1794–6), used the medical term "sensorium" to describe the relation of brain to perception. Franz Joseph Gall regarded the brain as a systematic organ; he published a series of physiologies of the brain from 1808 to 1825, including an attempt to discuss the relation of brain anatomy to soul and spirit in 1811.

The emergence of the brain as the biological source of thought, feeling, and sensation complicates the presumably idealist air of Romanticism, British Romanticism in particular. Brain science made both Romanticism and psychology materialist affairs, not because it was mechanistic, but because it situated ideas in relation to the "sensorium." Keats's hands-on involvement with the sciences of the body has produced generations of scholarship preoccupied by the connection between his emphasis on sensation and his experiences as a surgeon actually holding the material of his own metaphors. The British climate was particularly rich. David Hartley's *Observations on Man* (1749) is the best link between sensory philosophy and the beginnings of the science of the brain. Galvani's contemporary, Hartley already regarded physiology as the basis of psychology. Like Galvani's "electricity," Hartley's "vibrations" connected physical stimulation with events in the mind by using "association" to understand the way sensation, ideas, and feeling were linked. It is not Hartley's associationism that was new. The "associationist" bond between sensations and ideas was familiar from David Hume. What was new was the connection between associations and vibrations, the latter understood in a strictly medical sense: as an "active" power, as Hartley put it, in the "medullary substance" (1749, 1: 4). Hartley gave Hume's associationism an explicit neural foundation that was already implicit in Hume's own precursors, John Locke, like Hartley also a medical doctor, and Bishop Berkeley, whose early work included a short treatise on the physiology of human vision (1709).

Phrenology is also the precursor to the development of the first scientific discussions of perversion and criminality later in the nineteenth century. "Low" intelligence and "low life," as Luc Sante calls it (1991), are linked. Poor judgment does indeed lead to sin, with science replacing religion with the authority for saying so. Cesare Lombroso and Max Nordau play the most significant European roles in this parallel or adjacent history of "high" and "low." Lombroso's *Criminal Man* (1876) argued that sexual and criminal delinquency were "atavistic," deriving from the return of primitive instincts ordinarily superseded by evolutionary development in the "normal" individual. The pioneering Lombroso was often photographed with a skull in one hand and a cranial measuring device in the other. For Nordau, in the enormously influential *Degeneration* (1892) – the book was dedicated to Lombroso – skull types and facial characteristics

4

were direct indices of human character. For Nordau, no measuring was necessary; the state of affairs was self-evident:

> When under any kind of noxious influences an organism becomes debilitated, its successors will not resemble the healthy, normal type of the species, with capacities for development, but will form a new sub-species, which, like all others, possesses the capacity of transmitting to its offspring, in a continuously increasing degree, its peculiarities, these being morbid deviations from the normal form – gaps in development, malformations and infirmities.... Degeneracy betrays itself among men in certain physical characteristics.... Such stigmata consist of deformities, multiple and stunted growths in the first line of asymmetry, the unequal development of the two halves of the face and cranium; then imperfection in the development of the external ear, which is conspicuous for its enormous size, or protrudes from the head, like a handle, and the lobe of which is not involuted; further, squint-eyes, hare lips, irregularities in the form and position of the teeth; pointed or flat palates, webbed or supernumerary fingers (syn- and poly-dactylia), etc. (1892, 16–17)

Between Lombroso and Nordau come the first scientific sexologists, Richard Krafft-Ebing and Alfred Benet. Krafft-Ebing was not only the first psychiatrist, or "alienist," to study sexual difference with reasonable objectivity, particularly homosexuality and the perversions. In the obvious premonition of Freud, he did so by assuming that sexual characteristics were acquired in early development by chance associations experienced by the child in relation to his or her body. For perverts and hysterics alike, memory joined objects, whether through fetish triggers or hysterical ones, with the infantile affects associated with them. Thanks to sexology, phrenology was revising its own primitivism by becoming, like Hartley's before it, a physiological psychology.

As pop metaphors for intelligence and stupidity, however, "highbrow" and "lowbrow" do not enter English and American vernacular until early in the twentieth century. They are examples of what H.L. Mencken calls "loan-words" in *The American Language*, his compendium of American English, first published in 1919 and revised over the years (1919, 104). He dates the first use of highbrow and lowbrow in America to 1905, although he calls it "a guess" (186 n.3). It is a good guess, since it provides a generation's time for the scientific origins of both terms to make their way into general conversation. Lawrence Levine's *Highbrow/Lowbrow* (1988) dates the emergence of these terms in popular usage a bit earlier, although Mencken notes that highbrow and lowbrow in the modern sense do not get recorded in the *OED* until the 1908 Supplement, by which time the meaning of the terms in our current sense has already been stabilized in science.

In early twentieth-century America, as Mencken notes, the influence of phrenology produced not only the popular opposition between high and low. The emergence of the term "middlebrow" testifies to how much the terms high and low were already taken for granted as idiomatic usages. By the early twentieth century, as Joan Shelley Rubin reminds us in *The Making of Middlebrow Culture* (1992), the term "middlebrow" had been coined in order to describe the kind of mean or average cultural market that represented normative American taste in relation to these extremes. Van Wyck Brooks had included his essay "Highbrow and Lowbrow" in *America's Coming-of-Age* in 1915, calling the use of both terms "derogatory" (1915, 3), and recommending a middle path. Being a referee, as the "middlebrow" wished to be, meant that there was a conflict to police. The same was true in England. By 1926, *Punch* was using all three terms in the sense that they still have today. By 1927, Leonard Woolf had grown so exasperated with such debates about taste and intelligence that he devoted a pamphlet to the subject, anatomizing "the natural history of the highbrow," as he put it, with a Latin morphology designed to show just how much of a "lowbrow" even the "highbrow" was (1927, 11).

The specificity of these usages of "high" and "low" becomes especially clear when compared to their meanings before the twentieth century. No such sense existed for "highbrow" and "lowbrow." To the extent that the terms were used at all, they meant something very different, sliding up only gradually into the sense in which the terms are used now. Milton (1642) and Pope (1717) both employ "low-browed" to describe the ominous look of rocks in a brooding landscape.

6

Sheridan, in 1775, in *Duenna*, uses "lowbrow," but it is a residual borrowing from animal husbandry, and a metaphor still not associated with either the human face or the face's status as an index of the soul within. For Johnson in the *Dictionary* (1755), "brow" still meant "eye-brow," as it had for almost 800 years in English. For Johnson's rival Pope in *The Dunciad*, "brow" included the whole forehead (1742, 4: 141). Not until Wordsworth (1802) and Byron (1817) does the word come to signify the disposition of an entire person. By then, the wider usage had begun to emerge, but its cultural valuation had not, even when employed by a poet like Browning in *The Ring and the Book* (1868–9, 6: 669), whose sardonic use of bland physical metaphors would otherwise have been the occasion for lampoon. The reason is simple. Simmering but not at a boil, phrenology had not yet entered popular, or non-scientific, European vernaculars.

"Folk" and "Soul"

A physicalist or primitivist – an "atavistic" – notion of what is "low" had also slowly emerged in ethnology over the course of the nineteenth century. It begins with the early nationalist theories of Fichte and Herder in Germany, whose notion of *das Volk*, or "the folk" – peasants and their association with the land – initiates a tradition of thought that defines nationalism to this day. What else is nationalism but a theory of the "pop" – of, quite exactly, "the people"? Mazzini's abstract and liberal notion of Italian nationalism in 1830 shared with Fichte and Herder's the notion of a "whole" people joined together by place and custom. In England and in Scotland, similar developments occurred. Nationalism was a doctrine of the soil in Scott, although it was also, in its high philosophical exponents among Romantic writers such as Coleridge and Wordsworth, a theory of time and cultural usage. Spirit of place in Romanticism was not mystical; it was associationist, and in a ruggedly sensory way.

By the second half of the century, however, this abstract nationalism had become a physicalist one. A misreading of the theory of evolution was one of its principal justifications. In a premonition of future imperialist apologies for Britain, Herbert Spencer first applied Darwin's theory to society, with "social Darwinism" as the result. Capitalist society, too, was a matter of the survival of the fittest, or seemed to be. Those who sunk were those who could not swim. As with "degenerate" behavior, "high" and "low" as social stations followed phrenology in lockstep homology. Late in the century, the nationalistic link between the land and its customs also became a link with the language one speaks. This next step in the history of nationalism ensured its physicalist, or phrenological, foundation. Liberal nationalism had become organic nationalism. Place and custom give way entirely to soil and the blood, which also have supernatural overtones. For Heinrich von Treitschke, chief historian of the "Prussian School," "the State" is "primordial," and "no less essential" to life than "speech" (1898, 1: 3). "Nature," he says, showing how ideal this naturalism is, is a "lofty necessity" (1: 10). Houston Stewart Chamberlain is organic nationalism's most notorious exemplar, an Englishman who moved to Wagner's Bayreuth and who had accelerated the liberal nationalism of the early nineteenth century into a vicious racial and physicalist kind of nationalism in *Foundations of the Nineteenth Century* (1899):

> Never before have the nations stood opposed to each other so clearly and definitely as antagonistic unities. It has, however, also become a century of races, and that indeed is in the first instance a necessary and direct consequence of science and scientific thinking.... Scientific anatomy has furnished such conclusive proofs of the existence of physical characteristics distinguishing the races from each other that they can no longer be denied; scientific philology has discovered between the various languages fundamental differences which cannot be bridged over; the scientific study of history in its various branches has brought about similar results, especially by the exact determination of the religious history of each race, in which only the most general of general ideas can raise the illusion of similarity, while the further development has always followed and still follows definite, sharply divergent lines. (1899, lv–lvi)

Chamberlain's argument is, as he notes, also the burden of Victorian philology. Developments in philology toward a view of language expressive of a national spirit or folk accompany the ethnocentric shift in politics, eventually coming to justify it, first in the ethnology of colonialism, and then in the discourse of Nazi eugenics. Hitler's justification in 1939 for making the German-speaking portion of the Czech Republic a part of a greater Germany is chief among its direct practical consequences.

Even in the United States, an ideology of high and low had developed. It was not only medical; it was also racial. Weir Mitchell's Western rest-cures for East Coast neurasthenics were the therapeutic counterparts to the belief that the closer one was to nature, the healthier the result. The history of the Essalen Institute in Big Sur, California was part of this tradition long before Essalen became famous as a meditative retreat in the 1960s. Thomas Slate first used Big Sur's hot springs in the 1870s for his arthritis, eventually turning the site into the first Big Sur tourist business in the 1880s. Essalen was among the rest-cure stops for Eastern pilgrims of nature. The 1960s was part and parcel of this longer tradition.

So was its taste for rock and roll. Paralleling the development of ethnology in Europe was the development of minstrelsy in the United States. The cultural labor that it performed constructed not only American racism in its classic negative form. It also prepared the ground for the presumably positive American notion of "soul." Eric Lott (1993) is the best guide here. "Black" and "white" are two sides of the same sheet of paper. American ethnicity before 1830 was a welter of immigrant rivalries – Irish, Jewish, Hungarian, and so on. Lott's argument is simple. To produce a single kind of ethnicity – "white" – to unify these tribalisms, American culture actually produced a double one. It used the "blackness" that the popularity of white minstrelsy both parodied and admired as a foil or counterpoint – as a scrim – against which to prop the new illusion of "whiteness." The functional, and usable, difference in minstrelsy between performer and what was performed was the difference between white and black. Without its contrast to blackness, white ethnicity threatened to collapse back into the fragmentary turbulence of immigrant tribalisms. "Blackness" was the defense against it. Whiteness, like everything else in American history, was born on the back of black labor.

9

It is W.E.B. DuBois, of course, who introduces the term "soul" into American usage in its popular sense. Its roots, however, are distinctly German. After receiving his MA from Harvard in 1891, DuBois matriculated at the University of Berlin from 1892–3. There he attended Max Weber's lectures and read deeply in German philosophical texts. DuBois developed his notion of "soul" among rural blacks in the United States from the German idealist belief in the connectedness between land and identity signified by the notion of *das Volk* or "the folk" in the tradition of Fichte and Herder. DuBois's term "soul" is a redaction of "*Seele*," the traditional German word for soul. DuBois's German doctoral thesis was to have been a comparison of black and German peasant life, although the German part of the project never materialized, and the thesis itself disappeared (Lewis 1993, 139–40, 142). This manifestly racist estimation of human beings, destined to serve as propaganda for the Third Reich, also served to underwrite a doctrine of black American freedom (148–9). DuBois had wished to remain in Berlin to complete the PhD, but political difficulties with his fellowship forced him to return to Harvard to complete the degree there. DuBois's Harvard dissertation, on the slave trade, became his first book, *The Suppression of the African Slave Trade in the U.S.A.* (1896). *The Philadelphia Negro* (1899), a sociological study of urban blacks, was his second. The German dissertation, lingering in his mind, became his third, *The Souls of Black Folk*, published in 1903.

Dante's Republic

But one should really begin with Dante. Literary history, much earlier than scientific history, invents all the categories for the origins of high and low as ideas. The notional apparatus is already in place in Dante, even if it will take until the nineteenth century for the phrenological "brow" and "the folk" to organize Dante's argument into something that it both is and is not. Dante, of course, is the first epic poet to use the vernacular; he is also the first critic to defend the use of the vernacular as a literary practice. Indeed, Dante's defense of the vernacular, *De vulgari eloquentia* (1303–5), becomes important in Dante studies only in the nineteenth century because it appears to be a premonition of nationalist ideas about "the folk" and of criminological justifications for suppressing the "atavistic." The *Vulgari*, however, is actually the beginning of a scrupulous, non-idealist assessment of the relation between language and reality – a post-medieval and a post-Platonic one – that is less shocking and more familiar when it emerges in full bloom in the Enlightenment and in Romanticism. It is not an argument that separates the pop or the vernacular from the high or the learned. Rather, it reconfigures their relation.

Hilariously enough, Dante's defense of the vernacular is written in Latin. The unfinished *Vulgari* is a rough-and-tumble text, full of both persuasiveness and surprise. The vernacular is the language that people speak in their native places. It therefore signifies not only a greater proximity to what is real and specific to a community, but does so because of a community's pragmatic identity with the language it speaks. This is not a physicalist argument but a cultural one. Speech is a principal part of life itself. Speech, and language as a whole, are chief among life's actual components. For Dante, life, including the language of real life, is inevitably reduced by an idealizing Latin, even in learned discourse. The vernacular is a more vivid mimetic instrument. This is because it is not mimetic. In the *Vulgari*, language – vernacular language – is not conceived of as standing apart from its object. It is its object. It is continuous with it. It refers to elements in its own signifying chain. This is why the vernacular is "more noble" than the "artificial" languages (1303–5, 3). It is the language of daily experience, full of its immediate delights and its despair. It is the language, says Dante, "originally used by the human race" (2). "Originally" is "*prima*" in Dante's Latin (2). "Originally" means that language itself is a "primary" fact of experience, the reason for its having a direct relation to things. It is not a question of the vernacular having a quicker mimetic strength than Latin. The vernacular is our "primary language" (5) because it is a "primary" example of the kinds of things to which language refers or with which it is identical. It is identical with its object because its object is language. Language is an actual part of primary experience. It is "that which we learn without any formal instruction, by imitating our nurses" (3).

11

Language is also primary to experience for another reason. It is wholly material, part of the solid existence of things. The signs, or "signals" (7), as Dante calls them, of language systems can only be conveyed by means perceptible to the senses. Language "is perceptible, in that it is a sound, and yet also rational, in that this sound, according to convention, is taken to mean something" (7). This is already Saussure's materiality of the signifier, including a doctrine of the signified that is, like Saussure's own, conceptual, social, and psychological. The signified occupies the speaker's mind; its token is the perceptible materiality of the acoustic or the graphic signifier, which is also social. The signified is also material – it inhabits the self as a "mnemic trace," to use Freud's vocabulary – and it is also, inevitably, arbitrary in relation to its meaning except, of course, socially and historically.

Dante – it is important to be frank about it – is at pains to reconcile this nascent semiotics with the many linguistic myths to which his faith also requires him to adhere. The *Vulgari* is in this sense a text of competing trends, often at odds with itself. Dante does what he can, however, to bend myth to the uses of semiotics. Even the myth of Hebrew's status as the first language aids Dante's purpose. Hebrew's durable authenticity is proven by its willful maintenance as an "artificial language." The authenticity that is proven is that of faith, not of truth – a faith of the user, a vernacular faith. Prefiguring Johnson, Dante is, to use Johnson's own word for the popular, "modern" in this precise way. The durability of Hebrew is a function, not of its sacredness, but of its status as a custom of learning.

Like Hebrew, Latin is also a language that is "immutable" over "times and places" (23) for the same unexpected and ironic reason. That is why it is not a polemical target for Dante either. Latin is, quite to the contrary, even better than Hebrew as a good foil against which he can develop his notion of the vernacular as something defined by change, custom, and locale. "We differ much more from ancient inhabitants of our own city," says Dante, "than from our contemporaries who live far off" (21). This is because the ancients spoke a wholly different language. Even if the regional dialects of Italy are different from one another, they are, unlike Latin, still part of a common system of cultural exchange that determines the daily texture of modern Italian life. This is not a Fichtean argument regarding an organic relation to the "ancient inhabitants" of one's "own city" based on a mystical spirit of place. No such argument is to be found anywhere in Dante's account. In contrast to Latin, Italy's many vernaculars present a "cacophony" (27), but it has a rich potential for poetic use. Dante finds opportunity where there seems to be only restriction. This "cacophony" is the source of the "illustrious vernacular" (35) that Dante as poet wishes most to justify and defend for literary purposes. It is the language of the *Commedia*. This vernacular cannot be the result of choosing one or another regional dialect to use as the basis of a literary Italian. It requires the invention of a synthetic literary vernacular that is wholly Italian because it is the Italy simultaneously of no region in particular and of all regions combined:

> We can define the illustrious, cardinal, aulic, and curial vernacular in Italy as that which belongs to every Italian city yet seems to belong to none, and against which the vernaculars of all the cities of the Italians can be measured, weighed, and compared. (41)

This is both an ideal and a material Italian, ideal because it exists nowhere, and material because it exists everywhere. Dante's linguistics is not only Saussurean; his ethics are positively Marxist: "Literary Italian is common to all yet owned by none" (43). The presumably high – the literary – is in fact "common" and orphan. It is, however, still a regulated system, since it has a soul to keep, even if it is only a performative one that it creates through vernacular speech. Literary Italian is not so much the Latin or Hebrew of vernaculars, but the vernacular of vernaculars, a language as much about Italian itself as it is about the things to which it refers, which are mostly Italian. Dante now needs to "teach," as he puts it, "a theory of the effective use of the vernacular" (45) for literary purposes.

Book II of the *Vulgari* does this. To begin, Dante dismisses any but procedural differences between poetry and prose (47). Both are, psychologically and materially, functions of the same language system in any given tradition. Language and thought are reciprocal. "Language,"

13

says Dante, "is nothing other than the vehicle indispensable to our thinking"; "thought" is inevitably bound to the "words" that convey it (49). This new poetics goes hand-in-hand with Dante's new literary Italian. Its "illustrious" vernacular is the "best of all vernaculars" (51) simply because it is fitted to more uses. The argument is quantitative, not qualitative. It is fitted to more uses because it comes from more usages. The contrast with Latin is vivid. Literary Italian is more plastic, more available to stimulation and reciprocal referencing than the vernacular of one specific place or another because it includes them all. To combine all these elements in a greater Italian is to produce an expansion in artistic flexibility and strength. After all, "the noblest" writings "are those that most fully exploit the technical possibilities of the art" (55). Even ethical and artistic value, like linguistic value, are the function of judgment on a comparative scale:

> Degrees of worthiness, greater and lesser, can be established by comparing them with each other, so that some are great, some greater, and some greatest. It follows that some things are worthy, some worthier, and some most worthy.... This comparison of degrees of worthiness is not applied to a single object, but to different ones, so that we can call "worthier" what is worthy of greater things and "most worthy" what is worthy of the greatest (because nothing can be worthier of the same). (51)

Like his ironic handling of the authority of Hebrew and Latin in Book I, Dante's use of the tropological and metrical categories of the ancients in Book II to describe his "illustrious Italian" is filled with humor. The defense of the *canzone* is, of course, Dante's goal. It is the mechanism of how one decides the form's rules that is most interesting, and most of a piece with Dante's wider critical project. The key, once again, is comparison and its inevitable twin, contrast. Between them, they set up a hum.

The use of a group of vernaculars solves the most basic problem of all: how to relate the musicality of poetic structure to its semantic structures. This is the particular source of the new sensual power of vernacular writing and what gives it its decided advantage over composition in the learned languages. This sensual power has a clear if complex source: the orchestration of signifiers from different vernaculars – vernaculars shaded or graded in relation to one another – in relation to a bed of psychological or conceptual signifieds that is largely the same. A lexical or inevitably "national" Italian of the signified is internally graded far less than the play of the different regional signifiers to which it is linked. Italian is always already different from itself because of its many vernaculars. The calculation of the difference between sound and sense in vernacular poetry is what makes Dante the real founder of vernacular literature, not only as its first poet, but also as its first critic.

"General Converse": Johnson and the Long Eighteenth Century

Not until the Enlightenment does the next serious defense of the vernacular come, this time from the emergence of the novel as a form. Even the diction of the great vernacular epic poets who follow Dante – Ariosto, Tasso, Spenser, Milton – is "artificial" compared to the language of prose fiction. Eighteenth-century poets like Pope feel so pressured by this artificiality that it grows into an object of parody and attack. It grows into self-attack and, finally, self-erasure in *The Dunciad*. The heroic couplet is its tool for parody, just as prose is the novel's tool for an equivalent kind of swerve from the seriousness of epic even as a vernacular project. Before Wordsworth once again adopts the vernacular to epic use in the century following Pope, it is Samuel Johnson who stabilizes the new authority of the novel by means of a reassessment of the relation between language and the world reminiscent of Dante's own.

Johnson's word for the "popular" is the "modern." Johnson's praise of "modern fiction" goes hand-in-hand with the fact of his praising it in a new institutional form of writing, the newspaper. The praise and its instrument are, in a familiar structure, once again two sides of a single sheet of paper. This extraordinary identity of technological form and thematic content is a reflection of the deeper epistemological

15

break to which Johnson gives expression, and which makes fully explicit what in Dante remains masked in the institutionally learned form of Latin. Life is a text; there is no difference between representation and representing, between language, which is always in search of standardization, and the precariousness of life, which is also always in search of stability. The reason is clear: Life and language search for each other. Language is not only the world that writing refers to; writing and the world are, empirically, very often one and the same thing. Much of the world is speech.

Johnson's argument for the legitimacy of modern fiction, and of modern prose in general, lies in the changing position it represents in relation to the time-honored superiority of poetry. Modern fiction can, as he puts it, "keep up curiosity" – keep the reader reading – "without the help of wonder" (1750, 175). Unnecessary is the supernatural machinery of epic or of religious backgrounds, even the mock-heroic machinery of Pope. Why is this so? For a technical reason. "The task of our present writers," he says, "is very different" from that of past writers. It "must arise," he says, "from general converse." The phrase is a memorable one. The "general converse" is what "everyone knows." It is "the original" – it is what Virginia Woolf will call "life itself." No wonder the reader "can detect any deviation from," in the well-known phrase, "exactness of resemblance" (175). This may appear to be a familiar classical argument for and about mimesis – that art simply imitates life, as Johnson himself appears to contend here – but it is not. It is a theory of reference, not a theory of mimesis. Readers can judge "resemblance" not because of an equivalence between language and object but because language and object are of a piece. Something is knowable because it has its roots in the satisfaction of the requirements of its semantic inventory and its means of production. Language's objects are all drawn, inevitably and irresistibly, from the "general converse." How many of Bakhtin's arguments are based on an elaboration of what is really a Johnsonian discovery. Novelistic discourse in Bakhtin is as a rule one example or another of the direct representation of speech acts. The popular mind – "minds unfurnished with ideas" – is "easily susceptible of impressions" because "impressions" come to it with the direct force of new ideas (176).

16

The structure of language as a system is psychological. Johnson's philosophical counterpart, Hume, is the clearest exponent of this breakthrough. Literary language refers not only to colloquial speech, or *skaz*; it refers to whole states of mind constructed out of linguistic complexes, particularly in the building of the individual's unconscious. Thought and feeling for Hume are tiers of association that form "connexions," as Hume puts it, between "impressions" and "ideas." We are only a step away, surprisingly, from Wordsworth.

The Preface to Johnson's *Dictionary* (1755) gives us the reasons for this. Like the life to which it presumably only refers, language is in a perpetual movement of adjustment to its own usage, particularly in relation to its multiple origins. Language, in other words, is part of the reality it describes. The question is not how well language represents reality; the question is how well language represents itself:

> As by the cultivation of various sciences, a language is amplified, it will be more furnished with words deflected from their original sense; the geometrician will talk of a courtier's zenith, or the eccentric virtue of a wild hero, and the physician of sanguine expectation and phlegmatic delays. Copiousness of speech will give opportunities to capricious choice, by which some words will be preferred, and others degraded; vicissitudes of fashion will enforce the use of new, or extend the signification of known terms. The tropes of poetry will make hourly encroachments, and the metaphorical will become the current sense; pronunciation will be varied by levity or ignorance, and the pen must at length comply with the tongue; illiterate writers will at one time or other, by public infatuation, rise into renown, who, not knowing the original import of words, will use them with colloquial licentiousness, confound distinction, and forget propriety. As politeness increases, some expressions will be considered as too gross and vulgar for the delicate, others as too formal and ceremonious for the gay and airy; new phrases are therefore adopted, which must, for the same reasons, be in time dismissed. (1755, 525–6)

Words are life because life is language. There is no gap between representation and represented, or between a standardized language and the regularities of life. Both are standardized in relation to one another.

17

Composing the *Dictionary*, as Johnson well knew, was to compose, in the emotional sense of calming, the texture of English life. The consequences are stunning. The relation of high and low, the learned and the popular, is not hierarchical. The popular – the low – and its literary representative – the presumably high – are actually on a level field. Both are instances of language, in a constant exchange rather than in a hierarchical relation. Indeed, this is the very difference between feudalism and the new marketplace culture of which literary journalism is itself an example.

Swift parodies mimesis in *Gulliver's Travels* (1726) by having the inhabitants of Lagado research the possibility of carrying objects around rather than having to refer to them with words. "Since words are only names for *things*," says Gulliver, "it would be more convenient for all men to carry about them such *things* as were necessary to express the particular business they were to discourse on" (1726, 183). This is one of fiction's best emblems for the view of language left behind in Johnson's "pop" revolution. One unlikely consequence of Swift's joke about mimesis is that these objects – clocks, for example – do indeed have a status that words alone have only more remotely: a manufacturing and exchange value. Like the English soon to be standardized by Johnson's *Dictionary*, Swift's objects in *Gulliver* are parodies of mimesis among other reasons because the objects conform first and foremost to their descriptions. This is Oscar Wilde before the fact – life imitates art – but it is as much an economic proposition as an epistemological one. In order to have "value" in the Saussurean sense – in order to have "meaning" – objects must conform to the semantic inventories that underwrite them as the objects they are supposed to be. This does not mean the object in itself – there is no such thing – but the object understood as the product of the history of its production. The social and economic background of the object – its raw materials and the means of its production – are part and parcel of what the object is. Debates as to the quality of commodities when mass production begins to replace handicrafts in the eighteenth century reflect this shift from mimesis as a way of understanding linguistic reference to an understanding of reference as the relation of objects and language to one another. Like industrial production, intertextual reference is what guarantees the quality of the object-world. Like handicrafts, mimesis privileges language, like the worker's hand, as exercising a control over something different in substance and apart from it. Swift and Johnson both propose a theory of industrial reference, or mass production, rather than a theory of reference as one of correspondence between language and thing. Language and objects function at their best – have their best quality – when beheld fully in the light of the histories that produce them.

Swift's allegory about language and its objects is not only anti-allegorical. It is also an allegory about allegory, since it is an allegory about production as a whole. Objects and language alike – there is no longer a difference – are the products of a historical chain of construction, both always philological as well as linguistic, historical as well as self-present. Virginia Woolf, Johnson's best disciple, frustrated by her father's positivism and the mimesis that accompanied it, gives us the best example in all of English fiction for this expanded notion of both language and object in *To the Lighthouse* (1927). Mr Ramsay's philosophical work, she says, speaking of her father and demystifying his philosophical point of view, is best understood as "a kitchen table … when you're not there" (1927, 38). The object relies for its being not simply on its perception but on its history of production. A "kitchen table" is a "kitchen table" not only because one or another person beholds or even uses it, but because it fulfills, objectively, its own requirements, both semantically and historically, to be what it is. It is made of a certain material, and therefore has a particular manufacturing history; it has its requisite specifications, such as being high or low enough to sit or stand at; it has its requisite uses, such as being a surface for eating; and it is made a certain way.

This is the case in a world of mass production that begins in Johnson's time and reaches crisis proportions in the twentieth century and beyond. It is, however, also the case, one should remember, for pre-industrial civilization. It is unwise to fall victim to the belief in a "dissociation of sensibility" before the Renaissance. The Middle Ages has the selfsame epistemology of the pop, although in a very different register. Dante's revolution is less a revolution than it is a simple illumination of the "pop" intertextuality of medieval culture itself, especially of the medieval *plenum*. Dante can be both a religious poet and a semiotician because the bond of faith and the bond of language are not dissimilar. The *plenum* is full, harmonious, and present not because the world and its institutions reflect and embody the word of God, but because the "general converse" believes this to be true in the associative structures of its shared assumptions about the world. The truth of religion – I will remind the reader of this self-evident truth more than once in these pages – is a popular truth not because it is true or false but because its forms are shared. Bob Dylan, as I will show later on, completes this revolution by turning its whole history back upon itself two centuries later on in a stunning and self-conscious manner. No wonder the late eighteenth century sees a rebirth of medievalism in a renovated form. It is a reminder that the medieval and the industrial are facsimiles in their ability to produce consensual truth. Shifts in feeling characterize the new industrial age just as surely as they characterize religious ones. There are the Graveyard Poets, the preoccupation with ruins, and the cult of melancholy, new threads or trends of literary preoccupation that become central to English Romanticism.

Accompanying this drift toward the neo-medieval or the "Gothic" was the overtly "popular" invention of "trash," as Walter Kendrick describes it (1991), by Horace Walpole, himself the principal inventor of Gothic fiction. Walpole's collections of bric-à-brac at his Strawberry Hill estate are closely related to his Gothic project as a novelist. Both were "fake," as Kendrick puts it (1991, 73), and both had the same end: the production of frightening effects. *The Castle of Otranto* was the first "Gothic" novel, published on Christmas Eve in 1764. Its medieval setting, like the wallpaper at Strawberry Hill that looked like granite, was designed to elicit "a delicious, melancholy little chill" (42). This "Gothic surprise," in Kendrick's words, constituted a revolution, not in historical awareness – the great medieval cathedrals were built many centuries after the Visigoths sacked and pillaged Rome in 410 AD – but in taste. The earlier name, through a historical error passed down over the centuries, came also to designate the later architectural style. What was not classical in design, like Rome, was given the name of Rome's ancient enemy. The difference between "historical accuracy" and "the cultivated feeling of pastness" (76) was the difference we call "pop," or that Kendrick calls, more simply, "entertainment":

> There was something outrageous about the taste Walpole chose to make his own. For a century and more before the transformation of Strawberry Hill, Gothic architecture – not to mention the habits of thought associated with it – had been disdained by most cultivated people. They found it crude by comparison with both the Classical style and the Renaissance neo-Classicism that went to ancient Greece and Rome for its models. Walpole was not the first to proclaim the merits of Gothic, nor did he single-handedly engineer a change in these older, deeply entrenched attitudes. But thanks to his high social position and impeccable connections – also, no doubt, to the sheer gusto with which he publicized his preferences – he lent respectability to a style that had been curious at best, vulgar at worst. Very seldom does an individual achieve such pervasive, long-lasting influence: To a remarkable degree, Walpole can be held responsible for a shift in Western feeling that altered everything from the design of public buildings to the way we fall in love – and scare ourselves. (41–2)

"Similitude in Dissimilitude"

Wordsworth completes what Dante begins. Wordsworth's subtleties as a psychoanalyst and semiotician of the presumably simple life of the countryside are too often lost in handlings of what Romanticism is in both the nineteenth and the twentieth centuries. Like his German counterparts, Fichte and Herder, Wordsworth is famous for being misread on the subject of nature and on the subject of what the ties are that bind communities together. Ruskin condemned Wordsworth for giving nature a human voice; he introduces a term to criticism, the "pathetic fallacy," to signify his contempt. Jerome McGann's *Romantic Ideology* (1983) is the best contemporary academic example of regarding Wordsworth as a pantheist. McGann sees even the extraordinarily careful "Preface" to *Lyrical Ballads* (1800–2) as a naturalist manifesto.

Wordsworth's emphasis on simple life and on the poet's wish for calm in the *The Prelude* counters the entire tradition of epic by seeking both value and interest in what Whitman will call "the daily housework" in "To Think of Time" (1891–2, VI: 66). Wordsworth sweeps aside the heroic action of epic from Homer to Dante and Milton in favor of an emphasis on the quotidian that also defines the emergence of the novel as a form. His only precursor here is Dante, who paints the underworld in the colors of Florence. But even Dante simply retells customary mythic events in a vernacular tongue and from a more personal point of view. For Wordsworth, the materials themselves change. It is this emphasis on the details of custom that is Wordsworth's real focus in the "Preface." It is the way the machinery of custom rather than of myth functions that is his real concern. "Nature" does not speak, as Ruskin claims it does in Wordsworth; it speaks, as it were, with the voice of the customary machinery that motivates populations who represent nature to themselves for the purposes of labor. The beggar or milkmaid is not superior to the bourgeois because he or she is less repressed and therefore more at one with the creation. They are superior as poetic subjects because the social or psychological machinery that motivates them is easier to see. It is a quantitative proposition only. The urbanite or aspirant landowner – the suburbanite – is encrusted by more numerous, and contending, systems of custom compared to his rural counterpart. "The natural" – "the popular" – is significant for the clarity of its machinery rather than for its lack of machinery.

Like Dante's *Vulgari*, Wordsworth's "Preface" may seem to have physicalist tendencies, but, like the *Vulgari*, it actually criticizes and cautions such tendencies with its structural rather than naturalist view of language and culture alike. Poetry may be, in the immortal phrase, "the spontaneous overflow of powerful feelings" (1800–2, 246), but the "overflow" comes, Wordsworth reminds us, "from emotion recollected in tranquillity" (266). The cautionary note is struck even when the natural "expression" involved is the exemplary one of poetic utterance. The "origin" of poetic utterance is the recollection, not the emotion itself. The buffering of the immediate comes at a double remove: "tranquillity" following, presumably, passion or sensation, and recollection following event. This is hardly the aesthetic precursor to Kerouac's "spontaneous bop prosody" of 1958, even though it is

22

Kerouac's antiquarian source. As I will show in Part II, Kerouac's misreading of jazz is indeed akin to the Victorian misreading of Wordsworth as a poet of nature. Wordsworth is a different kind of poet than we think he is. Like Dante, he gives us an extremely scrupulous account of what the popular is.

This scrupulosity comes in two registers, a thematic one and a philosophical one. As with Johnson in the "Preface" to the *Dictionary*, what is important to Wordsworth in the "Preface" to *Lyrical Ballads* is that the reader sees that writing itself is made up — at least with the birth of the novel and with Wordsworth's own poetry — of "the real language of men in a state of vivid sensation" (241). Like the language of both prose and poetry, "the real language of men" and literary language are "of the same substance" (253). The material metaphor — "substance" — is noteworthy. Like the words of an eighteenth-century novel or newspaper, or like Wordsworth's own verse, endlessly revised until the end of his life in the case of *The Prelude* (1850), literary language and what it represents do not stand in a subject/object, hierarchical relation to one another. Literary language does not, from a summit, copy life below. Literary language and the life it describes are, as they are in Johnson, continuous. They are in "substance" one and the same. They are made up of the same material — "the real language of men," and, presumably, women.

Nor is Wordsworth's scope limited in the "Preface" to a thematic assessment of why rural custom provides, as it does in nineteenth-century French painting or in American modernists like Edward Hopper, a sharper picture than the city does of what the popular is and how it works. The case for the city is a labor left to Baudelaire to perform. Wordsworth's achievement here is dauntingly ambitious philosophically, and in a way that one does not expect from him. Like Hume, he provides us with an epistemology of perception, an epistemology of epistemology. No determinist, Wordsworth wonders "in what manner language and the human mind act and react" (243). This is really to ask what is the nature of the reciprocity between species and environment, in the human case a reciprocity, not between "mind" and "nature," but between "mind" and "language." They are, materially, of a piece, but it is their exchange that both creates and separates them. Indeed, it separates them by joining them, just as it joins them by means of their separation. Like Freud's *Beyond the Pleasure Principle* (1920), Wordsworth's "Preface" shows the organism emerging from the environment in a defensive posture. It does so in order to protect itself from the stimulation that continually breaches it. It becomes alienated in order to survive. "The primary laws of our nature" (245), as a seemingly naturalist Wordsworth calls them, are actually a system of exchange between species and environment, mind and language. The key is "the manner in which we associate ideas in a state of excitement" (245). Like Coleridge's, Wordsworth's philosophical origins are in the associative tradition of Hume and of Hartley. The relation between "ideas" and "sensations" (258), as nineteenth-century science will also call them, is precisely what custom structures. Custom structures nothing less than this interrelationship. "Continued influxes of feeling," says Wordsworth, are "modified and directed by our thoughts, which are" – here is the surprise – "the representatives of all our past feelings" (246). The formulation of a series of buffers is a refinement of Hume's doctrine of association, and a good example of it. Prior experience or predilection affects how we receive new feelings or stimulation. "Thought" – majestic "thought" – is no more than "the representative ... of all" – *all* – "our past feelings." The prophecy of Freud's equally surprising definition of "instinct" in 1915 is astonishing. The implication here is also astonishing, well before the Freudian fact. "Thought" is not only "feeling"; "feeling," necessarily, is also "thought." And custom – the new lord, custom – structures thought and feeling alike because it is custom that structures whatever historical interrelationship thought and feeling, sensation and idea may have.

The "pleasure" that poetry provides, then, is not a straightforward one. It illuminates the psychology of cultural "feeling" – of the "popular" – at its root, which is not direct, but infinitely mediated. Poetic pleasure, like any "feeling," "derives" also from an interrelationship: it is "the pleasure which the mind derives from the perception of similitude in dissimilitude" (265) – from beholding the tiny gaps in its experience which create its experience. This unlikely source is "the great spring of the activity of our minds and their chief feeder" (265).

24

Mental activity is the reaction not simply of the self to custom, but of the self's reaction to that reaction. It is a dialectics of the self. So audacious is the Freudian Wordsworth that this is also the "origin," as he puts it, of "the sexual appetite, and all the passions connected with it" (265). In domestic and sexual life alike, in other words, "the perception of similitude in dissimilitude" is the very engine of feeling, what brings it to life and quickens its pulse. Feeling is interactive, the difference between past and present, stimulation and defense, paradigm and practice. No wonder it is the "chief feeder" of our minds and bodies both. By likening the mental and the sexual, Wordsworth has also accomplished another Freudian deconstruction *avant la lettre*. The difference between mind and body has disappeared. As they inevitably are in psychoanalysis, mind and body are continuous with one another because thought and feeling, sensation and idea, self and language are continuous. The poetic depiction of these structures, says Wordsworth – the intimation of Pound's Imagist manifesto more than a century later is also surprising – is the production of an object identical in structure with what it describes: "a complex feeling of delight" (266).

Keats and Mediocrity

Keats's fear of mediocrity is the dread alternative to the new Wordsworthian grandeur of small things. Keats fears the small things that Wordsworth loves because they reflect his own anxieties about being low, poor, humble. Keats's biography is well known. Quite the reverse of Alice in the looking glass less than 70 years later, Keats sees a screen of his fears, not of his fantasies. The conversation he wishes to have is with the Immortals, as Hardy calls precursor authority in *The Dynasts* (1904, 1906, 1908), not with cottage maids, who remind him, too desperately, of his own memories of the girls he courted as a boy. If Fanny Brawne is Keats's idealized object-choice, classical models of women in a Miltonic style are his idealized poetic ones, particularly in the *Hyperion* fragments (1818–19/1820, 1819/1856). The combination of idealized poetic object-choices – projective identification is a better way to put it – is not a solution, however, but another symptom-formation in the world of Keats's melancholia or depression. Milton's prophylaxis of classical models for vernacular use – like Dante's a use of the Bible rather than of the ancients – is what Keats resents. Because Dante and Milton have already come up with the best solution for poetic belatedness – exchanging a more tractable Judeo-Christian authority for a more "artificial," but also more learned, classical one – no alternative is left but to rejoin Pope's more exacting sally with the ancients themselves. Without a sense of humor, it is impossible to win this battle. The loss is what ends up counting for Keats. He will, in the *Hyperion* epics-that-fail, insist on using the vernacular to resuscitate classical figurines, half of them dead on arrival in his story of the defeated Titans. Keats wants his writing to fail – in this labor lies a delicate filigree of grief, and pathos. He is bound to lose, a destiny that becomes his very subject.

Toxic metaphors are not inappropriate with Keats. They best describe his survival anxieties as both a poet and a person, and become entirely manifest with his illness. Anxiety, as Freud will describe it, is not unlike stimulation of any toxic kind, continuous with it on a material scale. Especially in the late, unforgettable fragment – "This living hand, now warm and capable" (1819–20/1898, 1) – Keats puts his body on, and in, the line.

What, then, does Keats add to the history of high and low? It is a surprising development, since it shows how it is the English canon itself that introduces the pop as a problem, not, as it is in Wordsworth, as a liberation. For Keats, failure is to be measured by falling short of the canonical authority. To leave it behind is not an option. In Keats's rule-plagued world, his singular musicality with established forms is his only escape from them. Keats invents the modern preoccupation with mediocrity, and with failure. This is the real source of what Christopher Ricks calls the "embarrassment" that Keats provokes (1974). No wonder Keats's friend Leigh Hunt largely invented, in his writings and in the homes he built outside of London, the notion of a baronial suburbia, even though the word in a simple descriptive sense goes back to Chaucer, in

"The Yeoman's Tale" of 1386. Hunt's is the social version of Keats's poetry, a *faux*-aristocratic defense of the successful bourgeois drone against the mediocrity that defines him. Assuming what Johnson and Wordsworth assume, Keats and Hunt both find an unlikely stressfulness in what is for their precursors a wholly positive eventuality. For Johnson and Wordsworth, measuring oneself against one's neighbors leads to a sense of community; for Keats and Hunt, measuring oneself against one's neighbors exposes a lack of self-esteem and the need to keep up with the Joneses. One nonetheless comes into being only by measuring oneself against what is already there. One's characterization of precedent as either oppressive or helpful is the difference between Keats and Wordsworth. If Wordsworth, like Johnson, finds the "popular" reassuring, Keats does not. It is a goad to his narcissism, which is deficient, and which, however gentle and alluring, is the baseline of his personality both clinically and poetically. In the process, Keats redefines the pop. He gives it an edge. It is a darkness into which one is bound to fall. Keats adds to the Wordsworthian glory in the quotidian a fear of abandoned gods. One should still fear them, in whatever form is available. We underestimate Keats's surpassing tackiness. The filigree is rococo. Idealization is everything for Keats. His anxiety is an anxiety about not being good enough. Keats as poet produces the specter of his own failure as the subject of his own quite new kind of poetry of visionary succession. The irony is as astonishing as the achievement. They are actually one and the same.

With Keats, "high" culture creates the problem of "mediocrity" by making the artist's struggle with outmoded forms the center of Romanticism. Shelley's glory is to succeed endlessly at this impossible task; Keats's is to fail, gloriously, under its weight. By initiating this artistic persona, Keats is rock and roll's original poet, the first Buddy Holly or Brian Jones, the man who died too young. Here Keats also joins with an unlikely contemporary to inaugurate the history of bohemia. Like Beau Brummell, Keats believed that anyone can, as Chesterton observed of Dickens (1906), do anything. If they succeed, they are tradesmen, or novelists; if they fail, they are poets.

27

Keats's preoccupations are externalized in the landscapes of his epic fragments, where the concern with lost power has reached, as it has in Keats's own body, a fever pitch. Keats's mid-career odes are already preoccupied with borders, their stability an ironic function of their ready violation by opposites on either side. It is a discourse, appropriately enough, of *contaminatio*, or "contamination." Melancholy and delight, past and present, ancient and modern, self and other, mind and body – the tightrope between these extremes is always on the verge of collapse, and the topic, as a rule, of his poems, which construct these polarities by contrasting them. Keats's world is not one of conflict, but of unsummoned differences. It is a world of constant foreboding because of the fear of their collapse. The melancholic current has won, psychosomatically devastating but poetically compensatory. It provides Keats with a freshly ripe subject. Keats gives us a new sense of loss – its imminence.

The presentation of Keatsian mediocrity is exact in the first *Hyperion* fragment. The poetic voice does not indulge in the first person, as it will in the second fragment, even though the scene is infected with narcissistic pathos. Keats's fallen Titans, crushed by the Olympians, sound more like Milton's devils in Hell than they do any classical precursors. They therefore lament their loss doubly – as story, and as a repetition of the diction of *Paradise Lost*. It is the landscape that is important:

> No stir of air was there,
> Not so much life as on a summer's day
> Robs not one light seed from the feather'd grass,
> But where the dead leaf fell, there did it rest.
> (1818–1819/1820, 7)

This is the world behind the world of the poem, its hidden, and toxic, garden, the place of growth that has lost its generative powers. Here the "leaf" – both the fact and the instrument of growth and dissemination – is "dead." "Not one light seed" can travel through the air because the air does not "stir." The "seed," or *sème* – the pill of growth, a pun with "*sème*," or "sign," as Derrida likes to remind us – is a dead letter.

28

The historical movement of this landscape and the way in which it is shared among the poets who follow Keats is what defines the movement of poetry in England later in the nineteenth century. The "seed" as a sign for the state of poetic imagination is everywhere. It is in Wordsworth well before the Keatsian difference from Wordsworth. Wordsworth, of course, has no difficulties when it comes to conversing with growing things in a landscape. But even Wordsworth himself falls into a Keatsian idiom when his focus is microscopic enough to require the discussion of the environment's actual mechanisms in *The Prelude*:

> Fair seed-time had my soul, and I grew up
> Fostered alike by beauty and by fear:
> Much favored in my birthplace, and no less
> In that beloved Vale to which erelong
> We were transplanted – there were we let loose
> For sports of wider range.
>
> (1: 301–6)

Not only are the seeds of the soul "transplanted" – the metaphor is consistent with Keats's, although, because it is Wordsworth, the metaphor is confident rather than depressed. The seeds are also "let loose," free to disseminate. They are not "dead," as they are in the constrained and defeated Keats, the English Bonaparte. For Wordsworth, the vernacular represents absorption in the "general converse." For Keats, by contrast, the vernacular is a fall. However "low" or resentful such an attitude may be, its carping tone produces by the reflex of its own fear of failure a self-sustaining "high" culture in relation to it. This condition is the fear of the pop into which the pop is always in danger of collapsing. It is how it produces a ghostly "high" culture forever at its side. It is a certain kind of pop, both gaunt and tawdry, like Keith Richards, and very unlike Wordsworthian pastoral. Like arena rock, Keatsian grandeur is the effect of something that must have been left behind. It is a braggadocio of losses. Longing creates its own object, despair its own hope. This is Keatsian space, and, as I will show in Part II, the space of rock and roll.

29

Compared also to friend Shelley's poetic landscapes, Keats's are indeed a fall. Like Wordsworth's, Shelley's voice is full. "Ode to the West Wind" (1820) is a transformation of "leaves dead" (2) into "winged seeds" (7). In the blink of an eye, Shelley's confidence, like Wordsworth's, can only animate landscape, even when the mood is bleak. Shelley's "Wild Spirit" moves "everywhere" (13). As with Wordsworth, the dissemination is unstoppable. For both, and no matter Shelley's classicism, it is a Johnsonian leveling of ground between language and object, sower and seed, sign and user.

Whitman, Shelley's only rival in pure poetic strength in nineteenth-century English, also flows from Wordsworth when he describes afflatus in "Song of Myself." So delighted is the poet that even the wind has been libidinized. Shelley's seeds have become, quite overtly, semen:

> Trickling sap of maple, fibre of manly wheat, it shall be you!
> Sun so generous it shall be you!
> Vapors lighting and shading my face it shall be you!
> You sweaty brooks and dews it shall be you!
> Winds whose soft-tickling genitals rub against me it shall be you!
> Broad muscular fields, branches of live oak, loving lounger in my
>   winding paths, it shall be you!
> Hands I have taken, face I have kiss'd, mortal I have ever touch'd,
>   it shall be you.
>
> (1891–2, 24: 537–43)

Late Romantic English verse is of a piece with this tropology, poet to poet. In Swinburne's "The Garden of Proserpine" (1866), the stance is Keatsian, even if the setting is Wordsworthian. Indeed, the relation between these literary settings is the poem's very subject. The sonorous conclusion to the poem converts Wordsworthian possibility into Keatsian defeat through a slow transformation from Wordsworthian to Keatsian topography. It is also reminiscent of the close of what we may now regard in retrospect as a rather Romantic *Dunciad*. As with Keats himself – and with an equally lovely irony – this dramatization of failure is also played out in the poem's technique. A consummate

poetic control takes its own loss of control over its subject matter as
its theme:

> I am weary of days and hours,
> Blown buds of barren flowers,
> Desires and dreams and powers
> And everything but sleep....
> And all dead years draw thither
> And all disastrous things;
> Dead dreams of days forsaken,
> Blind buds that snows have shaken,
> Wild leaves that winds have taken,
> Red strays of ruined springs....
>
> Then star nor sun shall waken,
> Nor any change of light:
> Nor sound of waters shaken,
> Nor any sound or sight:
> Nor wintry leaves nor vernal,
> Nor days nor things diurnal,
> Only the sleep eternal
> In an eternal night.
> (1866, 13–16, 67–70, 88–91, 93–96)

Hardy's likeness to Swinburne is well known. Note how exact the
likeness is in both tropology and thematic concern in an early poem
like "Neutral Tones" (1867), written only a year after "The Garden of
Proserpine":

> We stood by a pond that winter day,
> And the sun was white, as though chidden of God,
> And a few leaves lay on the starving sod;
> They had fallen from an ash, and were gray.
> (1867, 1–4)

The seeds will not even have a chance to die in this landscape; it is too
cold to allow anything to grow in the first place. Hardy invents his
way out of the Keatsian melodramas of his early poems with the

return to Wordsworth represented by his later verse, particularly its philological playfulness and its turn away from classical models in favor of native ones (Taylor, 1993). The three-volume *Dynasts* is a very different kind of late skirmish with Pope, over whom Hardy has the advantage of Romanticism. A play-poem about what authority consists in, *The Dynasts* lies behind Tony Kushner's *Angels in America* (1993, 1994).

Surprisingly, this same rhetorical environment is still in place in High Modernism. To find it at the start of T.S. Eliot's *The Waste Land* is especially surprising, since Eliot, presumably, is not a Romantic poet. When the Pound-edited *Waste Land* is completed and published by the Woolfs in 1922, much of its Romantic evocations of gloomy places had indeed been excised. But even what remains under Pound's supervision is, from the point of view of Keatsian landscape, still familiar. The scene of a technically astute poet navigating a drunken boat we now know is a conception not original with Eliot. The imagery of the poem's opening lines is also familiar:

> April is the cruellest month, breeding
> Lilacs out of the dead land, mixing
> Memory and desire, stirring
> Dull roots with spring rain.
>   (1922, 1–4)

The "land" is, as it is in Hardy and Swinburne, "dead"; the "stirring" of "roots" – we already know this, too – is impossible. For Eliot, as for all our poets, this presumable crisis in communication is actually an opportunity to have a new subject to write about: failure and loss. Keats's mediocrity – or, as Eliot likes to call it, "difficulty" (1921, 289) – is useful as both a technical and a thematic problem. Each one begets the other, and gives the poet a project. For Keats, the fear of mediocrity produces a new kind of grandeur – a cragged, pop grandeur, an old man, like Dylan, in a boy's body. For Eliot, the dull landscape provides him with a chance to bring it back to life as a poet, particularly as an urban poet overcoming the operatic tragedy of the Keatsian pop. As with Swinburne, failure as an object is a superb subject for poetic, or operatic, success. The Imagist snapshots that Eliot uses to transform the ruined landscape of Romanticism into, not a natural rebirth but a jeering carnivalesque, are the opposite of Hardy's choice to reanimate Wordsworthian spirit of place with the stately hum of dialects in play. These are two distinct ways of responding to Keatsian lamentation. Indeed, Hardy and Eliot provide the two heads from which the next 100 years of poetry in English will emerge: a loving accommodation of the vernacular, and a mockery and appropriation of it.

Culture and Anarchy in the UK

Matthew Arnold's early poems are, like Keats's later ones, defined by speakers who cannot compose themselves in gloomy natural settings. Empedocles, Thyrsis, the Scholar-Gipsy – all suffer from the dissolution of boundaries in the sand of uneasy symbolizations, particularly the symbolization of imagination's incapacity. Arnold as poet is a vivid example of the Keatsian paradigm despite his manifest dependence on Wordsworth. So overriding is the despair of these poems as to the possibility of any kind of imagination at all that they constitute an object of study in their own right. I tried to show this many years ago (1987), with the intent of also describing why Arnold, the dandy young poet of the 1850s, becomes the dour middle-aged essayist of cultural decline in the 1860s. Although Arnold continues to write verse – some of his late lyrics such as "Dover Beach" (1867) are among his best and most famous poems – it is with a different kind of voice from that of his youth.

This is, to be sure, a surprising way to introduce Arnold in these pages. As I noted in the Preface, he is a figure in many ways singly responsible as an essayist for the demonization of the pop. "Culture," so it goes, has succumbed to the "pop," or what Arnold calls "anarchy" (1869). "Culture" is now articulated as the foil of "anarchy." These terms give Arnold his famous title, which the Sex Pistols, more than a century later, will revise through negation. Anarchy is the confusion of realms, to use Richard Gilman's phrase (1969), brought on by the decline of religion and the disunity of society. The loss of a social center is the loss that Arnold's poems bewail. This sociological impetus is also commensurate with the depressive trend in poetic tradition that Arnold shares with Keats. It is not an explanation; it is part of the plot. Arnold's shift from poetry to prose is reflexive in a double way: The nobility of verse can no longer be managed in the crisis of culture that the new hegemony of prose represents. Only prose can strike back at prose; given the times, it is the stronger instrument. Given Arnold's own imaginative predicament as a poet, prose can also strike back at poetry. It is its replacement, even for Arnold. He, too, is of the devil's party. In either case, it is the failure of "high" culture that is Arnold's object of attack, whether the drift of England into intellectual "anarchy," or the Keatsian failure of his poems to produce heroes of sufficient strength to resist death. They die, like Keats, because of the devaluation of bardic form. Arnold had by 1851 become Inspector of English Schools. The task was a congenial one because it gave Arnold a nexus in which the political, the sociological, and the literary all found a place. The reason lies in something common to all three: the epistemological shift in the very conception of "culture" that Arnold brings to a head and to which he gives the fullest expression. The Romantic tradition provides Arnold with his immediate context, but, like his secret mentor, Keats, rather than like his official one, Wordsworth, it is Arnold's melancholic handling of what is a fall into the vernacular that gives him his recognizable tone.

Ever reflexive in all his modes of performance, Arnold is also the first Professor of Poetry at Oxford to give his lectures in English rather than in Latin. It is a reversal of Dante's *Vulgari*. In 1857, his inaugural lecture, "On the Modern Element in Literature," made the paradox behind the position plain. By lecturing in English, Arnold linked – as he also did thematically – the vernacular to the project of high culture. Both were now vernacular, and both were now presumably full of dignity. A new crisis had to be found so that the difference between high and low could return. This Arnold accomplished by calling in a new form of disorder whose threat to "culture" would sustain it as a categorical imperative. "Culture" required "anarchy" to exist. Arnold's own cultural authority required the endless oscillation between them for there to be both a crisis and a crisis manager. Like his poetic heroes, Arnold the essayist also ends up in a world of boundaries not stabilized but violated. Culture needs its delinquent twin, anarchy, as a prop against which to define itself. The productive play of this contamination of one category by the other takes a series of forms. They include the many compromises with the pop that is its antagonist, particularly the embrace of vernacular literatures as serious objects of study. Secondary school curricula and new degrees at Oxford and Cambridge in modern, vernacular literatures institutionalized these compromises. If Keats invents mediocrity, Arnold invents the very "anarchy" he bewails.

"Balance and regularity of mind" (1869, 409) are Arnold's chief concerns throughout *Culture and Anarchy*. The metaphor of regularity is a familiar one in Arnold's poems. There, its repetition is like a neurotic tic; its preoccupation with self-cleansing accompanies it as a defense mechanism. In *Culture and Anarchy*, the ideal is the same as in Arnold's early poems. Culture is "a study of perfection" (409). Its objects of devotion are the ancient and the modern classics, prose and poetry alike, that everyone should know, even if only in a vernacular language. Arnold is blunt about how he thinks "perfection" should exercise its authority – like a policeman in Hyde Park. "It moves by force" (410). The point is "to get the raw person to like that" (413). For Keats, "perfection" emerges only as the fraction between past greatness and present mediocrity. For Arnold, however, the situation is no longer a delicate one.

The kind of cultural regulation that Arnold has in mind, of course, is based on the model of religious institutions, despite their decline in the nineteenth century as intellectually vital. With faith in trouble in the Victorian age, Arnold puts culture, influentially, in its place. "Culture," says a pragmatic Arnold, "coincides with religion" (412). This does not solve the problem; it reconstitutes it in different terms. *Culture and Anarchy* is an unwittingly ironic text. Its own discordances are an instance of what it both laments and understands. Its harmonies are incidental; its real trends are double, and at odds, in different registers, and in jarring but productive counterpoint. Arnold's "religion of culture" may seem to resolve the opposition between culture and anarchy. It actually puts the opposition back in place. Arnold's resistance to anarchy has the constant counter-effect of inflaming the very condition to be eased. The book's other famous opposition also plays more than an allegorical role. "Hebraic" and "Hellenic" are additional masks for the kinds of differences whose resolution Arnold cannot achieve without also keeping asunder. It is a double-bind from which Arnold endlessly profits as a cultural manager.

Raymond Williams's vivid portrayal of the real historical conditions under which Arnold wrote is helpful in refining our sense of what Arnold brings, conceptually, to the idea of pop. For Williams, the wide cultural pressure for Arnold in the 1860s, particularly the rioting during attempts, politically, to expand the vote, forced him into an unlikely conservative position (1970, 5). It is the position we see in his cultural essays, despite his quite real reputation for being the father of liberal education. He is, as Williams also points out (7), the father, like his disciple Trilling a century later, of a new kind of cultural repression. Arnold's own fear of the "riot of ideas" in "Empedocles on Etna" is a premonition of the very real danger of riot in Hyde Park a decade later. Poetically and critically alike, Arnold is a reaction to Wordsworth, and an instance also of Arnold's anxiety about Wordsworth as a poetic influence. Born as a poet in the Wordsworthian tradition, he cannot live up to it. Hence the reaction in his criticism. The Keatsian laments about mediocrity in the verse, especially the late lyrics, is compensation, but it is not enough. Unlike Keats, Arnold is unable to tolerate paradox. Unlike Wordsworth – or Dante or Johnson – Arnold must smear the face of pop with the ashes of anarchy in order to glorify by contrast a "culture" to which it is opposed only polemically. After Dante, and certainly after Johnson and Wordsworth, there is no difference between culture and anarchy. To maintain it is sheer opportunism. It is what has ensured Arnold's fame.

One can trace Arnoldean conservatism into the twentieth century by any number of routes. At the turn of the last century, Arnold was on everyone's lips, and bookshelves. He was a defense against the "anarchy" of a rising bourgeoisie with dubious taste, and of a newly enfranchised working class with no taste at all. One telltale example is an edition of Arnold's prose published in 1898 in the United States by Lewis Gates, an instructor at Harvard with whom the young Frank

Norris had come to study after graduating from the University of California in 1894. Gates's enthusiasm for Arnold is fulsome and embarrassing. To Gates, the beloved Arnold is almost radical, "stylistically jaunty," as he puts it in his preface, and intellectually "Non-conformist" (1898, xv). Arnold's hostility to the established "Church of opinion" (xv) – Gates's own "jaunty" diction is presumably Arnoldean – is self-evident. How parochial established cultural values still are! Arnold's cultivation, by contrast, is liberal, not aristocratic. It sorts among "material facts" – it is "scientific" (xix) – not among prejudices to arrive at its conclusions. "Culture" (xxi), quite accurately, is what Arnold wishes to put, quite ironically, "before the popular imagination" (xxii). The cultural managing is to be done through non-recognition and enforced difference. This is indeed a good description of the structure of one's assimilation into "culture" in the classical sense, particularly as a manager or producer of it. The metaphor of Non-Conformism runs throughout Gates's preface and leads to another kind of irony. "The spiritual qualities of literature" (li), he says, are often presented with such a "strenuousness" of "moral purpose" (lix) that their own clarity becomes, from the point of view of Arnold's prose style, obscured by its muscularity. One has been here before. This is the structure of Arnold's influence. Whether it is presenting "culture" to the "popular imagination" or matching up the "ideal" with the "moral," Arnold is, as Gates shows, always on paradoxical ground. These are immeasurable differences because they can be measured in too many ways. If culture and anarchy, like black and white, are reciprocal products, so, too, is Gates's own Arnoldean distinction between culture and the popular imagination. Arnold's disciples, whether Gates at Harvard or, much later on, Trilling at Columbia, seek their own visions of culture by trying to balance the vicissitudes in Arnold's own.

"The Battle of the Brows"

Among the High Moderns, it is Virginia Woolf, not surprisingly, who sums up both the shape and the comic absurdities of the history of high and low before it once again becomes a glum one in the pages of *Partisan Review* in the United States. Woolf makes the structure of its terms pellucid. Woolf's moment of vision comes in 1932, in a letter to the *New Statesman* that she did not send (Cuddy-Keane, 2003). Published only posthumously, in 1942, it is a response to a nasty review of *The Waves* (1931). Woolf's complaint is that the reviewer fails to include the word "highbrow" among her vices.

Even in her humor, Woolf is a common reader, a Johnsonian. She regards the distinction between high and low with suspicion, but will use its terms for burlesque purposes. Here she inspects, not Mr Bennett, not Mrs Brown, but Mr Brown. Mr Brown is a bus conductor. Woolf studies him to see "what it is like" to be a "lowbrow" (1932, 178). "Lowbrows" are, she assures us, the material of novels, not only for Arnold Bennett, but also for Virginia Woolf. Everyone is a "lowbrow." The list of candidates to show "what it is like" to be one is a long list:

> … being the conductor, being a woman with ten children and thirty-five shillings a week, being a stock broker, being an admiral, being a bank clerk, being a dressmaker, being a duchess, being a miner, being a cook, being a prostitute. (178)

"Highbrows" – whatever that is – "need lowbrows," says Woolf, "and honour them." "Lowbrows," in turn, "need highbrows" (178). The history of high and low makes sense because the reciprocity of its two terms is finally described without prejudice. Woolf explains the chain of epistemological reciprocities that we have had to dig out of our earlier texts:

> The very donkeys in the fields do nothing but bray it, the very curs in the streets do nothing but bark it – "Highbrows hate lowbrows! Lowbrows hate highbrows!" – when highbrows need lowbrows, when lowbrows need highbrows, when they cannot exist apart, when one is the complement and other side of the other! How has such a lie come into existence? Who has set this malicious gossip afloat? (179)

History now has a police agent to enforce the distinction by being its "go-between" or mediator. This policeman's name gives Woolf's unpublished essay its title – the "middlebrow." The policeman is an undercover policeman.

> They are the go-betweens; they are the busybodies who run from one to the other with their tittle tattle and make all the mischief – the middlebrows, I repeat. But what, you may ask, is a middlebrow? And that, to tell the truth, is no easy question to answer. They are neither one thing nor the other. They are not highbrows, whose brows are high; nor lowbrows, whose brows are low. Their brows are betwixt and between. They do not live in Bloomsbury which is on high ground; nor in Chelsea, which is on low ground. Since they must live somewhere presumably, they live perhaps in South Kensington, which is betwixt and between. The middlebrow is the man, or woman, of middlebred intelligence who ambles and saunters now on this side of the hedge, now on that, in pursuit of no single object, neither art itself nor life itself, but both mixed indistinguishably, and rather nastily, with money, fame, power, or prestige. The middlebrow curries favor with both sides equally. (179–80)

"The point" to Woolf is "clear." The differential nature of taste ought to be recognized, and the tone of taste changed.

> The true battle in my opinion lies not between highbrow and lowbrow, but between highbrows and lowbrows joined together in blood brotherhood against the bloodless and pernicious pest who comes between. If the B.B.C. stood for anything but the Betwixt and Between Company they would use their control of the air not to stir strife between brothers, but to broadcast the fact that highbrows and lowbrows must band together to exterminate a pest which is the bane of all thinking and living. (184)

The "middlebrow," however, has come out on top. The policeman ensures both culture and anarchy, the punishment and the crime. The reciprocity of high and low is inevitable, and an enduring feature of the cultural landscape. It also allows the management of taste to occur.

"Kitsch"

The Arnoldean tradition of "high" and "low" reaches its historical climax with Clement Greenberg's essay "Avant-Garde and Kitsch," published in *Partisan Review* in 1939. Trilling's biography of Arnold, also published in 1939, made his own identification with Arnold very clear. As a group, *Partisan Review* upheld Arnoldean cultural values despite its political communism. Indeed, it prided itself on carrying both burdens at the same time, however awkward was the gait this required. This was also its most compelling, if inadvertent, moment of Jewish humor. It made Woolf's assessment of high and low as reciprocal equally amusing despite the New York insistence on keeping them separate, and keeping a straight face. This paradox has long been an object of consternation and of some study (Freedman, 2000), but its contradictions remain. These, too, are familiar. Like Arnold, Greenberg uses each term of the historical opposition in order, first and foremost, to invoke the other.

There is "a disparity," says Greenberg, even in "a single cultural tradition" (1939, 3). His example is both resonant and problematic: "a poem by T.S. Eliot and a Tin Pan Alley song" (3). What is the difference? Eliot is self-conscious and strategic; Tin Pan Alley is formulaic – deaf, dumb, and blind, like The Who's Tommy. He also, quite to the detriment of his own argument, reveals something he should not: that there is a "relationship between aesthetic experience as met by the specific ... individual, and the social and historical contexts in which that experience takes place" (3). As a historian of culture, Greenberg tells us just what Arnold does not. Values, historically, in art and culture alike, emerge through contrasts within specific contexts. Even value is "simply the latest term in a succession of orders" (4). The relationship between Eliot and Tin Pan Alley, however, is self-evident, especially so with a poem like *The Waste Land*, where their relationship is actually thematized, at once complementary or supplemental, and entirely distinct. Like Eliot, Greenberg is clever enough to see this supplementarity, but also policeman enough to be inclined to mask and control it.

This leaves the critic in an oddly free position. The critic may be like Virginia Woolf and refuse to fall prey to "contexts" when they police culture. The critic may also choose between these perspectives. Greenberg, of course, chooses, as Arnold does. He chooses to emphasize the contrast in the "disparity" between Eliot and Tin Pan Alley rather than the complementarity that puts both sides of the "disparity" in place. The praise this position allows Greenberg to heap on the emergence of avant-garde culture in the twentieth century, and on the bohemianism that is its ancestor in the nineteenth, is considerable. But his argument also has a downside: Art must lose its relation to life, at least to the life of the mainstream, or the "general converse." Avant-garde art seeks "the absolute" in "'abstract'" or "'non-objective'" art (5). What happens, then, to communism – to art's social status, including its many "contexts," which are social?

These contradictions do not elude Greenberg. Because "the absolute is the absolute," however, the ironic tone is muzzled. But it is still audible. "The poet or artist, being what he is, cherishes certain relative values more than others" (6). The result is a return to form – to comparative form – as a route *to* history rather than away from it. It is a formalist argument, but it is also a historicist one. All the "absolute" artist can do is to revise the history of the medium in which he works. Is this a formal or historical proposition? It is both. The artist "turns out to be imitating, not God … but the disciplines and processes of art and literature themselves" (6). But no sooner is history invoked than it is denied. "The world of common, extraverted experience" – the Jungian term "extraverted" is surprising to find in the pages of *Partisan Review* – "has been renounced" (6). Both modern painting and modern poetry "derive their chief inspiration from the medium they work in," not from "common … experience" (7). This distinction, too, is problematic. For Johnson or Wordsworth, art and experience are continuous. Art is part of experience, and the forms of experience part of art. Here, however, the question of the epistemological and the psychological relation between art and life remains unasked, even in a presumably "historical" formalism like Greenberg's own. "Avant-garde culture is the imitation of imitating" (8). Fine. But what is the link between the history of imitation and the way one sees experience? This latter also has a history that Greenberg only claims to care about. He doesn't have time. "Culture" is "threatened" (8).

Like Arnold, Greenberg has to invoke a foil for "culture" – his avant-garde – to battle against. "High" and "low" are still there, but with new names. "Where there is an avant-garde," says Greenberg, "generally we also find a rear-garde" (9). The name that Greenberg gives this "rear-garde" signifies all that is low, tasteless, and vulgar: "kitsch" (9). Tin Pan Alley remains chief among Greenberg's examples, and so do, surprisingly, "Hollywood movies" (9). Greenberg's "avant-garde" and "kitsch" are Arnold's "culture" and "anarchy."

So systematic are Greenberg's prejudices that he invokes the historical distinction between "formal culture" and "folk culture" (9) as an early version of avant-garde and kitsch. Universal literacy does not close the gap between high and low as it does for Johnson. It widens it. Kitsch is the "debased simulation of real culture." It is "mechanical and it operates by formulas" (10). The similarity to Adorno's condemnation of the popular is startling. Adorno himself has already weighed in on the subject, and finds kitsch useful as a historical measure. Recalling that the word derives from the English word "sketch," "all real kitsch," says Adorno, "has the character of a *model*" (1932, 501).

To say, as Greenberg does, that kitsch becomes "an integral part of our production system in a way in which true culture could never be, except accidentally" (1939, 11), is to miss the point. Kitsch, as Greenberg has said, is itself a theft of real culture. Kitsch therefore shows how fundamental a misreading of canonical culture is to its own maintenance. Culture at its widest depends on culture at its most elevated. Culture here is, as it is in Johnson, an endless series of misreadings of prior texts on a continuous field, not a "disparity" between and among qualitatively different things. "Kitsch," says Adorno, "is the precipitate of devalued forms" (1932, 501).

Greenberg fails to ask the really interesting question that now emerges: What is the exact relation between culture and kitsch that makes them require one another? Why, perhaps more interestingly, does it also make kitsch a function of culture? This question is not, however, Greenberg's concern either. The essay grows more polemical

42

and less analytic as it switches genre in its peroration and becomes the Arnoldean – and Eliotic – homily that it really is:

> All values are human values, relative values, in art as well as elsewhere. Yet there does seem to have been more or less of a general agreement among the cultivated of mankind over the ages as to what is good art and what bad. Taste has varied, but not beyond certain limits; contemporary connoisseurs agree with the eighteenth-century Japanese that Hokusai was one of the greatest artists of his time; we even agree with the ancient Egyptians that Third and Fourth Dynasty art was the most worthy of being selected as their paragon by those who came after. We may have come to prefer Giotto to Raphael, but we still do not deny that Raphael was one of the best painters of his time. There has been an agreement then, and this agreement rests, I believe, on a fairly constant distinction made between those values only to be found in art and the values which can be found elsewhere. Kitsch, by virtue of a rationalized technique that draws on science and industry, has erased this distinction in practice. (1939, 13)

Greenberg's blindness goes hand-in-hand with his insight. "If the avant-garde imitates the processes of art, kitsch … imitates its effects" (15). Here, in one sentence, Greenberg predicts the future history of reception theory and of psychoanalytic accounts of the relation between reader and text, putting reader and text on a single, sliding scale that is social and aesthetic simultaneously. This distinction between "processes" and "effects," if it is one, is astonishingly subtle, and provides a way out of the very difficult, and very absorbing, critical problems that Greenberg has raised. Here Greenberg's argument is closer to my own than it is to Arnold's. Form is central to Greenberg and has its own immanent history that is determinate and determining. This is true not only for the history of a given medium, but also for the way the medium in question affects the history of feeling and perception on a wider social scale.

But Greenberg is not interested. The Arnoldean laments obscure what is most perspicacious in his essay. Kitsch is bad because it is the enjoyment of art "without effort" (18). It is, in other words, a version of religion. It is pop at its mightiest. This is a fine definition of religion as a whole, and one to which I will recur throughout these pages. This means, of course, that Greenberg's own pleasure in modernism is not only a "difficult" one, to use Eliot's word, but, finally, one filled with the good schoolboy's self-regarding certainty that a thing is important because a show of effort is required to do it. This means that it is not pop. Greenberg's genealogy as a critic is clear when he punctuates the essay with one of Arnold's most notorious tropes for the laggard pop: "Philistine" (20). The use of the Arnoldean term is itself an example of kitsch.

The Myth of Popular Culture

The philosophical apogee of the resistance to pop comes in 1953. This moment is the infamous one we have been waiting for, the publication of Theodor Adorno's third essay on jazz, far more vituperative than his first two, in 1933 and in 1936, and far less accommodating than his encyclopedia article on jazz in 1942. Together with "On Popular Music" (1941) and the *Introduction to the Sociology of Music* (1962), "Perennial Fashion – Jazz" (1953) contains Adorno's central criticism of pop culture as a whole, and, more to the point, his particular, and very useful, reasons for it. Adorno provides, however negatively and indirectly, the philosophical basis we need with which to clarify and classify the logical terms of virtually any resistance to pop. Adorno's argument describes equally well the early moments of this resistance in the history of high and low and, at its most contemporary, today's arguments by New Hipsters, for example, about whether or not the artist is required to be self-conscious about his or her appropriated materials. Right or wrong, Adorno at least provides a technical philosophical reason for why he thinks a difference between high and low exists. He may be in error – I will show that he is – but his procedure is at least a critical one, however unsound it may be empirically. His texts and contexts alike are beyond the grasp of his ability to read them. Friend of the worker, Adorno is nonetheless a brickheaded snob on the question of the "popular" in art and in culture. Confronting him on this subject is a belated version of storming the barricades. Doing so in a serious rather than sardonic way – Robert Miklitsch's *Roll Over Adorno* (2006) is a good example of such a bad sense of humor – allows one to retain the valuable dialectical machinery required for the job. Adorno's durable relevance, particularly when he is read dialectically, or "against himself," is clear in other recent estimates (Haverkamp, 2008).

If "Perennial Fashion – Jazz" is a good introduction to the larger problems presented by the *Sociology of Music*, "On Popular Music," written in English and published 3 years after Adorno settled in New York in 1938, is a good introduction to the problems of "Perennial Fashion." Here sociology and musicology combine to produce a theory of "pop" that is affirmative for the very reasons Adorno thinks they are negative. The difference between "popular" and "serious" music, of course – it comes as no surprise – is the difference between "lowbrow" and "highbrow" (1941, 441). The "tension" (441) that "serious" music produces between what is already known and what is newly presented to the listener is the source of its value. The differences it requires the listener to become conscious of, whether within the piece or between a given piece and other "serious" music, is precisely what popular music simulates but does not really secure. A motif in *Parsifal* remains "unmistakable and not exchangeable for anything else," whereas it is "repetition" alone that makes a pop song recognizable (447). It does not occur to Adorno that this is not a capitulation, unlike Stravinsky, to the "standardization" that "mass production" presumably introduces into modern life, but, rather, a way of addressing standardization as itself a basic dimension of social and musical reality. By calling pop music a "handicraft" masquerading as an "industrial" art (445), he makes two mistakes in one: that pre-modern life is somehow more immediate than industrial life, and that pre-modern life is not, despite the hegemony of religion in particular, also a standardized affair. Because of this illusion, "standardization," and its child, "stylization" (444), are both historical aberrations rather than aspects of actual historical process. "Mass production" simply shifts the standardization to a machine technology from a more laborious manual kind, which is psychologically more standardizing than the conformism promoted by industrial

45

mass production. Indeed, pop's "standardization of its own deviation" (445) from precedents it has itself created makes it an achievement not less but more impressive than the individuation of expression represented by Mozart or Beethoven in relation to the norms from which they more happily deviate, whether in relation to past music, or to prior moments in their own. Adorno's Nietzschean word for this dialectical operation in "serious" music is "transvaluate" (440).

This dialectical transvaluation is also what pop does, although against a transistorized background. Pop's deviation from its backgrounds is more microscopic than is Beethoven's. Like modern art and sculpture, it is minimalist. It saves more of the past in less time and space than does "serious" music, different from it not in kind but in degree. "It is precisely the relationship between the recognized and the new," Adorno says, "which is destroyed" (453). In point of fact, it is precisely this relationship – a decidedly dialectical one – that pop heightens. Individuation in Beethoven is clamorous; individuation in Benny Goodman – Adorno does not yet have Miles Davis to use as an example – is, because of the narrowing of the field of difference from both the past and within given compositions, shockingly enough, more subtle. It is what Donald Barthelme, describing a similar technique in metafiction, calls "microminiaturization" (1970, 38). As Adorno's essay concludes, one wonders whether it is the pop listener who is full of unconscious "fury" and "frustration" (1941, 462), or whether it is Adorno who is. For Adorno, background and foreground are indistinguishable in pop dialectic. He has lost the German background familiar to him because of Nazism. As it is for any refugee, the foreground of New York is largely a blur.

The return to Germany in 1949, however, makes little difference. Adorno's typically Marxist contention that all popular music is lifeless and commodified actually derives from his Eurocentric measure of all things musical against classical time signatures and the authority of the maestro rather than the groove. Despite "the ostensibly disruptive principle of syncopation," jazz, he says, never really disturbs its "rudimentary ... formal structure," "the identically sustained metre, the quarter-note" (1953, 121). And yet before the essay's first paragraph is done, Adorno describes jazz structure in these very terms. The simple

46

fact of syncopation puts jazz in a call-and-response relation to classical music, which it revises at its most basic level, the articulation of time. Even in later jazz, distinguished for Adorno by its "commercial ... smoothness," jazz form is "so entrenched that an entire generation of youth hears only syncopation without being aware of the original conflict between it and the basic metre" (121). That is just the point. Adorno's criticism of jazz structure is surprising. It is not really a criticism. It is a good description, although with a wrong-headed tone. Every jazz enthusiast is aware of this "original conflict," however much it is taken for granted. Indeed, the more taken for granted it is, the more self-evident the distinction is in the lived experience of listening. This is also a fine example of Adorno's own notion of "negative dialectic." The "basic metre" – the maestro – is always present in every jazz utterance that violates its authority. Any act of defense carries in its wake the unconscious ghost from which it seeks to flee. This "double consciousness" – perhaps it is more accurate to call it a difference between consciousness and the unconscious in the listener – is what structures the very sound of jazz. It is to be found in the listener rather than in the textual object. Indeed, there is, as there never is, no "object." There is the listener's response, which is governed by unconscious knowledge, and which puts the object in place as a reaction to it. Like normative "high discourses," jazz discourse has an endless relation with tradition, in this case the history of classical music. Its appeal rests in a temporal doubleness based on expectation and denial. The departure, however "unchanged" (121) Adorno may judge it to be in itself, is nonetheless always a change at the level of principle and institution. Moreover, "the identically sustained metre" of "the quarter-note" is by definition impossible to sustain in a jazz environment in the first place. What Adorno himself calls the "original conflict" with classical time that defines jazz always introduces another fraction of difference into the simplest Tin Pan Alley reprise of a verse or a chorus. The conflict between the swinging and non-swinging quarter-note is endlessly revisionary. Difference results inevitably from sheer repetition. Hip hop is the best example.

To call jazz "static" (121) is therefore to miss the point. As Adorno digs into the sociological roots of jazz, he once again describes its double structure, this time in a historical key. But once again, he fails to grasp how well his material exemplifies his own notions of historical process at its most refined: "The Negro spirituals, antecedents of the blues" – this common assumption is, by the way, an arguable point historically, as I will show later on – "were slave songs and as such, combined the lament of unfreedom with its oppressed confirmation" (122). Adorno has no affection for his own very shrewd description of double structure in jazz procedure, especially the sedimented history it addresses and revises in its every gesture. Adorno is not, however, interested, any more than Greenberg is, in this kind of thing. His rich description of jazz is followed by this unlikely conclusion: "The perennial sameness of jazz consists not in a basic organization of the material with which the imagination can roam freely and without inhibition, as within an articulate language, but rather in the utilization of certain well-defined tricks, formulas, and clichés to the exclusion of everything else" (123). Jazz is not even "an articulate language" – slaves, after all, initiated its practice – even though its structure is no less than a rudimentary instance of the basic structure of any language: the use of "recipes" (123). "Contingent and arbitrary" (124) may be meant as negative; in point of fact, they are the exact preconditions of any language in the relation of its signs to time and history on the one hand – "contingent" – and to metaphysics on the other – "arbitrary." Despite his odd conclusions about them, Adorno's descriptions are accurate.

Nor is Adorno's essay without an overt connection to the history of high and low. Even jazz listeners are divided into high and low. There are aficionados and there are toe-tappers, avant-garde listeners and mainstream ones. Like Greenberg, Adorno believes avant-gardism to be the last fortress of culture in a fallen world of kitsch and stylization. Here come the familiar terms. "The organization of culture," says Adorno, "into ... low, middle, and highbrow" (127) cannot be "overcome ... simply by the lowbrow sects declaring themselves to be highbrow" (127). When all is said and done, jazz avant-gardism, too, is, alas, still lowbrow. Examples of "mass production" (127) such as jazz are not the same as the real avant-gardism of Eliot and Joyce. What mass production is and what its relation to modernism is do not, however, present themselves to Adorno as the next step in his assessment of pop, or of avant-gardism. Instead, Adorno's fury rises at the prospect that the difference between high and low may well collapse. It is the familiar Arnoldean position that I have described:

> Anyone who allows the growing respectability of mass culture to seduce him into equating a popular song with modern art because of a few false notes squeaked by a clarinet; anyone who mistakes a triad studded with "dirty notes" for atonality, has already capitulated to barbarism. (127)

The unlikely emergence of a sexual metaphor sums up not Adorno's psychoanalysis of jazz – it is an obscure one, anyway – but instead reveals Adorno's own unconscious fantasy in regard to jazz's African roots:

> Psychoanalytic theory alone can provide an adequate explanation of this phenomenon. The aim of jazz is the mechanical reproduction of a regressive moment, a castration symbolism. "Give up your masculinity, let yourself be castrated," the eunuchlike sound of the jazz band both mocks and proclaims, "and you will be rewarded, accepted into a fraternity which shares the mystery of impotence with you, a mystery revealed at the moment of the initiation rite." (129)

The heat of the argument eventually drives Adorno to a wholesale projection of his wish for jazz as an institution. In a chain of metaphors that links castration and Philistinism, Adorno draws together our history of high and low in a vision of prejudice and stupidity worthy of Pope's *Dunciad*:

> In jazz, the Philistines standing over Samson are permanently transfigured. In truth, the Philistines. The castration symbolism, deeply buried in the practices of jazz and cut off from consciousness through the institutionalization of perennial sameness, is for that very reason probably all the more potent. And sociologically, jazz has the effect of strengthening and extending, down to the very physiology of the subject, the acceptance of a dreamless-realistic world in which all memories of things not wholly integrated have been purged. (130)

49

"Physiology" indeed. We are back to phrenology. "Jazz," Adorno concludes – we are also back to Arnold – "is the false liquidation of art" (132). The collapsing of high and low brims with ironies too amusing for the glum and haughty Adorno to enjoy. There are avant-garde possibilities in music that do not occur to him.

But the crux of Adorno's dismissal of jazz and, by implication, of blues tradition as a whole, comes in an astonishing passage on the difference between "higher music" and "popular" in the *Introduction to the Sociology of Music*. I have quoted part of this passage in my preface; it is so poetical, and so useful, that it should now be quoted in full:

> The higher music's relation to its historical form is dialectical. It catches fire on those forms, melts them down, makes them vanish and return in vanishing. Popular music, on the other hand, uses the types as empty cans into which the material is pressed without interacting with the forms. Unrelated to the forms, the substance withers and at the same time belies the forms, which no longer serve for compositional organization. (1962, 26)

Adorno's description of dialectic is stirring – classical music "catches fire on those forms, melts them down, makes them vanish and return in vanishing." So, even by Adorno's own description, does jazz. If the history of jazz is anything, it is "dialectical." Far from using its "types as empty" – the metaphor is typically flattering – jazz and its musical heirs take the "forms" that enable them as their very subject. This includes the classical time signatures from which they depart. They "return in vanishing." Even the distinction between "form" and "material" in any kind of music is misleading, since music has no semantic plane that it signifies, only an endless series of "formal" ones. The "vulgarity" that Adorno assigns to "popular music" is unfounded. What is vulgar is the analysis and the presupposition.

The master dialectician's condemnation of pop music is central to the stance of the *Sociology*, since it gives its defense of a "higher" tradition in music a foil against which to measure itself and a prop against which to stand. The pop music fan is not "a good listener" (5). "A good listener," says Adorno, may not be an "expert," but has nonetheless "unconsciously mastered its immanent logic." Such a listener understands music the way one understands common language: "virtually or wholly ignorant of its grammar and syntax" (5). Adorno is at odds with himself. He has described the pop fan in the same way, despite denying the fact of jazz's own "immanent logic." Pop has no structures of immanence. It is not dialectical. The Freudian vocabulary of the *Sociology* is also severe, and for what seem to be obscure reasons. "Jazz remains imprisoned within narrow bounds" – the "syncopic" beat is, as before, the principal reason – because jazz is so entirely implicated in a "bondage to authority" (13). One way of regarding this is as dialectic. Another way – a very similar way – is Freudian. Their structures are the same, although Adorno does not note this fact. With jazz, he says, there is a "more … Oedipal touch in the Freudian sense: it is a kind of backtalk to the father in which readiness to knuckle under is already implied" (13). To be sure.

This is the perennial wager of freedom about whose terms jazz does not prevaricate. It is not only the essence, as it were, of jazz. It is also the essence, if I may put it that way, of dialectic itself. It is also Oedipal. It is a conversation with the authorities. Why does this not authorize jazz rather than condemn it in Adorno's mind? "Standardization" is what makes pop debased. Pop's "vulgarity" (27) derives from the fact of its "mass production" (26). As I noted before, this assumption suggests, now as before, that other forms of music must not be mass produced, this despite their avowed and, for the sake of sense, necessary systematicity. The production of cello players in the nineteenth century and of jazz musicians in the twentieth is an institutional difference, not a difference in kind. Adorno the dialectician has a double rhetoric; he suppresses the fact of jazz dialectic in order to create his own dialectic with the tradition of resisting pop. As a descriptive critic, however, Adorno is once again shrewd: "Standardization" is simply the regular structure of the pop song with its many variations of "32 bars with a 'bridge,' a part initiating the repetition, in the middle" (25). Of course, this "repetition" – the chorus – is never really a "repetition," especially when a bridge is involved. The fractioning of the beat, as Adorno has already observed, opens up its presumable formulaicism to endless potential differences from itself. Chorus and bridge alike are always different when heard again. After their first statements, each subsequent hearing amends the one before it when the listener experiences its repetition. Attack, mood, and orchestration all guarantee empirically this musical inevitability. The addition of lyrics heightens it. Repetition is never repetition, not despite but because of the "narrow bounds" that Adorno regards as only negative. It *is* negative – negatively dialectical.

2

Pop Culture in the Spectator

Poems of the People

Adorno's double or ambivalent stance is a mirror of our own ambivalence – perhaps a necessary one – in maintaining unconsciously the difference between high and low. Here the dialectic of father and son, master and slave, inscribed in jazz syncopation, finds an exact and refined character in the formal precondition of jazz as a medium. Dialectic is an inevitable function of the pop song's own temporality as a given object as well as its precondition as a new, post-classical form of music for which syncopation is the frame. This is not taken up by Adorno at all; its very possibility is dismissed. Pop may set up a system of "conditioned reflexes in its victim," he says, but "the crux" is so negligible that it "is not even" – not even – "the antithesis of primitivity and differentiation" (1962, 29). This, of course, is an especially insulting instance of the difference between high and low in all its ancient garb.

The secret finally comes out. Everyone does indeed know better. Properly speaking, there is no difference between the "popular" and the "higher" for a simple reason: All traditions are dialectical. Jazz is, as Adorno himself has shown. So is dread television. Whether it is the relation between *Mary Tyler Moore* and *The Dick Van Dyke Show* or between *I Dream of Jeannie* and *Bewitched*, the revisionary ratios are manifest for any viewer interested in the history of the medium. I will take this kind of dialectical behavior as the organizing principle of my histories of three pop forms in Part II. Behaviorally, or empirically, the

53

ceaseless transfigurations in the history of "popular culture" reveal something else, too: the presence of canonical figures who manage historical overdeterminations and anxieties of influence. Canonicity must be our next business. It is what determines what texts are paradigmatic for practice, and what texts we study, in any field. Canonicity is the agency of history. Canons are not imposed and they are not elitist. Nor are they the work of "authors" in an intentional, biographical, or even phenomenological way. They are, as Barthes says, functions. They are simply instances of this necessity, and of their own readability. Chuck Berry's transformation of big-band boogie woogie into the jump sound of rock and roll guitar is what makes him canonical, not the imposition upon him of a "moral" or "thematic" role from outside the terms of his medium. He is canonical because he transforms material, to use Adorno's own vocabulary, dialectically.

In *The Cowboy and the Dandy* (1999), I argued that canons and pop formations had a dialectical and causal relationship. From my description of Adorno's very different intention, it is clear, despite his polemic, that this remains the case. In Adorno's formulation, the dialectical implications for the reader's active participation in discourse are also plain. What better way to organize a notion of popular culture, particularly consumer culture, than through dialectic? Faced, for example, with the uncanny familiarity of the alien invaders in Byron Haskin's *War of the Worlds* (1953), the mind drifts to David Smith's *Tanktotem I* (1952), an avant-garde sculpture with considerable influence, although only within the presumably confined precincts of "high" culture. Smith's sculpture and Haskin's Martian warships look the same. In *War of the Worlds*, the influence of "high" culture makes its way to the neighborhood screen.

The example of Shakespeare, however, is always best: Shakespeare is the most popular way of displaying one's erudition, and the most erudite way of displaying one's knowledge of what is enduringly popular. Shakespeare is high and – as one never forgets to say – also endearingly low. He is everything. Here alone, with the exception perhaps of religion, does pop get a proper hearing. Shakespeare dialectically processes all past canons, and becomes the dialectical soil for all future English writing. The plays always outstrip any generic occasion they may stage, simultaneously banishing authority and letting the repressed return. This dynamic is thematized in Shakespeare's very plots, which collide or overlay generic states in persons as well as in poetry, in situations as well as in sound. Shakespeare is the best example of Adorno's dialectical effect. According to Walter Benjamin (1928), Shakespeare is the actual inventor, historically, of the kind of reconception of history that Adorno describes as dialectic. Shakespeare's use of his historical raw materials, says Benjamin, is the *sine qua non* of how dialectical texts produce their particular effect. Anselm Haverkamp gives an excellent description of Shakespearean process from this point of view:

> Every new observation in a text, brought from its latency into a manifest state, does so thanks to a radical de-contextualization, which must occur before interpretation can become fertile again in the light of historical details and produce a new historical context. Every new reading of literature allows history to be rewritten. This is what makes it literary: that it allows the old stories in history to be reconceived and rewritten. As part of its ongoing legacy, Shakespeare's theater revolutionized this rewriting of history, and re-conceptualized the function of literature – its ability to reconceive of history – in the epochal sense of a Copernican revolution. (2006, 172)

Dialectical behavior may be sharpest in Shakespeare, but the history of religion remains the *locus classicus* for this dialecticism at its most paradoxical. Is religion "high" or "low" culture? The term "canon" comes from the medieval church, whose intellectual elite formulated doctrine carried out in the practice of daily religion among the masses. Even the new direction medieval studies has taken toward an interest in an independent peasant Christianity and also in a women's Christianity (Bartlett, 1995; Elliott, 2004) traces less a departure from the movement of canon into practice than it does another, more radical and more structurally complex form of dialectic: a reaction to the "canonical," also determined by it, though in an antithetical rather than disseminative way. While not feminist, and very familiar, the Reformation is, of course, the best wide-scale example, with the many subsequent reformations within Protestantism instances of its own principal energies. The Levellers, who come to deny the need for Jesus in the search for a direct relation to God, are when the options finish running their course. Even this is to be naïve. Religion is the kind of formation that Foucault calls a "discursive practice" rather than, as one might expect, a "transdiscursive" formation, which involves simply following the rules (1969, 131–2). It feeds off repartee and revolt, consternation and conversation with its sources. Even carrying out instructions involves a shift from *langue* to *parole*, ideal to real, normative to exaggerated. The structure of obedience is also, epistemologically, a structure of difference from itself. The secularization of the believer's direct relation to God is the invention of Romanticism. Romanticism is secularized religion, when religion disappears by crossing the bar into culture as a whole. This is also the historical moment, as I noted in my preface, at which "culture" in the modern sense is invented. It unifies society afresh, and makes it religious in a new way – by splitting the world into good and evil again. This is the burden of Matthew Arnold's labor. In this sense, all of Anglophone culture is Protestant, and all of Protestant culture, *mutatis mutandis*, is an endless facsimile or misreading of Roman Catholic culture. When pop culture revives the world of Gothic iconography early in the twenty-first century, this continuity reasserts itself with renewed vigor and self-evidence.

Religion as an institution and as a practice breaks down the line between high and low that, even in the Roman Catholic model, it also maintains. The difference between canon and parishioners, priest and penitent is the linguistic one between competence and execution, model and function. This is the structure of Dante's vernacular, a cross, as it were, of the ideal and the specific. To use the Renaissance term for the representation of Jesus, it involves the "humanation" of the divine. This is why the *Commedia* is the greatest of the Christian poems. Dante's pilgrim is humble, wholly in possession, through a local language calculated to receive a divine truth, of this broken line, of the lack of distinction between high and low. Only the terms of Dante's strategy are new; the dialectical strategy is not. In its origins, Christianity dialectically transforms the Greek canon from a generic point of view, using the measured narratives of Athens to reshape the visionary narratives of Jerusalem into a single, combined Greek narrative. Jesus's "low" or pastoral biography is recast or redeemed as tragedy by his suffering and death. An "elevated" Greek genre revises the meaning of a "low" one. A grand effect emerges at its end to redact its humble beginnings. It produces divine truth on the backs of donkeys. Christ's pathos derives from deferred action. The Passion throws its shadow back over the earlier part of Jesus's biography. It has a coherence and a trajectory only in the light of the suffering and death that completes it. We know this effect as typological.

Canons and "Camp"

Thus a view of popular culture based in canons ensures a place – a constitutive one – for the reader or spectator. It is the reader or spectator, says Barthes, who produces the author, retroactively, but also as proof that readership has occurred, with all its stability and coherence. We know from German literary criticism in recent years that the reader is, to use Wolfgang Iser's term, necessarily "implied" by the text (1974). The reader completes, realizes, or, indeed, performs the text, which is otherwise without being, and certainly without effective cause. Only a reader can stir a text into life by activating its messages – by providing it its addressee. How does the reader do this? In the same way that the writer writes, or the painter paints, or the guitarist plays. The "author" is a reader, too, and responds to tradition with that very active form of readership called artistic production. Without it, the author remains a person and the world surrenders a text. If cultural products function by screening an earlier "high" form with a later "pop" form, what is it that the reader reads and who is it that the reader is, or will become? Texts place themselves in contexts in order to be readable. Readers are placed in contexts in order to be citizens. Readers are invited to organize the texts they read by seeing or hearing the overlay. Readers are inscribed into canons, and canons live because of the life that readers give them. Despite its difference in stance and tone, this is Adorno's own definition of the relation of low culture to high – that the former is, to use William Jennings Bryan's phrase, a "leak through," or "trickle-down," effect of the latter. Revivals of Bryan's phrase from his "Cross of Gold" speech at the Democratic Convention in Chicago in 1896 by Herbert Hoover and Ronald Reagan are examples of it. Although Bryan does not believe in it, his own influence, like his own rhetoric, testifies to the notion's reality in the sphere of superstructure or ideology (Michaels, 1987). This model reverses the familiar one proposed by Raymond Williams (1973), in which the "residual" idiolects of "dominant" ideology are replaced over time with newer, "emergent" ones. It is actually the other way around. One recalls Greenberg's surprisingly generous belief in 1939 that kitsch – a fair synonym for what Adorno means by the "popular" – derives from high-culture products.

Adorno's sense of how hegemony operates through kitsch is, as it is for Greenberg, the best model we have for understanding it. Kitsch is a fine example of the "trickle-down" effect. Greenberg is willing to concede kitsch a place on the map, but as an outmoded and useless cultural form. He underestimates the value of this uselessness. Adorno, however, is willing to grant kitsch the more active status it really has. This is because kitsch has a decidedly functional role to play in history. Derived from the English word "sketch," kitsch, one remembers, is, in Adorno's words, no less than "the precipitate of devalued forms." It is also unconscious, or "subconscious," as Adorno usually puts it when using a psychoanalytic vocabulary. Kitsch is a kind of pop unconscious. This pop unconscious, or kitsch "precipitate," is full of significance. "All real kitsch," says Adorno, has "the character of a *model*" (1932, 501). This "model" is invariably an exaggeration of some kind, public, fossilized, embarrassing. This is what Bakhtin calls "stylization," an exaggeration of any kind at all. Art and experience both possess funds of kitsch, or "stylization." Psychologically, they come mostly in the form of identifications, as Frantz Fanon points out (1952). These are the unconscious precipitates that serve as "cultures," if I may pun, in which new life and new art can develop from the husks of the old.

The history of television's dialectical relation to past forms is a particularly familiar example of this trickle-down effect, and a vivid example of the way even the rudest of pop forms has a constitutive relation to precise canonical precedent. Unlike film, television, despite its visuality, comes largely from the history of theater. *The Honeymooners*, with its own disciple in *The Flintstones*, derives from a misreading, in

Harold Bloom's sense, of its own period context in American realist theater, especially Arthur Miller. Ralph Kramden is the farcical repetition of Willy Loman. The dialectical wit is considerable. Willy Loman is already a farcical repetition of himself. Seinfeld's farcical relation to inherited forms even includes a relation to Miller whenever he calls George "Biff." The allusion identifies George for what he is – a repetition of Ralph Kramden – and *Seinfeld* itself, with neighbors coming and going in a New York apartment house, a repetition of *The Honeymooners.* As a comedian, Seinfeld's own dialectic includes a revision of the tradition of Jewish stand-up; it is a revision in tone. Perplexity leads no longer to anxiety, as it does in Jack Benny, Lenny Bruce, or Woody Allen, but to insouciance and the postmodern decision that the requirements of form are neither here nor there. They are simply given. To say that the scrim for *Seinfeld* is really Beckett is not only to give this history of situation comedy an almost self-evident "high culture" counterpart; it is also to suggest a dialectical source for this "low" form of ghetto lamentation in avant-garde art. The final episode of *Seinfeld,* showing the four principals in a jail cell, makes explicit the fact that we have been watching a Beckett play from the very start. Says Seinfeld in an earlier episode, espousing the "trickle-down" effect: "My entire knowledge of high culture comes from cartoons."

Of course, I have not yet asked the most obvious question of all. Is the relation between high and low itself a dialectic? The answer is simple. Of course it is. I have noted the reciprocal character of its terms throughout their history. I have also noted how dialectic, deferred action, and the Oedipus complex are all similar in structure. Now I should also note that the difference between high and low as a trope is a *chiasmus*, or a crossing over, a *contaminatio*, or contamination, of the categories employed. "High" needs to distinguish itself from "low" in order to be what it is, and, given our enthusiasm for a "pop" culture distinct from a "high" or learned one, "low" or "pop" also needs "high" to have its own presumably separate identity. The pop is a function of high culture, not its antithesis in any but a dialectical sense.

This notion of pop is Susan Sontag's, the product of her revision of Greenberg in "Notes on 'Camp,'" which also appeared in *Partisan Review,* 35 years later, in 1964. "Camp" is kitsch revised. At first blush it seems little better. It also assumes that someone has a superior perspective. While Sontag refuted Greenberg's position, she also enlarged it. The essay has a curious mixture of purpose, holding, as Woolf's letter does, the poles of the opposition between high and low in suspension. Like Woolf, and quite unlike Greenberg, Sontag wishes to discover an alternative to "the battle of the brows." She wishes to oppose something else to high culture than kitsch. It is "camp." No longer is the relevant opposition one between high and low, but one between high and camp. Most important is that this opposition it not an opposition. It is not a condemnation of high, and not an appreciation of pop. It is neither and it is both. "Camp," says Sontag, has "a witty meaning for cognoscenti, more impersonal – more non-existent – for outsiders" (1964, 281). Camp is not a style; it is a taste for style. The "logic of taste" that camp exhibits is one of "stylization" (277). It relishes exaggeration; not style, but the style of style. It is a dialectical pleasure.

Camp is the instrument that allows the ironies of the history of high and low to be balanced with reasonable grace. Camp is, in a phrase that gives us the picture of Keats that we have been looking for, "a seriousness that fails" (283). The failure is not, of course, a technical one. Despite Eliot's objections, *Hamlet* is a good play, and Keats a formidable poet. But in both cases it is the failure of seriousness that wins the day, and in a deeply serious way. *Hamlet's* own relation to Keats is an example of it. Keats is the play's biographical and poetic impersonation 200 years later – its human invention, as it were, its trickle-down effect. Camp's failures of seriousness are stacked under these kinds of overwhelming and exemplary ones. With camp, Keatsian failure and the reasons for it become the new center of attention. It is the thematization of failure that counts. It is the reversal of Beau Brummell's chronologically simultaneous thematization of success.

But camp is not the pop, even though camp can appreciate the pop at its best and at its worst. Like everything else, including "high" culture, camp is an exaggeration of a dialectically "vanishing" paradigm. Camp walks a tightrope of "double sense" (281). Camp is an example of the reciprocity rather than the rivalry between high and low. High and low alike can be – indeed, are, after Romanticism – camp. Camp's "double sense" is based, not on seeing oppositions, but on seeing something else. The reciprocity of high and low, of success and failure, spells doom for the faint of heart. Camp finds "pathos," not in tragedy as an accepted genre, but in tragedy as an unacceptable genre. Tragedy's moral seriousness cannot survive the pressure of its own moral interrogation when that interrogation is taken to its extreme. How can any genre be taken seriously, particularly tragedy, when it requires an exaltation of the sufferer to reach its aim? The tragic hero's exaltation through suffering is not true to life. Aristotle is quite wrong when he says that tragedy is the function of the hero's "error." Tragedy is the function of contingency, or mere accident. "The whole point of camp," writes Sontag, "is to dethrone the serious" in this precise way (288).

Is Sontag's essay itself an example of camp's "double sense"? It institutes a new ethics of meaning even if it is, as Sontag maintains throughout, an aesthetic one only. Of course, no opposition between ethics and the aesthetic is at work here. The assumption of an indifferent universe makes them one and the same. What remains is their reciprocity. *Hamlet* is both a serious and a popular play. It teaches above all that the language of the heart is likely to appear, as everything else does, "in quotation marks" (280). That is why the play's cadences are, as they are in Henry James, "excruciating" (287). The tale drives the character; the character's resistance to this fact, beginning with Hamlet himself, drives the tale.

Sontag's difference from Greenberg is clear, and very significant. With Sontag, a focus on form provides a return to a relation with real life; camp finds a new and accelerated relation to it. Art is not autonomous; it is everywhere. To point this out is what both pop and canonical form do at their most dialectical, and most democratic. One generation's canon is the next generation's camp. The two are, from the point of view of the reader, intertwined, and in a temporal dialectic. Canons are functionally inevitable. Canons require revolutions against them to produce the shadow of their own vanished authority, and to produce future histories.

M.M. Bakhtin's work (1929, 1975), so helpful in recent years in describing how central the reader is in text activation, is also a good example of a dialectical understanding of the sociological effects of kitsch. These latter I have already noted in relating Bakhtin to Adorno. Bakhtin's notion of "stylization" is also very close to the notion of

61

camp. Like camp, stylization is an exaggeration. But Bakhtin himself is also an example of kitsch. Bakhtin's work and his methods are double witness to the way that the canonical becomes the mythological. How? Bakhtin's own numerous intellectual agons are each kitsch allegories. His struggle with Soviet methodological orthodoxy is one example. His agon with Russian formalism – in its way also a sprint from Soviet materialism – is another, although it is a mask for the first. Bakhtin is indeed a socialist thinker from the point of view of a formalist poetics. Bakhtin discovers his view of the reader by turning Shklovsky's "defamiliarized" or "uncanny" reader (1917) into an intertextual or "dialogical" one. The chief evidence for Bakhtin's parallel struggle with Marxism is, of course, terminological. "Dialogical" is a misreading of "dialectical." It removes from dialectical thinking an interest in the generic or ideational forms that organize and direct the reader's journey through texts as wholes. One thinks of Lukács (1920). Bakhtin's insistence on textual polyphony is obviously true, but his inattention to the shaping allegorical assumptions a text requires of its reader on the macrocosmic scale are never objects of his scrutiny. The dialectical intentionality of texts, even – especially – if it is unconscious, is the topic whose avoidance wins Bakhtin a formalism empty, finally, of politics. It wins him his freedom from Marxism and his present global appeal, particularly in the West.

If it is Shakespeare, as I pointed out in *The Literary Freud* (2007), who, surprisingly, eludes Bakhtin among Renaissance writers – Shakespeare exemplifies the shift from epic to novel that is Bakhtin's chief historical quarry – then it is Henry James who, just as surprisingly, eludes Bakhtin among modern writers. Dickens is more fit for Bakhtin's purposes. In Dickens, the carnivalesque overwhelms the generic at every turn. It renders even Dickensian melodrama kitsch in relation to the energies of both Dickens's prose and Dickens's democratic belief in the ability of the individual to overcome the determinations of birth and circumstance alike. Like Conrad's, James's complex prose upsets its wider generic platitudes. James, however, is dialectical in a different way. The generic questions return, as they do not in Conrad, as questions of and about value. James's chief preoccupation is with the formation of the tasteful subject both as a character and as a reader. Each is a mirror of the other. Jamesian character seeks a mode of speech and pleasure that its market of readers shares with it. One reads James to join this world. Psychological subjects are also linguistic institutions. The quality and nature of their speech already contain, materially, as language, the sensory constituents of the selfhood and scenery that language, in a novel or in life, presumably only conveys. In the "modern" novel – in the Jamesian novel – language and the world are one and the same. The novelist's real subject is not simply language, but language in action – taste and value as language implants them in us. This is the way that what we call taste endows character with a sense of its own value. This social narcissism, if I may use an oxymoron, is what most preoccupies Jamesian character; it is already the decisive unpleasantness in "Daisy Miller" (1878). The inverted commas that appear with suspicious regularity in James's texts early and late are unavoidable examples of what Sontag calls seeing life in "quotation marks." No wonder James is "excruciating." He resists the camp that he describes. His heart is too pure for it.

My preoccupation with James is not a pleasant one. James fretted over the question of the relation between popular and "high" or canonical forms and did not mean to be pleasant about it. Herein lies his importance. The use of inverted commas in both narration and in the free indirect narration of his characters' states of mind testifies to a deep ambivalence, surely grounded in his American origins, about the status of speech acts in relation to different kinds of cultural value. The distinction in James is, to be sure, less judgmental than it is descriptive, but that does not take away from its "excruciating" difficulty. Son of Cooper and Melville, James had no trouble with cowboys. He had trouble with the sound of an English sentence. He could not decide how it should sound. James is the exponent of the difference between high and low from one who does not believe in the difference. It will never go away because it always does. Poor James's characters as a rule reflect their master's productive ambivalence. Caught between any number of impossible choices, Maggie's decision in *The Golden Bowl* (1904) to remain friends with her faithless friends is a case in point. She has no choice except loneliness, and loneliness of a particular kind – loneliness for a life of "high" or leisured culture without which James's cosmopolitan characters have no identity. The quotation marks highlight and identify this difficulty, and why Maggie can only choose to remain with her "cultured" companions. The quotation marks allow character and narrator alike a way of distancing themselves from vulgar expressions that they can look down upon even as they use. This kind of dialectical or, really, dialogical play between character and itself – and between reader and text – shows how acute the problem of high and low remains even under modernism, especially Jamesian modernism.

The moment at which the canonical becomes the bourgeois is the particular moment of anxiety, and the very focus of the story. James identifies the endless drift of the "high" into the "pop" at every turn of conversation or nervous thought. This is why we continue to value James. In the process, of course, the Jamesian narrative persona has the job of commodifying what it regards as vulgar. It does so by pointing out this exact game, and putting a price tag on it. In James, readership and commodification become one and the same thing. The exertions of James's reader to stay afloat reflect the exertions of Jamesian character to do the same. The quotation marks function as totems to protect character and reader alike from the fetishistic temptations of conventionality. A sense of self-worth is the necessity common to the successful functioning of both. Neither character nor reader wish to succumb to the pop or conventional for the purpose of having a bogus self-regard. One hesitates forever in James in order to find another kind of self-worth. No mode of discourse is free in James, even that of the narrator, from this reciprocity or contamination of one realm by the other. If the pop is a function of the canonical, then the canonical is also a function – especially among the leisured – of the pop. James's real subject is the self-esteem of his reader.

Base and Superstructure, Soma and Psyche

The wider philosophical question behind the reciprocity between reader and text, particularly between pop reader and canonical text or lifestyle, is the question of the subject's relation to social formations in general. This, of course, in one way or another, is also the central preoccupation of almost all contemporary criticism, even Harold Bloom's dialectic between poetic generations and canonical schools as they structure between them a series of historical conversations. The vast synthetic edifice that structuralism, deconstruction, psychoanalysis, and Marxism have bequeathed to us now makes any critical work possible, especially if we use Bloom's model of influence (1973) as a way of describing the temporal mechanism that converts canons into popular mythologies, and that popular mythologies, thanks to camp, convert into renovated canons.

Bloom, ironically, is the solution to the question of "agency" that Jean-Paul Sartre asked of Foucault, and, by implication, of the structuralist enterprise in general (1966). What is its historical mechanism? That it is necessarily dialectical is, from a Sartrean point of view, hardly surprising. What is it? The difference between base and superstructure need not concern us after Althusser – their mechanisms are shared no matter what hierarchy we assign them from the point of view of "first" cause. As Althusser has shown (1964), the priority of "base" is a retroactive effect of the presumably secondary effect of "superstructure." Without superstructure's promoting the material conditions of the economic base to be maintained in – let us be generous – "consciousness," "base" as such cannot exist. Like superstructure, base is the function of a difference that is also a dialectic – superstructure allows base the hegemony it plants in the heart. To use the Freudian term behind Althusser and Bloom alike, systems construct their own agency out of deferred action. Keats is Miltonic because he shows us what is Keatsian about Milton. Agency – cause – is a reciprocal effect, or dialectic.

This synthetic or dialectical assessment of the relation of base and superstructure is at work in Freud himself, in an environmental way. Deferred action is, of course, its mechanism. It accounts for species' adaptation to environment, much as Marx accounts for the adaptation of superstructure to base. Neurology and economics are homologous. As I have noted, dialectic and deferred action are, functionally, one and the same mechanism. This, too, is among the collateral effects of "theory" – to join Marx and Freud, and Hegel and Freud. In its grandest moments, psychoanalysis also thematizes this dialectical prompting. Read neurally, Freud's soma and psyche are, structurally, Marx's base and superstructure. More palpably than Marx, Freud lays the canonical foundations, as it were, for our understanding of the subject's enabling relation to popular forms, beginning with those of family life and of social custom. Structuralism and neuroscience combine to produce the richest reading of psychoanalysis. Lacan's dissertation (1932) is the centerpiece for this way of regarding subject formation. Here the pop star's importance to the unconscious identifications of the ego is already apparent. No wonder for Freud the child is from the start both a repository for and a reaction to the forms of popular life, or the life of popular forms. Freud's fear in *Group Psychology and the Analysis of the Ego* (1921) that identification would come to structure subject formation through the identification of a group's members with one another rather than with prior or "canonical" figures is premonitory. This new hegemony of popular culture is what Lacan's dissertation will register exactly. It is not so much the end of the Oedipus complex, *pace* Deleuze and Guattari (1972), as it is the democratization of the displacements to which the Oedipus complex is itself subject. With great irony, the Oedipus complex is never more than an example of itself. The father represents himself in a chain of authority that is itself a chain of social signifiers rather than natural signifieds. The father's authority, too, is a symbol of itself. This is the principal burden of Lacan's reading of Freud.

Neither biologist nor solipsist, Freud theorizes the sociality of subject formation as early as the 1895 *Project for a Scientific Psychology* and as late as the 1920 *Beyond the Pleasure Principle*. Subject formation is social because it is first and foremost ecological. Freud's environmentalism, of course, is the principal sign of his own descent from Darwin. Among Freud's overdetermined and overdetermining influences – literature, philosophical psychology, Hegelianism – Darwin's is the least studied and perhaps the most important. It is the influence that James Strachey had in mind, without naming names, in the General Preface to the *Standard Edition* when he described his image of Freud as that of an "English man of science of wide education born in the middle of the nineteenth century" (1966, 1: xix). For Darwin, the key to evolution is not the environment's determining effect upon the organism – that is Lamarck – but the organism's reaction to the environment. Heredity is the history of these adaptations. What is social and historical in all species is also material. Sociological diversity is also organic. The same species, Darwin found as early as his account of the voyage of the *Beagle* (1839), reacted to similar environmental forces in different ways. An ecological or "hereditary" feature of the global landscape is also a social one. Heredity and ecology are one and the same thing. Deleuze and Guaratti's *A Thousand Plateaus* (1980) is a superb if silent elaboration of the environmental implications of the *Project*, much as the earlier *Anti-Oedipus* is an elaboration, as I once suggested (2007), of the ironies surrounding the presumable sovereignty as the father in *The Ego and the Id* (1923).

Social formations are evolutionary formations from the point of view of organic defense. Evolutionary formations are therefore social ones because they collect group adaptations to danger, and endlessly recalibrate the defense mechanisms of the organism by means of the social history of the species. To argue that a habit is social or biological is to overlook the fact that in both cases habit is really like – or is – a tic: a reflexive or unconscious response to anxiety when anxiety rouses the organism to defend itself. To survive, the organism creates higher and higher levels of habit or "crust," as Freud calls it in *Beyond the Pleasure Principle* (1920, 18: 26), a crust identical on a species scale with "civilization" or "culture." Adorno's "precipitate" is a good synonym. Ecological and neurological, material and sensory, this interactive relation between species and environment separates the two as a defense against their interdependence. The structure is the same as the structure of high and low, which follows as a later ecological history stratified or propped upon this "lower" or more primitive one. Even an account of the history of social formations is structured by the terms of its history.

3

Pop and Postmodernism

The Social Self

This sounds familiar. Why? Because the performative or reciprocal relation between art and spectator, environment and organism is what we typically call postmodernism. Postmodernism's globalism politically is continuous with its performativity aesthetically. It programmatically breaks down distinctions between subject and object, consciousness and the unconscious, oppressor and oppressed, high and low. This is why an appreciation of pop has as a rule been identified with postmodernism as a practice. It is another way of describing the reader's active if unconscious role in the construction of the pop out of the canonical, and in the saturation of the field of language by pop and its many systems. As I have noted, this is little different from the workings of a religious culture, particularly medieval culture, which, whether Christian, Jewish, or Islamic – "unified cultures," to use Wole Soyinka's term (1976) – ensure continuity of life through continuity of form. Postmodernism, by all accounts, makes overt what in Adorno remains largely hidden – the reader's or the spectator's participation in the dialectical conversion of canonical into pop form. Postmodernism, like pop itself, teaches that a reciprocity between a reader or a spectator and his or her "references" is the fulcrum not only of social life, but of the structure of subjectivity. The subject is a social affair even in its origins.

Here it would be irresponsible not to note the Freudian cast of postmodernism's notion of gender as the correlate or effect, not the prior cause, of subjectivity. This is true even in the case of presumable disagreements with it such as the renegade Irigaray's, who misreads Melanie Klein in order to misread Lacan. Gender, like high and low, is the cultural consequence of a defensive scenario in species history. This is by no means prehistory, since it involves symbolization. Gender is the infantile or Imaginary reaction to the merely anatomical distinction, as Freud puts it, between the sexes. In seeking to account for it, the child, of either sex, creates a version of high and low in "male" and "female." For this, of course, we have Judith Butler to thank (1990, 1997), and, before her, Juliet Mitchell (1974). We should also remember that the movement of Freud's own career is a movement from "modernism" to "postmodernism." Freud's first "topographical" phase, ending during the theoretically transitional years 1914–17, is a landscape of surface and depth. It posits a "low" or prehistorical notion of the unconscious from which the "high" or civilized functions of consciousness derive. Freud's second "structural" or "economic" phase, beginning in 1920, is without spatial characteristics except for its ecological functions, which include its location. Here the psyche is pictured as an apparatus. Its place is determined, not by its division into high and low, or consciousness and the unconscious, but by the individual's gradual separation from the environment, which it protects itself against by shunning. It externalizes the environment by internalizing it, as a memory or image. The organism comes to have an inside different from the outside world only over historical time. "Low" no longer produces "high" so much as "high" derives from a "low" that threatens it.

The most familiar theorizations of postmodernism make its continuity with psychoanalytic estimates of the subject very plain. Even Jean Baudrillard's notion of the simulacrum (1981) is an excellent way of describing the passage of "high" into "low" in a manner that emphasizes their reciprocity from a psychological point of view. Baudrillard has, of course, been appropriated by what I will call "prescriptive" postmodernism, or postmodernism *maudit* – a polemical misreading of postmodern artistic *praxis* that regards postmodernism as a lamentation for a fugitive real whose loss makes us inauthentic, or "simulated" (Hassan, 1987; Bersani, 1990). Postmodernism *maudit* is a diagnosis of the ills of a world dominated by images and mass production, and – no matter its own technical virtuosity and playfulness – says that we should cure them. Readership becomes a kind of green community. Even a preoccupation with toxicity such as Don DeLillo's in *Underworld* (1997), however, features a parallel narrative of making environmental art out of old fighter bombers. David Foster Wallace is the best example of this tension in postmodernism *maudit*, preoccupied, on the one hand, by addiction and the production of compulsive texts – one recalls *Infinite Jest* (1996) – and, on the other, pleased to topple his own pronouncements by virtue of their dialogical presentation.

In point of fact, Baudrillard's notion of "simulation" puts postmodernism *maudit* into question. A "simulation" is not a false copy of a true original. It is like the movement of canon into kitsch, or identification into stylization or exaggeration. Where is the line between them? There is none because they are not subject and object, representation and represented. They are reciprocal functions in structures best described by Saussure's axes of language, or *langue* – an absent and ideal whole – and speech, or *parole* – a present and real moment in time. The original is language, the simulation is speech. All speech is simulation, an exaggeration or stylization of an ideal that does not exist as such. It is the simulation that puts it into place, not the other way around.

Like Baudrillard's "simulation," Jean-François Lyotard's "postmodern condition" (1979) is a descriptive term, not a negative one. For Lyotard, the subject is also a simulation. This may be accentuated under late capitalism, especially because one grows aware of it, but it has always been true. Postmodernism is not a wake for the alienated subject. The subject is alienated by definition. The defensive symbolizations with which the subject bundles itself up are what make the subject a social being. This does not prevent a nostalgia from developing, even though it has no basis in Lyotard's argument. To be sure, he defines postmodernism as "incredulity toward metanarratives" (1979, xxiv) – toward all those arts, sciences, and religions, including household practices, that give one a way of knowing, and of being, in the world (9). But rather than emptiness, this "incredulity" puts new kinds of narrative, or knowledge, in place. It puts in place explosive, ironic, amusing postmodern "metanarratives." A "constant process of dispossession" (75), to use Lyotard's words, becomes a new kind of "possession." Painting's "dispossession" of itself becomes an example of what postmodern painting is. Duchamp's "ready made" (75) establishes this tradition of "dispossession," which will climax, as it were, with Robert Rauschenberg.

And then there is Fredric Jameson. Jameson's sepulchral *Postmodernism, or, the Cultural Logic of Late Capitalism* (1991) is mournful in the style of Leslie Stephen. Its moralism, however, is Marxist. It is the best example there is of postmodernism *maudit*. As he always is, Jameson is also a superb reader. His assessments of negative dialectic in popular culture are both psychologically and deconstructively sound despite the allegory of loss and redemption with which he wishes to recontain them. The collision of Marxist genre and active sentence in Jameson's own prose resembles the collision he describes in Conrad's in *The Political Unconscious* (1981). The restless tension in Conrad between language and genre mirrors the tension between subject and ideology in Baudrillard. This is, of course, Jameson's point, although it displeases him to say so. The tension is provocative and productive, not, as it might appear to be, inhibiting and wasteful. It is certainly not, as Jameson puts it, a "fundamental mutation both in the object world itself – now become a set of texts or simulacra – and in the disposition of the subject" (1991, 9). World and subject are always mutations by definition. What is real is the difference from a norm or ideal that exists only paradigmatically. This is "specificity." The subject's formation by ideology makes the subject a simulation, like it or not. There is no human essence before human existence. History is everything, including natural history. We intermix with it because we are part of it. Pop is no more a coercion than anything else, since everything is coercion.

Andy Warhol

Andy Warhol is postmodernism's chief avatar. He is the *locus classicus* for the deconstruction of "mass production," and the figure who summarily disrupts every distinction there is, especially the difference between high and low. This latter distinction, like all the others, collapses at the end of the domino row that it begins by setting up. Mass culture imagos like those of Marilyn Monroe or Geronimo initiate a series of differences from one another that among them make up what object there is. Each has a retroactive effect on the one, and on the series, that precedes it. Like images of Jesus in the Renaissance, pop images in modernity organize the spectator, not the other way around. This, Lacan calls "the gaze," the points of view – specific, social, historical – by means of which culture situates and stabilizes its citizens unconsciously. This is theme for Warhol. The pattern of its effects is Warhol's technique, which doubles theme: The work of art may appear to choose its subjects from the cultural field, but it is really the other way around. The cultural field chooses the subject matter of the work of art.

Warhol's art is particularly sensitive to the ground of its own presumably mimetic presuppositions. Technique in Warhol ensures this by taking the problem as its real subject. How does it do so? Silk screen is the clearest way to see it in operation: Warhol produces a series of copies – all signed – for which there is no original. The silk screen's "original" is simply the press into which colors are variously and perhaps arbitrarily – or not – squirted. There is an "original" only to the extent that it is the first step in the process of the work of art's production. The origin is not a free-standing, real object, whether natural or made, that the subsequent work copies or reflects. Rather, the work does no more than recall the history of its own production. Deconstructing "mass production" and "existence" are actually one and the same thing. The "original" exists only as the retroactive effect of its "copy." One is hesitant to use the vocabulary of existence here. One is less hesitant to recall Dante, Johnson, and Wordsworth, hardly postmodernists, at least by conventional definition, but very clearly among Warhol's own precursors in the history of poetics. Language – or paint, or film – does not copy life. It is part of life. It achieves its verisimilar effects by means of self-confirming references within a familiar social field. Warhol simply makes this overt. As in religion, deferred action is everything. The first or "original" event – the "original" upon which the mimetic work of art is presumably based, and of which it turns out to be not a copy – gains its founding status only later. It is the effect of an original that it puts in place after the fact. This deferred operation guarantees the object's primariness because the stability of a perilously belated spectator depends on it. It allows the spectator to borrow his or her "ground" or primariness from the object's.

The difference from a religious structure of belief is once again negligible. At least here one can see it. The real model at work is typological. Typology has the same job, that of guaranteeing the "fallen" or belated subject's redeemed or "saved" stability. Passover's freedom is the original of Easter's redemption because Easter's redemption is the proof of Passover's truth. Warhol is on Christian ground. It will require Dylan in Part III for me to describe the deconstruction of typology at its fullest.

The clash between what everyone knows about Warhol and what "prescriptive" postmodernism says he means has always produced a strain on our critical terminology, even when it is simply descriptive. This, I suppose, is part of the point. The criticism of postmodernism behaves like postmodernism itself. It stages the irrelevance of its own drama regarding the presumable loss of essence. Warhol's art challenges not only mimesis in visual representation, but also mimesis as a way of thinking. It also shows, as Derrida does, that we have no choice but to fall into this error, inevitably, and forever. Language, like representation generally, requires among its own functional necessities the belief that it refers to something outside or beyond itself. This is not to say that it does or does not. It is simply a defensive feature of human adaptation. One continues to believe in the object. For reasons of survival one must. Warholian representation, or, rather, presentation describes this process, and takes part in it.

"Hey, Rapunzel, Let Down Your Hair"

No "postmodern" novelist better dramatizes the doubleness of postmodernism and its deconstructive playfulness better than Thomas Pynchon. In Pynchon, grand, often mythic structures collide with ordinary language and its vicissitudes. Ordinary language is defeated by myth in the early texts; myth is overwhelmed by conversation in the later ones. In *V.* (1963), *The Crying of Lot 49* (1966), and *Gravity's Rainbow* (1973), Pynchon's exuberant seekers grow grim without the key they think they need to unlock mysteries that are not there. That, of course, is the point. In *Vineland* (1990) and, most especially, in *Mason & Dixon* (1997), this changes. Dialogue invades the world of Pynchon's narrator from the outside, decrying his conspiratorial myths, if that is indeed what they are, in the early novels. The later novels throw a different light on the earlier ones. The narrator's infectious hipster cadences are replaced by a give-and-take which undoes the greatest plans, even those, as Mason and Dixon reflect, of Manifest Destiny. From this fresh perspective, Mucho Maas, a disc jockey, and Oedipa's husband, becomes the decisive figure in *The Crying of Lot 49*. He shifts the focus away from Oedipa, the quester, and onto his own skill, not in questing, but in spinning the many tunes, or conversations, that questers speak. What Pynchon's novels really require is a mode of organization that allows all their trends to circulate at will. This, the model of the DJ provides. The quester is old hat. Balancing "incredulity toward metanarratives," or quest, with an implacable fascination with it, Mucho the DJ splits the difference between them. He rocks to platters that he endlessly remasters by replaying them again and again. This difference is postmodernism, and also pop. Sampler, mixer, cool king of reference, allusion, and appropriation, Mucho is Pynchon's muscular dialectician of pop. "Hey, Rapunzel," says Pynchon of myth, "let down your hair" (1966, 10).

Pynchon's alternative, more carnivalesque notion of the postmodern has, of course, prevailed over postmodernism *maudit*. It is the wider philosophical frame within which the understanding of popular culture should proceed, a landscape of ecology and neurology as well as of images, all in dialectical play or suspension. Postmodern art neither copies nor criticizes the discourses available to it. It participates in them. Text and world, language and object are continuous. Epistemology is no longer a question of sign and referent, but of signifier and signified. Pop and postmodernism are two sides of the same coin.

Part II

Dialectics of Pop

4

The Death of Kings: American Fiction from Cooper to Chandler

"Paleface" and "Redskin," Cowboy and Dandy

Philip Rahv's influential reading of American fiction in "Paleface and Redskin," published in 1939 in the third issue of the *Kenyon Review*, is suspiciously familiar. Rahv divides the energies of American cultural life, and of American literature in particular, into two camps: the "paleface" – the wan, Eastern, or Anglophile strain – and the "redskin" – the robust, savage, or "native" American strain. Rahv is very clear about the exclusiveness of his "types": They are "polar" (1939, 1). There is the "lowlife world of the frontier" (1) and the "thin, solemn, semi-clerical culture of Boston and Concord" (1). Emerson is at one pole; Whitman is at the other. No matter that Whitman is Emerson's great poetic heir. No matter that Willa Cather tells her sister in a letter of 1912 from New Mexico that the cowboys there carried pocket volumes of Emerson in their jeans (Lee, 1989, 87–8). "Paleface" and "redskin" are a "dichotomy," not a dialectic; a "dissociation," not a reciprocity (1). The difference between paleface and redskin is the difference between the "refined" and the "vulgar," the "snobbish" and the "spontaneous," the "patrician" and the "plebian" (2). The paleface – can there be any doubt? – is "a highbrow," says Rahv, and the redskin "a lowbrow" (2).

Paleface and redskin are our old friends "avant-garde" and "kitsch," dressed in frontier garb. Published in the same year, "Paleface and Redskin" and Greenberg's "Avant-Garde and Kitsch" proceed from the same New York intellectual milieu. Rahv had founded *Partisan*

Review with William Phillips in 1934, and, like Greenberg and Trilling, sought to encourage a division in American cultural life that their progressive politics sought, as I have mentioned, to overcome.

"Paleface" and "redskin" reinforce numerous distinctions in addition to the distinction between high and low. Their policing powers are more substantial than their dialectical ones. They recall the structure of minstrelsy, using the "red" man instead of the "black." "Red" and "black" are both surrogates for what is "low," in Lombroso's exact physical sense. The white man is "high," or on top. Rahv does not give the racism of his metaphors a second thought. Even Philip Roth's parody of Rahv in "On *The Great American Novel*" (1973), substituting the emotive pairing "redface" and "paleskin" for the racial one, exchanges the racial opposition for a psychological distinction between normality and deviance that is also familiar. It is Nordau's distinction, with the sexologists as his source, and the opposition between health and neurosis as its result. It is the difference between highbrow and lowbrow in phrenology.

Rahv's polemic is unrelenting. James and Whitman are Rahv's great examples of the difference. It is one, not of "education" (2), he says, but of sensibility. It is a "mutual repulsion" (2), "a kind of fatal antipodes" (2). No matter that James and Whitman both address, in different ways, the same American preoccupation with convention and conventionality. No matter that the defining issue in American life is the problem of high and low. Rahv is ambivalent. "Paleface" and "redskin" are projections of this ambivalence. He wants American literature to be original, but he also wants it to be legitimate.

The essay's direct precursor is Van Wyck Brooks's 1915 essay, "Highbrow and Lowbrow." Rahv's own stance as a critic, midway between the university and the street, is a belated instance of Brooks's own. Rahv's "polarities" have their source in Brooks's "fixed … poles" (1915, 5). In America, says Brooks, shrewdly, they derive from the difference between Jonathan Edwards and Benjamin Franklin. Brooks sought to find, or to make, a relation between them. Rahv, however, does not wish to do so, foreclosing the next step – an exchange between his "polarities" – that Brooks recommends. It is Rahv's dialectical response to Brooks.

There is, of course, no need to recommend an exchange. It already exists. It exists in Shakespeare; it exists in Johnson; it exists even, *contra* Brooks, in America – in Whitman and in Twain, in Melville and in Norris, in Thorsten Veblen and in William James. Brooks wished to collapse his "poles" by looking beyond them. Rahv wishes to defend his "polarities" by positioning himself between them. It is the easier mode of self-empowerment. His distinctions are dead in the water, and he likes it that way. It makes for a "breach" in literary tradition "without parallel" (3). It gives him his subject.

This is extraordinary. It is even more polemical than Greenberg's use of the same argument. It is also more mean spirited. And because it deals with all of American literature rather than with modern art alone, it is also more irresponsible. The history of criticism of American literature following Rahv's essay is a movement away from his fixed and ambivalent "polarities" toward a more unified view of American writing, and of American culture generally. Subsequent critical tradition is interested in what American culture holds in common, not in what divides it. F.O. Matthiessen's *American Renaissance* (1941) appears only 2 years after Rahv's essay is published. It is the founding text of American studies. Very different from Rahv's cultural approach, Matthiessen's New Critical methods lead him to produce a splendid book with almost no theme at all. Almost, but not quite. Emerson and Whitman are not "polarities," even though Emerson is from Harvard and Whitman is a "rough." Emerson and Whitman are the founding partners of America's literary maturity. They are not "paleface" and "redskin," but, as I once put it (1999), "cowboy" and "dandy" – both forms of knowing, different in style but not in stance or kind. Whitman is the poet that Emerson prophesies. The "common denominator" that links "even Hawthorne and Whitman," says Matthiessen, is "their devotion to the possibilities of democracy" (1941, ix). For Emerson, it is what Americans "share" that counts (8).

Matthiessen's critical disciples put meat on the bones of his abstractions. They return to Rahv's cultural approach, but with a difference. They look for what holds America together, not for what drives it apart. For Henry Nash Smith, American expansion over the course of the nineteenth century gains its power from the common belief that the American wilderness was an Eden, or "virgin land" (1950). For Smith, this Edenic ideal is at work in cultural contexts beyond literature alone. He finds it in both the "high" poets and the "low" hucksters whom he studies together. *Virgin Land* initiates the multidisciplinary approach associated with cultural studies today. Smith's contention is also true for subsequent students of American mythology, who go on to refine it. Not only is the American wilderness a paradise. For Leo Marx in *The Machine in the Garden* (1964), it is also a toxic paradise. It is besotted not simply by the advancing tide of industrialization. It is also corrupt as a notion because it relies on prior Christian myths, reinforced by British Romantic ones, in order to purchase America's status as a realm, not simply "beyond culture," to use Trilling's phrase (1955, 95), but before it. For Trilling, like his *Partisan Review* colleagues, this ideal was salutary. For Smith and Marx, it is wish fulfillment. The notion of America as a spoiled "virgin land" reaches its culmination with New Western History (Slotkin, 1973; Limerick, 1987), which catalogues the Eastern myths upon which the West constructed its beliefs to justify its colonialism. The pattern of this critical history is clear. Each moment in it finds a dialectic in its materials, and each moment in it revises the viewpoint it inherits in a reflection of that assumption.

Pathfinding: Cooper and Mark Twain

The American wilderness was not, of course, a garden, even in the beginning. It was, as James Fenimore Cooper constantly reminds his reader, already civilized, a land of surpassing Native American culture. Its "redskins" are not only "educated." They are also, in Cooper's world, the very opposite of what they are in Rahv's. They are "patrician." Their eradication *as* patricians is necessary in order for the myth of America to be real. This irony is central to Cooper, and to the history of American fiction that follows from him. Cooper's dialectic is with the myth of kings, the myth most at odds with American democracy, and whose form, particularly as encomium, is verse. Milton, particularly, had already disrupted this tradition on native English soil. Like

Peter Ackroyd's *Milton in America* (1996), Milton scholarship has acknowledged the deep affinity between Milton's republicanism and the American political enterprise (Stevens and Simmons, 2008), including the anxieties that led even Americans to be uneasy about Milton's own regicidal enthusiasms. By writing novels, Cooper overcomes this anxiety on a formal plane; by killing off kings, he overcomes it thematically. With the shadow of Charles's execution in 1649 falling across the long eighteenth century, Cooper finds in American colonialism a way of alleviating British anxiety about regicide by shifting the burden for it onto American shoulders. Shifting the burden has positive results for both parties. Tolerating this crime – one necessary, symbolically, for democracy – gives the United States a leg up on its colonial progenitor. It allows America to solve its own postcolonial anxieties about British precedent while also allowing England to begin to heal itself with the Restoration of 1688. Cooper accomplishes this through a double displacement. Kings may not be killed, even in America, but the death of Indian chiefs is another matter. It has a collateral yield in colonial real estate. This highly diplomatic solution is what Cooper's five Leatherstocking tales provide, particularly the second and most pungent of them, *The Last of the Mohicans*, published in 1826. The death of Uncas, the last of the Mohican kings, is a sanitized version of the death of Charles.

The phrase we customarily use to describe the epic fortitude of "savage" populations is, of course, "the noble savage." Dryden coins the phrase in 1672, in his play *The Conquest of Granada*. Says Dryden's "noble" hero:

> But know, that I alone am King of me.
> I am as free as Nature first made man,
> 'Ere the base Laws of Servitude began,
> When wild in woods the noble Savage ran.
> (1672, I, i, 206–9)

His autonomy derives from natural right, even though a complex rhetorical operation is required to ensure it. The natives of the American hemisphere are "noble" only by means of a contrast between

81

slavery and nobility. By the same token, however, the savage's "nobility" is a function, not of his difference from his oppressed comrades in color, but of an innate kingliness that precedes it in time. This, however, is also a contrast. Dryden needs both historical comparisons to give the "savage" his "nobility." Each comparison replaces the other, but both are won by a difference from black slaves, who suffer by either contrast. "Laws of servitude" is also an equivocal way to describe racial slavery. "Laws of servitude" characterize British feudalism also, with a population of serfs rather than slaves. So does the notion of innate nobility. It may look like natural right, but its terms here are those of divine right. Dryden's "noble savage" is actually a form of nostalgia for feudalism.

Cooper's "noble savages" are also an embodiment of feudalism, although not a nostalgic one. It puts the fate of feudalism in American hands. It remains "noble," but, in a democracy, it is bound to die. No wonder Cooper's "savages" are so superb. It is Cooper's way of being both non-racist and anti-British. Native American culture is valued in Cooper not only for the pathos of its vanishing aristocrats; it is valued for its scholarship or learnedness. For Cooper, unlike Rahv, the Indian's knowledge is just as profound and systematic as the white man's. It is different from it only in content rather than opposed to it in form. Rahv cannot account for American literature because defending the difference between "high" and "low" is really an Anglophile's defense of aristocratic privilege. Rahv's racism is a function of his Anglophilia. Cooper's anti-racism is a function of his Anglophobia. Cooper's wilderness, like its inhabitants, is no paradise. It is not only dangerous; it is also full of intricate systems. This is not Milton's Eden, although the "mazy error" (1674, 4: 239) of Milton's paradise is one of the chief characteristics of its own organization. In Milton, the "coy" Eve's "wanton ringlets" (4: 306, 310) forewarn the reader of the Fall to come. In Cooper, the Fall has come many times, and in many forms. Knowledge of the forests, woods, and waterways is Hawkeye's job. He is, like his Native American tutors, a pathfinder among them.

The Pathfinder, the fourth of the Leatherstocking tales, appeared in 1840. To call Hawkeye a "pathfinder" is an appropriate metaphor, among other reasons because it is not a metaphor. Hawkeye walks many paths simultaneously. His many names – Leatherstocking, Deerslayer, Natty Bumppo – are examples of how cultural identity is, like a settlement in the wilderness, one position or another along a signifying chain. Hawkeye is a rich composite of positions, unlike the less flexible and more stationary positions of Uncas and Chingachgook, or the Colonel and his daughters. Cora's hidden black ancestry is significant or not, depending on the context in which it is revealed. "Pathfinding" is also important as a trope for a reason beyond that of cultural identity. Its cognate will be Freud's word – "*Bahnung*" – for what Strachey will translate as "pathbreaking." Like Hawkeye in the wilderness, the brain's neural corridors are constructed by its traumatic encounters with what lies outside it. This is Freud's environmentalism, as it is Cooper's. Cooper's "pathfinding" is as much a psychiatric trope as it is a material and historical one. It joins the somatic and psychical experience of the individual with the material and ideological history of the culture in which he or she lives.

Twain follows Cooper with a dialectical response. He both preserves the structure of the "other" in Cooper, and revises it. The "other" in Twain is the Negro, not the Indian. As Lott has shown, "black" is conceptualized in the 1830s in order to produce as its effect a unified notion of "whiteness." The Negro gives the "paleface" something to stand out against in a new way. By 1830, a bustle of contending ethnicities complicated what a once-British "whiteness" needed only the "savage" Indian to support as its opposite. Twain both records and helps to invent the new fictional "other" required to institutionalize once again a uniform notion of "whiteness." Leslie Fiedler, Rahv's contemporary and *confrère*, does indeed regard Twain in this light (1948). Unlike Cooper, however – and unlike Fiedler – Twain doesn't simply use this opposition. He also deconstructs it. It is a constitutive difference, not an empirical "polarity." For Cooper, it is both. For Twain, it is neither. Negro life, like Indian, is also a learned discourse, different from "white," not simply its opposite. Unlike the fading discourse of the Indian, however, it is, Twain realizes, here to stay. It cannot be made into a myth; it must be absorbed. Like Hawkeye, Huck – his heir – peregrinates the differential line that positions all these identities as points on a chain. Unlike Hawkeye, however, Huck doesn't hide in the trees until and unless needed. He is, and will remain, a visible and integral part of life on the Mississippi. He is its emblem.

Although Hawkeye's demeanor is, like the red man's, stoic, his speech is recognizably white. Huck's is not. It is cross-pollinated with black diction, and gives Twain's first-person narrative its distinctive voice. This is the "double style" of *Huckleberry Finn* (1884), as Stephen Fender calls it (1981, 14). Twain's decisive achievement, says Tony Tanner, is to "supplant" the "official rhetoric" with "the vernacular" (1965, 127). The novel's speech acts are crucial, and critical. Twain is very clear about this in the "Explanatory" note at the beginning of the novel. There he details the "number of dialects ... used" in the book: "I make this explanation," he says, "for the reason that without it many readers would suppose that all these characters were trying to talk alike and not succeeding" (1884, 7). This is precisely the assumption that the novel does away with, leaving the notion of "success" in relation to "likeness" – a Keatsian notion of success – in the dust. "There was not a breath stirring," says Twain in *Tom Sawyer* (1876, 59), evoking the first *Hyperion* as a learned way of describing the dead world of book-learning when Tom is sitting in school, bored. Huck and Jim's itinerant crew of "false" European nobles is a good example of the novel's transvaluation of values. Their manner and speech are parodied by a style that is itself a parody of "official speech." The result is to make "official" speech itself parodic, inverting high and low in a precise way. Huck and Jim's own performances as Kean and Garrick also give the lie to their own presumably renegade status. Not only are they scholars of British theatrical history; their performance is so self-conscious that it is not simply critical, but metacritical: It is the performance of prior performances.

The novel's ironies are also more strictly formal. *Huck Finn*'s style – its sentences and their syntax – is recontained by its generic form as a romance. Jim is freed, the sufferings of Missouri redeemed by the green paradise of Kansas. This notion of narrative "recontainment" is Jameson's, as I have noted, in reading Conrad. Twain's wit garners a particularly sharp edge when the allegory is freedom and it is deconstructed. The energies of the Twainian sentence overwhelm even its freedom song. The prose takes too many directions at once to be bound by any of them, including freedom conceived of in a natural way. This, too, is a philosophical position, not a self-evident truth. In Twain as in Whitman, all "creeds," to use Whitman's words in "Song of Myself," are held "in abeyance" (1891–2, 10). The energy of Twain's sentence is itself freedom.

Like his transatlantic counterpart, Dickens, and like his transatlantic contemporary, Hardy, Twain also complicates and undoes the distinction between high and low. Tom's scheme to get others to whitewash the fence that he is obliged to whitewash as punishment for playing hooky is a case in point. In *Tom Sawyer*, he makes them feel it is a privilege to do so, and likens his scheme, *mutatis mutandis*, to the logic of aristocratic privilege in England:

> There are wealthy gentlemen in England who drive four-horse passenger-coaches twenty or thirty miles on a daily line, in the summer, because the privilege costs them considerable money; but if they were offered wages for the service, that would turn it into work and then they would resign. (1876, 21–2)

In *A Connecticut Yankee in King Arthur's Court* (1889), Twain makes a nostalgia for aristocracy the centerpiece of attack, mocking not only contemporary Victorian taste, but also Victorian taste at its source, in its preoccupation with its own principal nativist myth of kings, the myth of Arthur. Huck, rescued from the river by Southern aristocrats, flees their protection. He wishes instead to rejoin Jim, the runaway slave. In Twain, aristocracy has no attraction, and no uses. It is no longer a myth; it is the myth of myths.

To one's surprise, the earlier *Tom Sawyer* accomplishes this dialectical work as systematically as does its sequel. A frontier novel, *Huck Finn* takes on Cooper's ethnic oppositions. A domestic novel despite its mostly outdoor settings, *Tom Sawyer* takes on the even older opposition between high and low. It does so by imagining not only Huck's life on the Mississippi, but also Tom's life in Aunt Polly's house. Its vision of a new American domesticity does to high and low what Huck's life on the Mississippi does to black and white: It disrupts their coherence as contrasts. In *Tom Sawyer*, the center of the action, even if it is often only in the form of Tom's full stomach, is Aunt Polly's kitchen. If *Huck* negotiates the frontier in a vigorous confrontation with the elements, Aunt Polly's kitchen negotiates the relation between species and environment in the preparation of food. By virtue of her excellence as a cook, the difference between culture and nature – high and low – ceases to exist. Field and stream become all deliciousness. Like Whitman's "daily housework," Aunt Polly's kitchen is the site of the transition between population and environment. In the kitchen the distinction between nature and culture is produced, like the food that is consumed, as a function of its own disappearance. Well-nourished and decently dressed, Tom is, unlike Huck, "sivilized," as the boys call it. But Tom and Huck do not represent "high" and "low." They are not "polar." They are continuous despite their differences, dandy and cowboy rather than paleface and redskin.

Labor, Leisure, Love: Melville, James, Hemingway

Melville's dialectic with Cooper is, of course, earlier than Twain's, and it has a very different later result. It will lead to James. It will also lead to Hemingway. If Twain takes on Cooper by adding black and white to red and white, Melville adds a worldwide cast of color to the ethnic proceedings that Cooper programs and that Twain has already disrupted. Description alone does this labor for Melville in *Moby-Dick* (1851), especially when the descriptions are themselves the descriptions of labor performed by a multiethnic crew. This labor is Melville's globalism; it far exceeds his imperialism. The interruption of Melville's popular career following *Typee* (1846) and *Omoo* (1847) by *Moby-Dick* comes from this new and sustained emphasis on both labor and its performance in an integrated fashion. In the travelogues, work is segregated by color. White imperial crews and native populations both work, but separately. Questions about cultural difference abound, as do notions of what is true and what is not. *Mardi* (1849) and *Redburn* (1849) are likewise full of anxiety about class and ethnicity compared to *Moby-Dick*'s level eye. Published only 6 years later, "Benito Cereno"

(1855) reveals the unsettling questions about race and imperialism that *Moby-Dick* was designed to solve.

Moby-Dick's racial polemic also has a formal dimension. It is different from Twain's formal inventiveness, and provides the link to James that Twain does not. Twain is not interested in the seductions of generic allegory or recontainment. Melville, by contrast, the educated Eastern schoolboy, is preoccupied with the generic forms of allegory, tragedy chief among them. He reads authority in formal terms. Ahab's authority as a captain and his status as a tragic figure are one and the same. The novel describes, not heroic quest as such, but an assessment of heroic quest as a way of living and of writing. To witness, as Ishmael does, the death of a king is to shift the emphasis, at the end, to the response. Ahab's death is Uncas's death unplugged. Its full tragic dimension is now clear. One looks on again as Charles dies on the scaffold, the last dying light of the Middle Ages. It is the passage from feudalism to capitalism, to which Ahab's kingly kind of authority, like Uncas's, is unsuited.

Pierre (1852) is Melville's untidy attempt to come to grips with what is finally the epistemological trauma of *Moby-Dick*. There is no way of knowing the world except through the outmoded forms of allegory. Enter "Bartleby the Scrivener" (1853). "Bartleby" resolves the pain and confusion of *Pierre* with a simple response. Bartleby's notorious preference "not to" is a preference not only about the laws of genre but about the laws of syntax. It is that thoroughgoing. Syntax is transitive. There must be an object to which one refers in a sentence, or that one desires in the mind or the heart. Even the unconscious is structured like a language. Bartleby's preference is based, not on intransigence, but on intransitivity. His preference is intransitive because it has no stated object. It is pure negation. Bartleby refuses to recognize that there is any object that one may desire or to which one may refer. To do so is to capitulate to a law of language, not of experience. Experience conforms to language, just as meaning conforms to genre. Neither is acceptable. Bartleby's preference, negative and intransitive, is formally absolute. Transitivity – the securing of objects – is never possible to achieve, and the only achievement we are structured to want. There is no object.

"Bartleby" is Melville's premonitory version of James's "Beast in the Jungle" (1903b). Melville and James were both popular writers who became brooding, introspective ones. The reason for the shift is the same in each case, and makes James's career a startling repetition of Melville's own. James also does away with objects in a steady and relentless way. James's response to "Bartleby" is to reinvent the terms of the shift. They become psychological instead of absolute and without cause. "Bartleby" is the text of Melville abstract enough to appeal to James, and "low" enough in its subject matter to be sufficiently safe to function as a source without anxiety or fear of belittlement. Bartleby is a clerk, not a gentleman. James is a gentleman, not a clerk. This allows James to approach "Bartleby" without the danger of rivalry or competition, to absorb its teachings, and then to revise them by illuminating, as Melville does not, such an opaque inner world. The difference between rivalry and competition, will and nervousness, informs all of James. It is the difference between the feudal and the bourgeois, the "high" and the "low." This difference in taste, or, really, style of taste, is what preoccupies James early and late. James's interrogation of taste and his eschewal of the "pop" is what has already made him important in the history of taste. It is what requires those quotation marks.

James's career has all along been a quest to grasp objects – sexual objects – that turn out to be not really there. Not only does "The Beast in the Jungle" summarize this thematic preoccupation in James. It is also, as a portal to the late phase, a clear indication of what the "difficult" style of *The Wings of the Dove* (1902), *The Ambassadors* (1903a), and *The Golden Bowl* (1904) requires both James's characters and his reader to do. It requires them to give up objects altogether. Character must give up libidinal satisfaction. The reader must give up the satisfactions of prose romance, at which the early and middle James excels, even when he tells stories about disappointment, which has lessons to teach. It is another way of identifying how James wishes to distance himself from "popular" preoccupations in style and lifestyle alike. The late phase does not, however, require one to give up everything. Objects do remain in James's world, but they are not human objects, nor are they fetishized, either sexually or from the point of view of status. This is the world of income and commodities. This is the background in James's otherwise objectless world, from its beginnings in *Roderick Hudson* (1876). It is always taken for granted, even when it presents itself as the avowed object of dreaming by schemers like Giovanni in "Daisy Miller" (1878) or Morris in *Washington Square* (1881). James's hunger for the sexual and the socially intimate is very different, and scorns this kind of hunger for the conventional. Jamesian desire functions at a different level. Jamesian desire prefers people to things, even if the people, unlike the things, turn out to be unavailable.

This unavailability is epistemological. It is what Jamesian aestheticism comes to share with the Paterian aestheticism to which it is opposed earlier in James's career. Paterian aestheticism has no objects at all. Texts and observers are both "loosed" into a swarm of "impressions." What impresses whom, or who impresses what, is always, and quite amusingly, undecidable. So Pater announced in the famous "Conclusion" to *The Renaissance* in 1873. Indeed, when James saw the book for sale in the English book shop in Florence that year, he burned with rage, having read the "Conclusion" in the *Fortnightly Review* in its 1868 form. Pater had beaten him to the invention of aestheticism. This, of course, was never the case anyway. Pater's objects, like his subjects, are no more than shifting, molecular structures certain to die even if there is the momentary illusion of their liveliness or potential possession. Hunger for objects is out of the question in Pater. They do not exist as such. James's assumption that human objects are available can, in so smart a novelist, only come from the realist's belief in the tangibility of things, and in the well-to-do boy's assumption of an assured income among others of the same station, which grant them, except for medical problems, an unquestioned survival. When these objects are present and then disappear, whether because of Dr Slocum or because of Marcher's own stupidity, there is pathos. When these objects are never present, as in *The Ambassadors* or *The Golden Bowl*, the epistemological protest of "Bartleby" also becomes a social and sexual one. James's abnegation does Bartleby's one better. James prefers not to in a double way. He gives up people and objects both.

89

Hemingway fights off James by turning a different Melville against him. He uses *Moby-Dick* instead of "Bartleby." Like James, Hemingway accepts "Bartleby" because, like James, he accepts the loss of sexual objects. Like the Melville of *Moby-Dick,* however, Hemingway also accepts what James cannot – the inevitability of codes and commodities, even in an epistemologically featureless world. They are the only features the world has. Hemingway's reaction to James is very like our own reaction to James throughout these pages – James is the writer who puts his anxieties about being conventional, or "low," in quotation marks. In Hemingway, everything is in quotation marks. No one can avoid being conventional, especially Americans. It is Melville who grants Hemingway this peace. He uses it as the knowledge he needs to take Jamesian – and Melvillean – stoicism a step further. Though James is the exception rather than the rule in the history of the American novel – the turn away from the social is a turn away from engaging the "general converse" – his style embodies the rule from which he deviates thematically: It reflects an endless anxiety about taste. Hemingway's own style does something very similar. It looks like an attempt, as is Steinbeck's in a minor key, to purge language – unsuccessfully, of course – of the pretensions of the "high." In point of fact – and as its boomerang effect – it hastens an evocation of the "general converse," or the "low." The effect is intentional. One cannot escape it.

Jake's plain speech in *The Sun Also Rises* (1926) is actually dense with concrete detail of every kind, from fashion to food, and the brand names of liquor. Brands of liquor are a specific material narrative of the growth and packaging of the material whose distillation is tasted. Brands are compact symbolizations in a denotative or descriptive key of the material and epistemological chain that a thoroughgoing preoccupation with the "pop" should present – the entire means of production and mode of consumption of given products. This is how they become historical products, and how the individual preferences that distinguish one drinker in the novel from another are also produced. Jake's world of commodities signifies not so much artificiality as it does the feeling that somebody else has been there before. This is an American anxiety, not for reasons of status but for reasons of knowledge. It is true of both the plains settler and the otherwise "high" James, who is fearful of being repetitive or clichéd as a matter of taste. Like the settler, he wants free and first lease of his land, as a right of conception, which ownership includes.

For Hemingway, by contrast, conventionality has a wholly different status. This can be seen most dependably in the luxury of tradition in wines and spirits. There is no resentment of the precursor here. A known history ensures the consumer's enjoyment. Taste is a relishing of the rivalry of what can only be conventional because the reliability of brands comes precisely from their standardization of processes poorly negotiated by inferior brands. The conventional is good, not bad. This conventionality is the very conventionality that James takes for granted and never represents – the world of food, drink, and lodgings, and the waiters and servants who people it. This is also Melville's precise turf, at least the turf before "Bartleby," the Melville whom James negates, as does Melville himself. Hemingway returns to this earlier Melville who is concerned with the production chain. Hemingway gives us the consumer end of this chain whose other end is Melville's own: the direct representation of human labor upon the raw materials of the sea. Hemingway can combine a negation of James with an affirmation of Melville because his source is not "Bartleby" but *Moby-Dick*. The result is a prose as tough as Melville's and as nervous as James's own.

Dialectic is also at work within the Hemingway canon. Like Melville or James, Hemingway also revises himself. Although *A Farewell to Arms* (1929) follows *The Sun Also Rises*, it is actually the earlier text conceptually. Hemingway's presumable wish to cleanse language of the concrete takes its clearest form here. The desire meets with only partial success. Frederic and Catherine reach the sanctuary of Switzerland thanks to their heroic efforts, which are vividly portrayed in the astonishing escape across the lake. The achieved neutral ground is the counterpart to the neutrality of style that Hemingway achieves as a writer in the movement away from the detail-ridden *The Sun Also Rises*. In this sense, the later book is indeed a triumph over the earlier one. But the later novel also goes on to destroy its own achieved goals in the most drastic thematic ways: Catherine loses the child, and then loses her own life. The reconstitution of the family romance, despite the adventure of the lake, is not possible. In this sense, *A Farewell to Arms* is really a precondition for *The Sun Also Rises*. Because it sets out the conditions under which the earlier book proceeds, it is an earlier moment in Hemingway's dialectic, even though it succeeds it chronologically. The later novel narrates the unconscious of the previous one.

No wonder, then, that Jake Barnes is castrated. *The Sun Also Rises* is a text about why the wishes of *A Farewell to Arms* are doomed. The family romance is itself a fiction. The psychological reality of castration is the real truth about the unconscious. Frederic's virility and Jake's impotence are of a piece. Frederic's potency is also doomed. Hardly a sad event, Jake's castration is actually Hemingway's greatest moment of imaginative triumph. It represents – it is – the dismantling of patriarchy. The feudal, the "high," everything associated with what Lacan calls the Name of the Father, has ceased to function. Even new gender-oriented readings of Hemingway (Eby, 1998) do not go far enough in assessing the nature and the extent of Hemingway's own abnegations. They are revolutionary and democratic. Compared to James, and even to Melville, Hemingway, against all odds, advances rather than retreats. Without a penis, Jake can still function or "pass" as a man in all ways but one – the purely anatomical. Frederic's physical prowess in *A Farewell to Arms* leads to a sadness almost equivalent to Jake's own in *The Sun Also Rises*. In all other respects – even the sexual difference ends up making no difference – Jake remains a man in the fullest sense. He is an active connoisseur, a lively companion, a lover of travel and spectacle. Marriage to Brett remains an active question in their relationship. Full physical ability on Jake's part, one reflects, would still require him to accept an open marriage. In this way, too, the novel is democratic. No man actually possesses the feudal power of generation socially assigned to him. Paternity, to use Joyce's phrase, is "a legal fiction." Like Jake, Cohn, Michael, even Romero – all are compromised, each in a different way. Cohn is a fool who cannot be taken seriously. Michael is only valued sexually. Romero represents, not heroism as such, but the heroism of a man willing to expose himself to the worst kind of danger, the danger of castration that even athletic men face.

Rather than a triumphant recuperation of the primitive, bullfighting – like Jake's sexuality – provides the novel, not with climax, but with renewed disappointment. Fighting the bull is a dance with the endless possibility, to adapt Edmund Wilson's phrase about another kind of civil war, of patriarchal gore. Fighting the bull, like fishing in the Nick Adams stories or in *The Old Man and the Sea* (1952), or like big-game hunting in *Green Hills of Africa* (1935), is not a natural activity that returns the hunter to a primeval relation to nature. Hemingway's is not a pristine nature. Like everything else, Hemingway's nature is also ritualized. In the Nick Adams stories, the running streams are lively versions of Keats's gloomy ponds. The escape sequence of *A Farewell to Arms* is a merciless version of Wordsworth's boyhood adventure on the lake in *The Prelude*. In both cases, Hemingway's conversation with his poetic sources is muscular and productive. Romantic melancholy becomes momentary enjoyment; romantic fear becomes duty.

Hemingway's increasingly flat style over the course of his career is not simply the vehicle of his irony. It is its result. And it is no longer ironic. It is Hemingway's own next step, his revision of himself. In *The Sun Also Rises* and *A Farewell to Arms*, Hemingway succumbs to neither the Jamesian fear of a world without objects, nor to the Bartlebyan preference to engage the world – and the laws of syntax – no longer. The later Hemingway does both. He gives up both language and the world. There is, however, compensation even here. What is left in the later novels is a single code, one that even Bartleby cannot manage – the code of syntax, and of the objects that syntax provides. Hemingway's *écriture blanche*, the style of Camus and Blanchot, is indeed a narratological revolution, one that does away with high and low entirely because it does away with everything else. Everything, that is, but grammar. It is composed almost entirely of shifters, simple personal pronouns. Grammar, however, requires even shifters to function transitively, whether as subjects that take objects, or as objects that need subjects in order to be objects. It does not matter whether the subjects or objects are real or not. Language makes them so. Language is the code of codes, the grain of being, not something that gets in the way. Grammar is Hemingway's only inevitable reality. It is the philosophical version of the mortal body. To accept it makes him tougher than

Bartleby, whose preference is a fantasy. Language always requires an object, whether it is there or not. Handling the psychological aftermath that this material reality of the signifier requires is the real source of both Hemingway's stamina and sobriety. It is also the source of his influence.

Transatlantic: Raymond Chandler

How does American fiction reinvent itself after Hemingway? It does so from an unexpected direction that tests one's seriousness about pop – the detective fiction of Raymond Chandler. Even Chandler's defenders as a fully serious writer – Fredric Jameson is the best example, and Jameson is nothing if not serious (1970, 1982) – are casualties of "the battle of the brows." Making Chandler "high" rather than "low" is a question of identifying, not his dialogical powers, but his redemptive ones. It is hard to see why Chandler is remarkable if one's focus is on such a monological Chandler, whether it is the Chandler who ennobles the mean streets of Los Angeles by making them "epic" (Skenazy 1982, 33), or the Chandler who stirs up gender trouble behind Philip Marlowe's suits and ties (Legman, 1963; Mason, 1978; Wolfe, 1985).

No American novelist after Hemingway – not Mailer, not Ishmael Reed, not even Pynchon or Philip Roth – requires a dialectical reading more than Chandler does. No American novelist exposes the limits of Rahv's "polarities," which stack American writers neatly into two distinct groups without relationship, however seriously one takes either one. Chandler not only represents both these groups at once; he also puts them into unparalleled conversation. This conversation and its pleasures are the real subject of Chandler's novels, and the source of his appeal. Chandler's surprising stylistic resources are always the first thing one responds to in his fiction. Where they come from reveals the dialectic that structures his work. It is a dialectic that also sums up the wider dialectic, beginning with Cooper and Twain, of popular American fiction as a whole. It is the dialectic, not of "paleface" and "redskin" – these do not have a dialectic – but of cowboy and dandy.

Chandler is ordinarily valued as a "high" filigree of the "low" form of detective fiction. Though invented in the nineteenth century by the American Romantic Poe, American detective fiction devolves, in the hands of writers like Erle Stanley Gardner, whom Chandler studied closely, into a bland form of entertainment dependent entirely on story for its energies despite the allure of its principal characters, Perry Mason and Paul Drake. In a tradition quite distinct from the British one of Arthur Conan Doyle and G.K. Chesterton, the influence of Hemingway presumably reinvigorates the form in America and gives it a new seriousness. Here Dashiell Hammett is the chief witness for the defense. Chandler is typically conceived of as an enrichment of Hammett. The great style is at bottom bare-knuckled, like Hammett's, or like Hemingway's own. But it has a rococo element that gives it its specificity and that is the reason for its influence. This is the Chandler we know; it has become part of the mythology of cool, tough-guy speech in American fiction. But its origins remain hazy. They come from Chandler's earliest writing as much as they do from his study of the "pulp" Gardner.

Hammett – and Hemingway – are only Chandler's belated source. Before them comes Chandler's "dandy" English youth as a writer in London in the years before World War I. The source of his dialectical achievement is biographical. Born in Chicago in 1888, Chandler was raised in England because of his parents' separation. He was educated as a day boy at Dulwich College, a distinguished public school in London, where he excelled in classics. Chandler did not return to the United States until after World War I, when he settled in California and went to work in the oil business. He began writing "pulp" detective stories for *Black Mask* in 1933. His first novel, *The Big Sleep* (1939), published in the same year as Rahv's essay, is a departure from the stories because it is a departure from formula in both its lush style and its relative disregard for plot. This is not because Chandler excels where other "pulp" writers have not. It is because his American influences are at last joined with the British influences of his youth.

Chandler's "dandy" writings in London from 1909–11 are principally contributions to *The Westminster Gazette*, *The Academy*, and *The Spectator*, both as a poet and as essayist. Writing very self-consciously in the aesthetic tradition of Pater and mixing socially in the *demi-monde* of Bloomsbury's fringes, Chandler was an aesthete in every sense, particularly in his work. The rather moving "A Pilgrim in Meditation" (1909) is the best example. Like his poetic master, A.E. Housman, Chandler is preoccupied with landscapes and personations drawn from medieval romance. They are put to use, in a century-old Romantic practice, in psychological ways. Chandler's poetic persona seeks a connection between chivalric posture and secular desire. This is at bottom Keats. Chandler's voice as an essayist, however, adds another element to this otherwise Keatsian profile – how to connect, not chivalric romance with secular psychology, but the poet's receptive, aesthetic posture with the citizen's appreciative experience of city life. Chandler is in good company here. This prose tradition begins with Baudelaire in "The Painter of Modern Life" (1859–60), and becomes the characteristic posture of both Bloomsbury's Woolf – "Street Haunting" (1937) is the best example – and of Walter Benjamin, particularly in *The Arcades Project,* begun in 1927. Here is Chandler in 1912:

> Any man who has walked down a commonplace city street at twilight, just as the lamps are lit, can … exalt the sordid to a vision of magic, and create pure beauty out of plaster and vile dust. (1912, 67)

Not only does Chandler's prehistory as a novelist include the umbrella of Bloomsbury. Unlike his Bloomsbury contemporaries – the editor of *The Spectator,* St Loe Strachey, supported World War I and fired his nephews because of their objection to it – it also includes an experience of technology, particularly aircraft. This, too, the young Chandler found enjoyable; it prepared the way for his interest in the oil business, and augurs the cowboy side of his emerging dialectic. Chandler had joined the Canadian Army, and was later transferred to the Royal Air Force. No wonder Chandler was at home in California only a few years after the war. Technology, whether aircraft or oil, was another kind of aestheticism. As Chandler's London aestheticism already shows, the world of machines and of the visionary are supplemental, not opposed. "Realism" and "Fairyland" are Chandler's names for them (1912, 65). They are in conversation, not in conflict. This is not Marinetti's Futurism, which regards life and machines as antithetical despite the aesthetic – and neurological – explosiveness of their every meeting, especially in modern warfare. Chandler's is the very different play of cowboy and dandy. For Chandler, environment and machine are continuous because machines are built by people as a response to the environment. Technology – Chandler's screenwriting also shows this – is a highly evolved form of *aesthesis*, or perception, not its counterpoint.

No wonder Philip Marlowe's transactions with the environment are easy and superb in Chandler's novels. Even beatings are overcome with a glass of whisky and a nap, environmental responses – especially, as in Hemingway, the whisky – that testify to Marlowe's endless ability to adapt to any and all situations, physical, social, or both. Marlowe is a go-between among the various subcultures of Los Angeles. He is an industrial-age Hawkeye; his automobile is his "pathfinder." For Marlowe, there is no difference between high and low. In *The Big Sleep*, he is equally at home with General Sternwood and the gambler Eddie Mars. He moves freely among all spheres of California life. He has functioned, perhaps too well, in the District Attorney's office, from which he has been fired because of too easy a relation toward authority. He also functions easily in the world of books. He has the intellectual competence to impersonate a bibliophile thanks to a few moments in the library before visiting Geiger's shop for the first time. He is even comfortable with "high" reading. He discourses on murder in Shakespeare's *Richard III* in *Farewell, My Lovely* (1940), and offers to buy the chauffeur in *The Long Goodbye* (1953) a copy of T.S. Eliot's poems. That the chauffeur is black and already owns a copy of Eliot is good evidence of how Chandler programmatically levels cultural priorities. The "lowbrow" chauffer has "highbrow" taste. By the same token, of course, Eliot is well known for his derogatory use, among other American dialects, of black American speech. The moment is both a parody and a paradox. Chandler's style also recognizes no difference between high and low. It is a "double style" in the truest sense. It employs the vernacular of the underworld in complex rhetorical figures that only a boyhood student of classical writers would know how to construct. The famous style derives from the resources of the British schoolroom.

Why the detective? Here Chandler's double determination is particularly important. Chandler's combination of British and American, high and low, dandy and cowboy finds its most capacious site in the figure of the sleuth. In American fiction, the hero is a pathfinder first and foremost, a loner among the ruins, an explorer who knows the virgin land is actually haunted. In European aestheticism, the urban lounger, or *flâneur*, is, by definition, also a kind of detective, always interested in patterns, and in the details that both shape and upset them. Sherlock Holmes and Father Brown are the modest counterparts to their flamboyant cowboy doubles on the other side of the Atlantic like Kit Carson and Buffalo Bill, high plains drifters with eagle eyes. These impulses are one and the same. This is because pathfinding and perception are one and the same. Pathfinding, or "pathbreaking," as I noted with Cooper, is Freud's word for the structure of the organism's functioning in relation to the environment. Defending against the environment's dangers requires the organism to turn away from it. The result is the creation of an internal world that becomes the organism's buffer zone of survival, and its psychological space. Experience stores the traces of this endless history of buffering to produce memory and thought. No wonder Alan Bass retranslates "*Bahnung*" as "breaching" (Derrida, 1967a) – it underscores the doubleness of Freud's meaning. Like Marlowe, "breaching" – one also recalls Melville's whale – is at one and the same time a violent and a reflective site of experience. Outside and inside, environment and psyche, "low," as it were, and "high" – all three find a form of stability in relation to one another. They find, to use Freud's term, borrowed from Fechner's revision of Helmholtz, a state of "constancy." Strachey's translation of "*Bahnung*" from time to time as "facilitation" also recalls Chandler's comfort with both technology and the social world. "Facilitation" as a psychoanalytic metaphor is the historical source, thanks to the work of Strachey's disciple, D. W. Winnicott (1965), of the social-science use of the term "facilitation" to describe an individual's adaptive powers. It is also the source of the term "facilities management" to describe the administration of buildings and power plants.

Competence, of course, is Marlowe's only real value. His lament over Harry Jones's death in *The Big Sleep* is a lament about a failure in competence. Jones is Conrad's Jim in a very minor key, a sweet boy who does not react well in moments of professional crisis. He is insufficiently competent in his dealings with his chosen professional environment. Like the sea in Conrad – or in Melville – Chandler's Los Angeles is the widest possible environment, one with the most vicissitudes, and the most nuances and dangers. For Marlowe, specificity is everything. The details count most of all. "No matter how smart you think you are," says Chandler in *The Long Goodbye*, "you have to have a place to start from: a name, an address, a neighborhood, a background, an atmosphere, a point of reference of some sort" (1953, 110). Chandler's is not a regionalist fiction but an urban and cosmopolitan one. It is why Los Angeles appealed to the Londoner in Chandler, and why Marlowe is the Baudelaire to its Paris.

Reading Chandler as a transatlantic writer adds a considerably sharper focus to the reading of American fiction as a whole. It shows what American fiction really is historically – a particular form of post-colonial writing. The American relation to British culture from Cooper and Twain to Melville and James has always been an anxious one, even a foundational one. It is what American fiction reacts to. It is the customary moment of negation in its dialectic. Chandler reinvents the dialectical enterprise of American writing by finding its post-colonial anxieties in the exaggerations of the social world. Chandler gives the feudal repressed some room to operate. We see it in the power politics of Los Angeles, whether in Sternwood's baronial mansion or in the back office of Eddie Mars's casino. If Sternwood has a military title, Mars does him one better by bearing the name of the Roman god of war. The presumably distinct locales, and the two distinct personages, have the same style of authority, whether "high" or "low." Both men are feudal chiefs, rivals in a battle of wills to which Marlowe himself is only a spectator. Marlowe surveys feudalism with the neutral eye of the Epicurean. This coolness is his safeguard. The feudal unconscious is the unconscious of capitalism. Chandler's post-colonial fiction comes to terms with the feudal unconscious by coming to terms with what makes American fiction most uneasy – its British origins.

5

Knock on Any Door:
Three Histories of Hollywood

Ars Gratia Artis

How does Hollywood handle its own very considerable anxiety about
being "pop"? Like other pop institutions — vernacular poetry, the
novel, or, as I will show next, rock music — it does so by staging a relation to "high" culture particular to the histories that determine it.
Hollywood, of course, is no more egregiously "pop" than American
fiction. It is neither repetitive nor formulaic. It is structured by shad-
ows, pursued by ghosts. It is resolutely dialectical, even mournfully so.
And yet it tries to allay its nervousness about its radical specificity by
constructing an apologetic myth about itself.

Like American fiction or pop music, Hollywood is an art of democracy. It understands freedom as both relative and achieved, not as absolute and given. As I propose to show, freedom — of the film image, of
the director, of the actor — is always the result of context and comparison. It is always dialectical. So is its myth about itself. As in Shakespeare's
plays, Hollywood's materials are very often those of historical drama,
and very often the dramas of kings and queens, rebels and monarchies.
This thematic preoccupation has an exact institutional counterpart in
Hollywood's material base, or infrastructure: the studio star system.
Here base or infrastructure is also superstructure: Hollywood's stars
are its chief myth as well as its chief way of organizing its payrolls and
marketing. Like the kings and queens that they often play in movies,
the stars of classic Hollywood are a native aristocracy or nobility. They
are an industrially produced aristocracy. The studios made sure of both

100

their business and their mythological appeal. They were one and the same. Stars are a baroque or rococo – a *faux* or "stylized" – recreation of aristocracy. Hollywood stardom is another return of the feudal repressed in American culture. It is the sign, like Cooper's Native American aristocrats, of America's perpetual anxiety about British culture, and about the need both to express and expunge it. It summarizes America's post-colonialism.

The star system in America was founded in the silent era by Carl Laemmle in 1916 – he went on to start Universal Pictures – although the Canadian actress Florence Lawrence, who starred in 65 films, is credited with being the first "movie star." The word "star" in our contemporary sense was already used for the stage. It had been general since 1829 for anyone who "shined," as the *OED* puts it. It had not been fully exploited, however, by American silent film because silent film was considered a form of simple pantomime that hurt an actor's chances for obtaining work as a serious stage actor. Despite a richer theatrical tradition, however, there was already precedent for marketing silent films using "stars" in Europe, particularly in Italy. The Italian studios lost much of their financial backing with the increasing troubles of the Italian Discount Bank in the early 1920s and, in the process, moved away from the promotion and subvention of stars, especially as leading couples. The German film giant UFA had also marketed stars in the same period, but between financial problems of its own and the rise of Nazism, it also grew less focused in its marketing strategies. This left the star system a singularly American phenomenon.

The enthusiasm with which American audiences embraced the star system even in the silent era recalls the passions of American fiction. This is the wish or repressed element in American life to take one's revenge on England, not by displacing its institutions, but by outtopping them. No wonder Hollywood has such deep cultural persuasiveness. Despite its overwhelming dialectical achievement, it still wishes to be, in its own way, British, or aristocratic. It is the wish to be "high" rather than "low," learned rather than ignorant, powerful rather than oppressed. High and low, as in American fiction, is the difference between lord and serf.

Like the baronial glamour of the star system, the genres particular to the films of the 1930s, when the studio system reached its Golden Age, fill the screen with allegories about these unconscious fantasies. Each executes the wish in a different way. The lavish historical musical or adventure film represents the feudal unconscious as such. The gangster film is the king of the films of Hollywood for a good reason: The gangster as hero is a trope for Hollywood's own presumably illicit hegemony. It is the thematization of its own sense of itself as powerful but illegitimate. Stars and directors write this story with extraordinary lucidity, particularly in the case of Grace Kelly and Alfred Hitchcock. Kelly's transformation from American girl to Princess Grace of Monaco is Hollywood's greatest myth of what an aristocrat the star really is. But Kelly only completes the dialectic that Hitchcock begins by emigrating to Hollywood from London in 1939. Her marriage to Prince Rainier takes place in 1956, the same year that Hitchcock, the Englishman, becomes an American citizen.

MGM's seal is the best example of all. Designed for Sam Goldwyn by Howard Dietz in 1924, the MGM seal features a text around the lion's head that reads "*ars gratia artis*" – art for art's sake. It is the summary emblem for Hollywood's wish to be "high" rather than "low." "*Ars gratia artis*" is Latin for something very familiar, and a striving, unnecessarily, for the effect of a smoothness or polish that Hollywood already has. The phrase is a translation into a learned language of a phrase coined in French – a vernacular language – by Théophile Gautier in the "Preface" to *Mademoiselle du Maupin* (1834–5): "*l'art pour l'art.*" "*L'art pour l'art*" was translated by Pater as "art for the sake of art" in the "Conclusion" to *The Renaissance* in 1873. It came to be called, popularly, in the 1890s, "art for art's sake." MGM translates two vernacular phrases into a learned trope from which neither derives. This is not unlike the use of Latin names to designate British university degrees. In the case of MGM, it has a double rather than a single result. The first is a reversal of Dante on his own ground. Second, "art for art's sake" is a doggedly anti-conventional cultural stance, one that relies on individual perception and a sense of community derived from bohemian contexts, unlike the highlife world of Hollywood that Goldwyn wishes it to legitimate. Objects dissolve and reconstitute themselves in aestheticism; Hollywood studio films do – or seem to do – no such thing. Hollywood film, however, does this kind of thing very well indeed. Whatever Goldwyn's intent, his gesture is as radical as the Hollywood films he helped to create. Resolving this anxiety about high and low in Hollywood history is inscribed not only in the Goldwyn seal. It is also inscribed, as I will show, in the history of film criticism, in the history of film genre, and in the history of both Hollywood's principal directors and major stars.

Benjamin, Bazin, Eisenstein

Film criticism's central preoccupation has always been the epistemology of the film image. Walter Benjamin is the first to describe it in "The Work of Art in the Age of Mechanical Reproduction" (1936). He is also the first to show how the philosophical problems it presents are projections of social anxieties regarding taste. Everyone knows Benjamin's essay. Its lament is contagious: Mechanical art, especially the photograph and the film image, removes from art the "aura" (1936, 222) that customarily surrounds it. Although "in principle a work of art has always been reproducible" (218) – the woodcut, the painting, and the lithograph are Benjamin's sequential historical examples – photography and film complete this process, which results in a qualitative transformation in the nature of the art object: the "decay," as Benjamin puts it, "of the aura" (222). The "aura" Benjamin defines as "the unique phenomenon of a distance, however close it may be, whether a mountain range on the horizon or a branch which casts its shadow over you" (222–3). Painting preserves the aura because the "distance" of the artist's hand is, like the "distance" of what is represented, always – and ironically – near. The nearness of the distance is what gives the aura its razor-edge of emotion. What is chilling is not the loss. It is not the fugitivity of the thing that is the aura, but the palpability of the distance from the thing. Photography and film jeopardize the aura, according to Benjamin, and jeopardize its unique effects. Even more than photography, film brings this crisis of the aura

103

to a head. "The audience," he says, may "take … the position of the camera" (228) – a remarkable advance – but "the effect of … film" is the "forgoing of its aura" (229). Film and photography have, or appear to have, no aura; painting is superior. In sociological terms, the "aura" is a cipher for "high" culture – painting. The presumable disappearance of the aura in film and photography is a cipher for "mechanical" or "low" culture, both degradations of painting from the point of view of taste.

Things are not, however, as simple as they seem. Benjamin deconstructs his sociological opposition in his critical practice. It leads to a new estimation of what cultural value is. Benjamin does indeed think the photograph to be without the presumable "aura" of painting, its original sin, as it were. But, by the same token, the photograph also does what painting does, and in a more pointed way. Both have an aura. Most striking is his conception of acting. Consider his startling declaration that actors in film portray, not characters, but themselves: "What matters primarily," says Benjamin, "is that the actor represents himself to the public before the camera, rather than representing someone else" (229). Mimesis is no longer at work; a new material event has replaced it. That the actor "represents himself" has profound philosophical consequences. It topples mimesis as a way of understanding what the structure of film representation is.

The "low" or "mechanical" image is not a copy of something real that is, as the "auratic" or "high" object presumably is, fugitive. Rather, it is the record of something fugitive that is, as André Bazin will conclude in "The Ontology of the Photographic Image" 9 years later on, dead, or soon to be dead (1945). Benjamin's suggestion is made explicit by Bazin. For Bazin, photography and film possess a reconceived kind of "aura." Film and photography are chilling in a new way. They do classical mimesis one better. They do not copy the living. They "embalm" the dead (1945, 9). In film and photography, what Benjamin calls the "aura" is actually a more, rather than less, moving and funereal affair. The photographic image is "mummified." "Lives" – the lives of the actors – "are halted at a set moment in their duration," says Bazin, and "freed from their destiny" (14). This destiny, of course, is death. And yet, because of this "halt" or "freedom," the "lives" that are momentarily suspended become even more implicated in the inevitability of death than they were before being filmed or photographed. Because, as with the Egyptians, this kind of imagination – this "mummy complex" – is "aimed against death" (9), it is also in league with death.

For Benjamin and Bazin alike, the photographic image is wholly different from painting, and resolves an ancient split in painting's own history. Painting, says Bazin, has "two tendencies" – the wish to express a "spiritual reality wherein the symbol transcended its model" (9), and the wish to produce a "purely psychological" effect of "the duplication of the world outside" (11). These "tendencies" are really one and the same. The "effect" of "duplication" is the precise "spiritual reality" signified by the symbol's ability to "transcend its model." This transcendence is what one really means by mimesis, whose psychological effects are as a rule granted the status of a kind of spiritual enlightenment. The photographic image does away with this double-dealing because the photograph and the photographed "share," as Bazin puts it, "a common being, after the fashion of a fingerprint" (15). They are both objects in a conversation, each one taking the measure of the other. The question of mimesis, or the copy, does not have to be raised. Representation and represented are continuous, materially and epistemologically. The photographic image is "an hallucination that is also a fact" (16). It "rescues" time at the very moment that it accedes to it. The photographic image "embalms time" (14). It is a triumphant moment for actor and spectator alike. In point of fact, Benjamin's "aura" also represents a death. It is the same as Bazin's notion of the photographic image as an "embalming" or "mummification." When Benjamin says the actor represents himself and not a character, the actor's presence is no longer mediatory – no longer a mimetic vehicle for something it copies that is fugitive – but the sign of a real death always happening to the actor's actual body, again and again, every time his performance is viewed. What film shows is not the mimesis or representation of a living thing, but the brutal spectacle of the actor's imminent, or already real, death. The actor's mortality does not represent anything; it simply is.

The transformation of high and low into the uncanny "mechanical aura" of the film image is what structures the history of film criticism following Benjamin and Bazin. Its sociological reductions are identical with its epistemological radicalism. Each one of its principal moments is also a conversation with the moment before, each one centering on this transformation, and each one articulated in dialectical or revisionary contrast with the moment before it. In the 1940s, film criticism's distinguished history is heating up to a boil. In 1942, Sergei Eisenstein publishes *The Film Sense*; in 1944, *Film Form*. Both are composed of talks and essays from the 1920s and the 1930s. *Film Form* includes "A Dialectic Approach to Film Form" (1929), a dialectics of the film image. Eisenstein's dialectical materialism is thoroughgoing. There is no difference between high and low, not simply because of Eisenstein's egalitarian politics, but because of his epistemology. Eisenstein's epistemology is dialectical. It is a kind of deferred action or "screen memory." It is based on "a dynamic concept of things" (1929, 45), which arises from "superimposing on the retained impression of the object's first position, a newly visible further position of the object" (49). This is the effect that montage produces. It is the way we see anything. Things emerge as a function of their contrast with the things before them. Eisenstein's epistemology of "superimposition" is contextual, specific, differential. It includes rugged demonstrations of literary precedent for film technique in Milton (1942) and in Dickens (1944).

By 1951, Bazin has co-founded the *Cahiers du cinéma*, pioneering what will come to be called "auteurism," or the theory of the director. For Bazin, too, the temporal dimension of film is not only fundamental; it is, in Bazin's own words, also "dialectical" (1958, 35). Though their interests are different – Eisenstein champions montage, Bazin deep focus – Bazin's reasons for preferring deep focus actually elaborate Eisenstein's notion of film's ability to loosen the image into its component or "dynamic" parts, even in the single shot. Bazin turns preference into film history. Even though Eisenstein already has "a dynamic concept of things," Bazin regards this as something that emerges in film history only with Orson Welles. It is a good example of creatively misreading Eisenstein. Like Seurat's pointillism – a form of digital representation before the fact – Welles's deep focus is a cinema of pure context. By finding this Eisensteinian feature of film's dialectic in a single director, Bazin can, in his own dialectical fashion, step beyond Eisenstein. He invents a history of film based on Eisensteinian principles, but one that emphasizes, not montage, but its presumable opposite, deep focus. Welles's single shot is unique because it can achieve the effects of "superimposition" without benefit of montage, and without benefit of Eisenstein's theories. Welles allows Bazin to clear a critical space for himself after Eisenstein.

The critical reactions to auteurism are also dialectical. In film, as in fiction, dialectic is everywhere. The rise of structural film criticism in both France and the Soviet Union is a revisionary response to it (Metz, 1968, 1976; Lotman, 1973). Film semiotics focuses on the spectator of films, as does feminist film criticism (Penley, 1988), although it also returns, in good dialectical fashion, to film criticism's earliest preoccupation, the epistemology of the photograph (Barthes, 1964). No matter the quality of a given film, its narrative structure requires no director, simply a camera, and no need conceptually for positing a director. The most striking feature of Star Studies a decade later is its own kind of revisionary relation to film semiotics (Dyer, 1979, 1986; Sklar, 1992). Rather than focusing on the film grammar available to anyone with a camera, it restores to film criticism a presence – the presence of the actor. As Benjamin and Bazin point out, this presence is, of course, no presence at all. The epistemology of the actor in films is actually the most radical and complex of film's economies.

Robert Warshow's collection of essays on popular culture is an early and rich moment in the battle for taking Hollywood seriously in America (1962). It places any discussion of Hollywood history very plainly within the wider history of high and low, not only from the point of view of taste, but also from the point of view of the assumptions that classically structure conceptions of taste within that history. They, too, are epistemological in nature. Warshow's struggle with them shows how much movies challenge the history of high and low. Warshow makes no distinction between the gangster film of the 1930s and the film noir of the 1940s and '50s in his classic essay "The Gangster as Tragic Hero," first published in *Partisan Review* in 1948. The essay is striking less for its explanation of film noir than for its failure to recognize the changes it has wrought in the genre of the crime film.

These changes are dialectical. It is the history of high and low that prevents him from seeing this. The crime film, he says, is an "unspecific" form of expression (1948, 129); it is monolithic, unchanging, archetypal. It is ahistorical. It repeats the same formula "indefinitely" (129). The gangster is "without culture," he says in his later essay on the Western (1954). The judgment is phrenological. The gangster is "without manners, without leisure." He is "crude"; even his "melancholy" is "inauthentic" (1954, 136). The cowboy has the advantage over the gangster because the cowboy knowingly pursues style, and style alone. He has a history. The gangster does not. The gangster allows one to identify with failure and defeat – the "low" – in a world where only success – the "high" – is valued. This is not only a phrenological estimation; it is also a sexological and "degenerative" one.

No wonder Warshow represses film noir. The insinuation of the psychiatrically pathological into the middle class disrupts the clarity of the opposition between normal and healthy, high and low. This is Rahv talking, and this is Greenberg. It is certainly not Benjamin, Bazin, or Eisenstein. In 1948, the crime film has experienced a transformation that implicates bourgeois heroes and expands the notion of what it means to be a criminal. The terms of the classic crime film – high and low, good and evil, auratic and mechanistic – are now, with a slight adjustment in focus, in conversation rather than in contrast, interdependent rather than distinct. Coined by Nino Frank, an Italian-born French film critic, in 1946, the term "film noir" designates a major shift in the crime genre that defines its later history, and that troubles the difference between high and low as surely as it does the difference between the auratic and the mechanical. *The Godfather* (1972) summarizes these changes. The character of Don Corleone rests in a combination of politeness and murder, a living synthesis of high and low, and a revision of earlier, less refined images of the gangster hero. Such dialectic is also true of the film's visual technique, which recalls, by turns, the soft richness of Caravaggio's oils and the blunt and uneven camera of Rossellini. Even noir plot is dialectical. Noir thematizes its revisionary relation to sources by employing plots that are very often plainly Oedipal ones. Killing the husband by an adulterous couple is the core of much noir melodrama, such as Billy Wilder's

Double Indemnity (1944) or Tay Garnett's *The Postman Always Rings Twice* (1946). Wilder's *Sunset Boulevard* (1950) will feature a triangular family romance, with William Holden as the insurgent son, Gloria Swanson as the seductive mother, and Erich von Stroheim – silent director and actual emblem of early film – as the indulgent father. Here, in a summary way, the king is reduced to a chauffeur. The *Shaft* cycle of films in the 1970s will complete noir by literalizing it. Not only is the detective's world noir; the detective himself is.

Noir's dialectical relationship to the history of the crime film is a familiar and only limited example of the wider dialectics that constitute Hollywood history as a whole. Whether we focus on film's semiotics, on directors, or on the actor, there is dialectic at work in numerous ways. When the star and the director are one and the same, the dialectical machinery, particularly the reimagination of the "aura," is enhanced.

Dialectics of Directing: Hawks, Welles, Scorsese

Benjamin, Bazin, and Eisenstein not only set out the epistemology of the film image. They also provide a thematic direction with which to organize a dialectical account of Hollywood history. As film noir only begins to show, the history of Hollywood actually narrates the epistemological trauma to which Benjamin and Bazin respond, and to which Eisenstein gives easy and simple expression. Hollywood films narrate the epistemological transformation that Benjamin and Bazin both describe – the disruption of mimesis by death. This is not only a psychological challenge for the film spectator. It is also a test of the actor, a test about whether or not one can adjust to this new kind of psychological and aesthetic reality and tolerate it. Even its moral and pedagogical structure is dialectical. The test is not about giving up prior realities, but about giving up prior assumptions about reality that turn out not to be true. When, in George Cukor's *Dinner at Eight* (1933), John Barrymore and Marie Dressler, both in the role of silent film stars whose careers have faded, sit next to each other staring in terror into the space before them, they are looking at their own deaths. The biographical component adds extra truth and compassion to the scene. They look at dying, as the spectator does, looking at them. It is the cinematic image that allows this to happen by immortalizing or embalming them. Their success is failure, and their failure success. As a form, film enforces the reality principle, not, as do the other arts, the principle of pleasure.

Canons will tell the tale, whether of directors, stars, or both. Even the semiotic structure of films shows how dialectic, in Adorno's sense, produces them. Most familiar is Bazin's history of directing. As I have noted, it is, in his own words, "dialectical." His aim is to provide a "dialectical … history of film language" (1958, 35). In the composite essay "The Evolution of the Language of the Cinema," first published in the initial volume of *What Is Cinema?* in 1958, Bazin lays out his well-known scheme in clear detail. It is the standard account of film history through directors. Orson Welles is the fault line. In 1941, Hollywood reacts to itself with *Citizen Kane*. Welles "challenges" the normative editing style of 1930s Hollywood:

> It was this fashion of editing, so admirably suitable for the best films made between 1930 and 1939, that was challenged by the shot in depth introduced by Orson Welles and William Wyler. *Citizen Kane* can never be too highly praised. Thanks to the depth of field, whole scenes are covered in one take, the camera remaining motionless. (1958, 33)

Citizen Kane at one and the same time changes the medium technically and occupies a key moment in the history of Hollywood institutionally. Welles always sought total control over his own motion pictures, and became more and more unable to get it. Welles's invention of tracking and deep focus is simultaneous with *Kane*'s production at a moment that is both the stunning apex of the studio system and the arguable beginning of its decline. The revision the film accomplishes technically is a reflection of the unmooring of assigned positions under a single gaze that the studio system is, or was, as an institution or a bureaucracy before Welles. The anxiety that the Wellesian character, beginning with Kane himself, typically feels is equivalent to the anxiety that participants in the film industry began to feel in their actual lives in the movie business.

Welles's revisionary technique is also reflexive in regard to viewer expectation in watching a film. Expectation relies on historical assumption, and it is the history of viewer assumption that Welles's camera addresses. This assumption is that films are narrated through the technique of montage, with a particular emphasis on characters' faces and on objects. Disappointing and "challenging" its viewer by upbraiding this assumption, *Kane* invokes past film history by negation. The spectator's mind becomes a storage space for both the history of Hollywood and one's reactions to it. Welles's camera produces this archive in the spectator.

Nor is Welles's inventiveness entirely original. It simply returns film to the other technological option in its history besides montage – the sustained shot of early directors like Flaherty, F. W. Murnau, and Erich von Stroheim. According to Bazin, even D. W. Griffith, who "invents" montage, is no more original than Welles, who invents deep focus: "Welles did not invent the in-depth shot any more than Griffith invented the close-up. All the pioneers used it" (1958, 33). Welles's "in-depth" shot may negate Griffith, but as a negation or step backward, a return, with a difference. Flaherty and Griffith already establish the medium's two kinds of direction long before Welles, and even before Eisenstein, who only later on becomes the chief spokesman for montage. Montage is quick, close to the actor and things; deep focus is expansive and at a distance from personages and things. Although Eisenstein describes historical events in his films, his technique is highly personal in its close-ups, very concerned with time and anxious in its cutting. Although Flaherty describes personal suffering, his technique is highly distanced because his camera simply observes Nanook, for example, fishing, waiting in the moonlight. Welles returns to one father to help him slay another.

Howard Hawks is a fine example of the classic Hollywood style that Welles overturns, and probably the best director with whom to compare Welles as the norm from which Welles departs in his dialectical revolution. Hawks is not, like his friend and contemporary John Ford, a director who uses the combination of long-shot and montage that Bazin regards as the convention from which Welles departs. In point of fact, Welles moves away from the severely Eisensteinian

111

montage of Hawks. If Welles recalls Flaherty, then his adversary must be Griffith, whose own disciple is Hawks. In good dialectical fashion, history is always a battle, not of fathers but of sons, of disciples fighting each other in order to take their revenge indirectly upon their fathers. Hawks has flattened even Eisenstein's limited use of depth of field into almost parodically flat sets, juxtaposed only occasionally with shots of city streets or of physical plants like airfields or race tracks.

It is the thematic difference with Welles, however, that is most important, a difference that also shows how much Hawks resembles Eisenstein, and, by contrast and implication, how much Welles takes aim, not at the combined style of Ford, but at the montage of Hawks, and at its theme of cool judgment by characters who ensure the stable functioning of groups. This theme Hawks also shares with Eisenstein. Hawks's films span a period from the silent era to the Technicolor of the late 1960s. As Andrew Sarris has remarked (1968), Hawks's films, early and late, always have a common theme: the work of a crew, and a preoccupation with questions of competence. This is the Russian Revolution recast in capitalist terms. Social justice in Hollywood is about the quality of one's professional skill.

This theme is also reflexive. Turn the camera around and one sees a film crew shooting a story about the work of a crew – an aircraft company in *Only Angels Have Wings* (1939), a newspaper staff in *His Girl Friday* (1940), the governance of a Western town in *Rio Bravo* (1959) or *El Dorado* (1966), a big-game safari in *Hatari!* (1962), or a stock car crew in *Red Line-7000* (1965). In the tradition of Conrad and Chandler and its preoccupation with professional competence, Hawks's films are highly precise in their use of montage, particularly to tell the story. The sequencing of discrete scenes is very clearly what structures story as a whole. Story has many potential sequences in Hawks, but, thanks to the cutting room, the spectator is shown only one story among many possible ones, and only one ending. The master of reassembling scenes into narrative, Hawks reduces narrative to scenes. Hawks himself is quite clear about this in his autobiography:

> In *Rio Bravo*, Wayne was the sheriff, and his deputy was a drunk. In *El Dorado*, Bob Mitchum was the sheriff, and *he* was the drunk, and the

deputy was perfectly sober. We changed it from Wayne being a sheriff to Wayne being a gunman. You had Dean Martin as the drunk in one, Mitchum in the other. They're two different people. There are always two ways to go, you can go any which way, and we knew that both ways were good. We just turned the whole thing around. (McBride, 1982, 133)

Here a history of directing becomes a semiotics of film in the blink of an eye. Hawks is a splendid structuralist critic of his own work. A synchronic reservoir of scenes – Saussure's paradigmatic axis – may be variously arranged on the diachronic axis of the film's plot – Saussure's syntagmatic axis. Here, by the director's own testimony, narrative is spun from the play of synchronic and diachronic, paradigmatic and syntagmatic, scene and sequence. The narration of a presumably stable and separate story is achieved by what is really the use of one narratological axis by the structure the other one brings to it. The Saussurean mechanism of Hawks's narration is, from this point of view, identical with the mechanism of the relation of individual speech to language. The master of reassembling scenes into narrative, Hawks also reduces narrative to scenes.

Because Hawks's career continues after Welles's has begun, this strategy can be seen in films released not long after *Citizen Kane* such as *Air Force* (1943). The Conradian history of moral failure and redemption that John Garfield's story represents there is itself an example of how narrative is a function of the editing of scenes already available to memory. Part of the film's work is to put the viewer in possession of the bitter memory that Garfield and the captain share from cadet training, when the captain washed Garfield out of his candidacy to become a flyer and an officer. Garfield endlessly replays in his own mind the story of his failure and his knock-down back to the rank of enlisted man. When, as gunner on the *Mary Lou*, he has to fly the plane at the film's climax because the captain is wounded, he redeems his earlier failure. The irony is both technical and thematic. At the moment this history is expunged for the characters, it is put in place for the viewer. The viewer is contaminated by it at the very moment that the characters experience its dissolution. Whether Garfield regards this redemption as anything more than showing the captain that his earlier judgment of him was foolish, or whether he has learned something about honor that he had not learned before, remains an open question. This question is one that the viewer and Garfield share. *Only Angels Have Wings* is similar. Thomas Mitchell fails as a flyer when his captain, Cary Grant, is injured. Mitchell breaks his neck trying to fly when he is, as Grant puts it, "not good enough" to undertake the kind of risky mission at which Grant routinely excels. Embarrassed by his tears, he asks Grant to let him die alone. If he cannot fly solo, he can at least die solo. This, presumably, is a very clear kind of moral redemption. Mitchell is so ashamed of his failure that he will not allow Grant to cradle him as he expires. And yet what is right and what is wrong in such a situation escapes the ethical codes at work in the film's brutal masculinist ideology. As if to highlight the flexibility of montage and of the potential re-editing to which any story is always subject, Hawks shows that there are always many films possible within one film.

It is against this kind of moral, and narrative, open-endedness that Welles's revolution is ironically directed. The deep focus of *Citizen Kane* may provide a greater freedom for camera and spectator alike in witnessing a wider and more flexible cinematic world than does montage direction. By the same token, deep focus actually produces a less challenging and more determined world. The choices have already been made. In this paradoxical way, Welles's own obsession thematically with media masters and industrial authorities like Kane or the Ambersons is also a reflection of his directing. They are simultaneously powerful and unprepossessing. These figures move in and out of focus, now foreground, now background. This, too, is part of Welles's revolution. Welles changes the very texture of the cinematic environment by shifting it to a pointillistic graininess. The emergence and dissolution of characters and things within it constitute the real rhythms of Wellesian *mise en scène*. The screen becomes a kind of molecular theater or neurological laboratory for spectator and character both. Even the powerful man is subject to its tides. Theme and technique in Welles are one and the same.

A later director like Martin Scorsese revises Hawks and Welles alike by combining them. Scorsese's moment in the history of directing also relies, as it does in different ways in Hawks and Welles, on a heightened emphasis on the semiotics of film production. Scorsese synthesizes montage and tracking into a single filmmaking style. He is the dialectical synthesis of Hawks and Welles. He combines, as no other director does, the moving camera and brisk cutting. The tracking shot in *Goodfellas* (1990) that leads the viewer, without a cut, from the kitchen entrance of the Copacabana to a table directly in front of the stage is a tour de force of Wellesian artistry. By contrast, the sinuous cutting once Ray Liotta and Lorraine Bracco are seated is a Hawksian tour de force of two lovers in a night club whose facial nuances can only be described by a series of superimpositions. Add to Scorsese's combined technique the inventive use of soundtrack, particularly the use of rock and roll, and the dialectical change is complete. Unlike Eisenstein's original Prokofieff scores, Scorsese's rock and roll is already familiar to his viewers – it is a soundtrack borrowed from their lives. Representation here is the representation of spectator memory from the start. In Welles, and even in Hawks and Eisenstein, the film works to produce the memory. In Scorsese, the memory works to produce the film.

Dialectics of Acting: Barrymore, Bogart, Brando

If there is a dialectic of Hollywood directors, is there also a dialectic of Hollywood stars? One can see Clark Gable, for example, behind Jack Nicholson; Nicholson's humor is a send-up of Gable's own inability to laugh at himself, hard as he tried. In European film, Yves Montand is a poor man's Frank Sinatra; Marcello Mastroianni is an even poorer man's Humphrey Bogart. Jean-Paul Belmondo is the stronger response to Bogart, Marlon Brando with a fedora like Bogart's own. The conversation with the past can be very self-conscious indeed. When asked why he is wearing a fedora in the bathtub in Godard's *Contempt* (1963), Michel Piccoli replies that it is an "*hommage*" to Dean Martin in Vincente Minnelli's *Some Came Running* (1959). These, however, are largely self-contained dialectics, dyads, not parts of a chain. They occupy the suburbs of cinematic grammar, not the streets

115

of its inner cities. Who is Welles's equivalent as a director among actors? Though Welles's own contribution to the history of acting is considerable – I will take it up in the next section – he does not anchor it in the way he anchors the history of Hollywood as a director. The shift in film from silent to sound after 1929 is the fault line that is useful here. It may have indeed seen the end of many careers – Tom Mix comes to mind, as does Harold Lloyd, Buster Keaton, and even Charlie Chaplin. But it did not end the career of John Barrymore. If anything, it enhanced Barrymore's reputation, and did so by inscribing the perpetual shadow of Barrymore's silent stardom into his even more compelling stance as a speaking actor. It turned Barrymore from a happy adventurer into a tragic figure. As I have noted, Barrymore's staring silence in *Dinner at Eight* remains its best example. This is because the silence is first and foremost a reminiscence of Barrymore's earlier silent career. His speaking career refers to it when he does not speak. It takes the spectator back to a past that has slipped away. It makes something dead alive again. It is pure Bazin, through the agency of Benjamin's notion that it is himself and not a character that the actor really represents.

Barrymore's definitive silences in a sound medium have a clear response and elaboration in the history of Hollywood acting – Humphrey Bogart. Bogart's career as a sound actor recapitulates Barrymore's own shift from silence to sound. Bogart's many conceptions of his own persona over the course of his career involve a technical relation to sound like Barrymore's, but played out through shifts in his notion of self-representation within a medium that now takes sound for granted. The relation to sound gains in motivation as a result. Bogart begins as a whining hoodlum who talks too fast and too much in films such as William Wyler's *Dead End* (1937) or Raoul Walsh's *The Big Shot* (1942). Once he becomes a leading man, he can still talk too much, and very often in a dull, conventional way, even as late as his role as a newspaper editor in Richard Brooks's *Deadline U.S.A.* (1952).

No wonder Michael Curtiz's *Casablanca* (1942) is Bogart's real turning-point. Released within a year of *Citizen Kane*, it provides another kind of dialectically critical moment in Hollywood history. The change in Bogart's persona recapitulates the change that Barrymore

116

undergoes in his shift from an expressive silent actor to a largely silent sound actor. It both alludes to and cancels Barrymore at one and the same time. *Casablanca* marks the beginning of Bogart's own punctuated silences, the moment of the discovery by Bogart of his signature style. It is appropriated from his own, as it were, silent master. The better films that precede and follow *Casablanca*, from Walsh's *High Sierra* (1941) to Nicholas Ray's *In a Lonely Place* (1950), document an intensification of the Bogart of *Casablanca* who emerges from under Barrymore's shadow.

Bogart's principal disciple is Marlon Brando. Brando is hesitant to talk as a precondition of his persona even as a youngster. He becomes increasingly silent as his career proceeds. Once again, the transaction with the medium of sound film is basic and decisive, although in Brando's case the relevant shift is not from silent film to sound, but from theater to film. Brando's early fame as a stage actor in Tennessee Williams's *A Streetcar Named Desire* on Broadway in 1947 rested less on his speech than on the effect the paralysis of his speech by emotion produced. The Broadway audience, legendarily, thought he was having a seizure during the performance on opening night. In an early, and definitive, film such Lazlo Benedek's *The Wild One* (1954), his authority as a renegade biker rests on his sunglassed gaze. His voice, when he uses it, is a surprisingly soft one. As with Elvis Presley, as I will show later on, this is a feminization of male authority, which is why it is a renegade form of authority. It is an indictment of patriarchy, and fair to keep under wraps, or drag. Whenever Brando is asked to speak a great deal – in Edward Dmytryk's *The Young Lions* (1958), for example – one is as a rule treated to an unrecognizable Brando. What recognizability there is in the famous voice lies always in its hesitation to say much at all. A principal exception is Gillo Pontecorvo's *Burn!* (1969), although here, even a stentorian Brando is unrecognizable because of his gorgeous British accent. Brando's characteristic penury in relation to sound does not find a fully appropriate thematization until *The Godfather*. Francis Ford Coppola makes sure to key the film largely on the rhythms, including the silences, of Brando's speech. Don Corleone is film's chief spokesman for the dangers of talking too much. Doing so gets you into trouble.

117

Brando's best disciple or revision is Robert DeNiro. DeNiro does to Brando what Brando does to Bogart, and Bogart to Barrymore. He recurs more and more to silence as the canonical films of his career proceed. Particularly decisive in this regard is Scorsese's *Taxi Driver* (1976). No wonder the film's best-known scene is that of DeNiro looking at the camera and asking, "You talkin' to me?" It makes DeNiro's sense of himself in relation to speech the film's very center. Here character exceeds itself by reflecting on its own improbable excess, something only a film can show. DeNiro will speak only in response to someone else's speech, even if it is his own. Barrymore, Bogart, and Brando all remain silent and depressed about what DeNiro grows maniacal about: the need to speak at all. It becomes the very subject of the acting. In *The King of Comedy* (1982), Jerry Lewis, the talk-show host kidnapped by DeNiro and Sandra Bernhardt, is the king not only of comedy – he plays a character like Johnny Carson – but of talking too much. No wonder Bernhardt tapes his mouth shut when he is being held for ransom. Acting represents itself within the history of acting.

Blonde on Blonde: Harlow and Monroe

Dialectic in female acting is as plain as it is in the male tradition, and defined even more abruptly by canonical figures. Not only that. Female stardom is structured differently from male, as is gender difference itself. It is, to use Eisenstein's term, a "superimposition," a propping of one image upon another. It is the daughter's face against the mother's. The Hollywood difference reflects this difference. Here the canonical figures are really only two, Jean Harlow and Marilyn Monroe. They form a dyad similar to the pre-Oedipal relation between mother and child. This is a different kind of dialectic from the violent, totemic murders of the father in the Oedipal series that unfolds from Barrymore through the primal horde of his ungrateful sons. By the same token, any female representation that is not blonde is, by definition, a deviation from prototype, less significant because patriarchy privileges the blonde female. Gentlemen, as Hawks notes

118

in the title of his 1953 film with Monroe, do indeed prefer blondes. By contrast, Olivia de Havilland or Lauren Bacall are simply "quirky" or "interesting." Bette Davis, as Joseph Mankiewicz's *All About Eve* (1950) suggests, takes revenge on all of them. This is also why Garbo is so enigmatic. On which side of the blonde/brunette line does she stand?

Technically, however, the terms of the female tradition are very similar to those that define male stardom, particularly Bogart's revision of Barrymore. If Barrymore and Bogart are the twin pillars of the male tradition, then Harlow and Monroe are, blonde bias aside, the twin pillars of the female tradition. Like the relation of Barrymore, Bogart, and Brando, Harlow and Monroe's relation is – and is about – the play of silence and sound. Endlessly talky – or "talkie," as it were – Harlow will not, as a rule, shut up. Her stardom begins at the very beginning of sound film, in Frank Capra's *Platinum Blonde* (1931). Her voice is, presumably, an endearing and comedic trait. It adds both an additional luster and a blister or blemish to her beauty, much as her full face and ample hips do. Hesitant to speak, and soft-spoken when she does, Monroe's relation to the camera is structured by her relation – or lack of it – to the loudmouth Harlow. This is Monroe's revision of the blonde bombshell prototype. Brash and trashy, Harlow is nonetheless engaging and adorable because of the smile and softness of heart that underwrites what is really a good and open soul. Her sins are those of enthusiasm, not of fraud or faithlessness. As with Barrymore, *Dinner at Eight* is probably the performance that presents her at her fullest, thanks also to Cukor's direction. It not only presents Harlow at her most characteristic, but also thematizes the conditions of her persona. What beauty Harlow projects visually is undercut by her cheesy accent and the strident pitch and volume of her voice. Difficulties regarding class and money are what *Dinner at Eight* is about thematically. Not only does Wallace Beery snatch Lionel Barrymore's old family business out from under him. Harlow, Beery's trophy wife, serves as his sounding board as he constantly calls her out – as she does him – on the subject of social ambition. It is her wish to be among aristocracy that reigns supreme in her mind, a wish that Beery, whose wealth comes from outdoor work, finds absurd.

119

Monroe's revision of Harlow is one based on cutting out, with great precision, the incongruous element in Harlow herself – the briny voice. Monroe represses it, leaving herself clear of its weight both morally and from the point of view of fashion or taste. It is, however, an imperfect correction of the "low." She "superimposes" herself on Harlow with less of a difference than she wishes. Monroe's pathos, like the pathos of the centerfolds and the porn stars to whom she gives rise (Meisel, 2007), results from her misconceived longing to be "high." Monroe reads Harlow's anxieties and does her best to change them, first and foremost by allowing the voice no accent, and a very limited range of expressiveness. A mid-American accent helps wash away Harlow's harsh tonalities, but even this is not enough. The depression in Monroe's character comes from this repression or internalization of what Harlow exuberantly acts out. When Monroe does speak, she has transformed all enthusiasm into a complex mixture of hesitation masked as grace. Nor is this for reasons principally of gender – Brando's is actually a more transgendered persona – but for reasons of class. Monroe wants to make sure – as she did biographically, more than once – to marry that millionaire. Her millionaire, however, unlike Harlow's, is very different from the crude Beery. He is Joe DiMaggio, the Yankee Clipper, or Arthur Miller, the tragic playwright. Monroe's encounters with working-class loners and drifters like herself – Don Murray in Joshua Logan's *Bus Stop* (1956), for example – strike the spectator as more logical if also more painful to witness. The original title of *Bus Stop* was in fact *The Wrong Kind of Girl*. Her perplexity about potential detective lovers like Richard Widmark in Roy Ward Baker's *Don't Bother to Knock* (1952) leads to her unmasking as a criminal. The tension between high strivings and low realities defines her throughout both her career and her life.

The school of blonde actresses who flow from the Harlow/Monroe line is a series of swerves from Monroe's own swerve from Harlow. Lana Turner, even when her lover is the working-class John Garfield in *The Postman Always Rings Twice*, remains on the tidy side of the street; Shelley Winters remains on Harlow's less fastidious side as Turner's contemporary and wholly different kind of disciple of Harlow. Grace Kelly revises Harlow so fully that, as I have noted, she is propelled out of the star system altogether and into the ranks of real European royalty. Of all Hollywood's stars, she alone becomes a genuine star by becoming a real-life aristocrat. She succeeds precisely where Monroe falls short, although Monroe remains the more paradigmatic figure because of this. As later disciples striving for autonomy, Kathleen Turner and Sharon Stone both require tough, criminal roles – Turner as hit-girl in Huston's *Prizzi's Honor* (1985), Sharon Stone as prostitute in Scorsese's *Casino* (1995), or as murderer in the two *Basic Instinct* films (1992, 2006). This is to free themselves from their genealogical relation to Harlow and Monroe alike. Though they are thugs, they are also elegant, confident women. This is to distinguish themselves from Monroe even more than from Harlow. Monroe's surpassing status as cosmic outcast makes her unique among all stars in history.

The play of sound and silence from Barrymore to Bogart and from Harlow to Monroe also recalls the play of presence and absence with which Benjamin and Bazin are concerned in the epistemological precondition of film as a medium. The presumably mimetic projection or expressiveness of acting becomes, from this point of view, a philosophical instance – an embodiment, quite literally – of the medium's own epistemological paradoxes. The history of Hollywood stars narrates the terror of what Benjamin and Bazin alike describe in the shift to film's cultural hegemony. Early death interrupts Harlow's career during the filming of Jack Conway's *Saratoga* (1937). Monroe, of course, is a probable suicide in 1962. It also shows how sound film always retains the shadow of its early silent period. Its prior condition as a medium becomes the decisive element in its representation of character in the sound era. It is the "talkiness" and "silence" of Hollywood acting as a whole that are its decisive oppositions. Whether cast as enthusiasm and gloom, optimism and depression, these poles in human expressiveness actually derive from the grammar provided by the history of the medium rather than by a mimetic impulse. Hollywood copies, and revises, not life, but its own prior representations. Each of our canonical actors, male and female, reduplicates as a sound actor this precise relation to silent tradition. It is also what gives film acting its absolute and unmistakable specificity.

121

Hang 'Em High: Welles, Lewis, Eastwood

When the actor is also the director, auteur dialectics and the dialectics of acting combine into a still wider dialectic. "High" and "low" become no less than life and death. Three figures predominate: the inevitable Welles; the unlikely Jerry Lewis; and the enormously efficient Clint Eastwood. The sequence they provide as actor/directors narrates nothing less than their own deaths, each in a different way. They provide a collective and unfolding allegory of film's ecological or Darwinian process as a medium, which is a battle for survival. Welles as hero dies in each of his films. Lewis can never really be said to be fully alive in his solo films after the partnership with Dean Martin ends. His spasmodics inhibit his psychological and even his physical wholeness. This begins with Frank Tashlin's direction of him even before he begins to direct himself. He is also the first actor to copyright his characters, as though he regards his self-representations as separate from himself and in need of mooring to the social – and financial – order. This is why Eastwood's constant ability to survive – quite unlike Welles's – is critical. In each of his films, he is still left standing.

Welles inaugurates this wider tradition, and not simply because of the change he brings to directing. He is also the first director in the sound era to direct himself as leading man. In the silent era, both Keaton and Chaplin direct themselves, with groundbreaking and, in each case, very different results. Keaton meditates on his own face; Chaplin meditates on his body. Welles's cinema of context – his pointillism – newly highlights the problem of the actor's very clarity on the screen as an entity. As a director, Welles does not even take the molecular stability of the body – or the environment – for granted. This is the ambivalence he shares with Ford, and one he resolves by being, not less ambivalent than Ford, who makes choices, but more ambivalent. Welles's is an undecidable cinema *par excellence*, for actor and director alike.

As an actor, Welles was famous first as a radio personality. Welles's *War of the Worlds*, his Mercury Theatre's 1938 radio docudrama, based on H.G. Wells's novel, quite literally sent its listeners into flights of genuine fear. The violent effects of which the new technology of arts like radio were capable was the real meaning of the anxiety about the invasion from Mars. The feared attack was not allegorical or fantastic – it was a fear of the invasion into people's homes of technology – of radio – itself. People had a right to be afraid. They had indeed let an alien into the house. The alien landing from outer space that Welles "reported" was entirely accurate. It was the landing of his own voice in one's parlor. It was a reflexive, interactive achievement.

This carries over directly into film, first and foremost with *Kane*, a film about a media mogul whose death sets off a hunt to clarify the man against the background. The film's theme, in other words, is identical with its technique. Knowing Kane is the interpretative equivalent to the perceptual or neurological challenge posed by the deep focus that leaves personages in obscurity, and makes the background the foreground. Welles's handling of himself as actor in his subsequent films follows suit. His presence only as the narrator in *The Magnificent Ambersons* (1942) almost refines him out of existence. Joseph Cotten predominates as Welles's Boswell or Marlow, presiding over an authoritative personality who is less evocative than he should be. That is why, as with Conrad's Kurtz, all the interpretation is necessary. Kurtz, like Kane, is "wanting," as Conrad puts it, in interest. As in *Kane*, the commentary in *The Magnificent Ambersons* has a more prominent role than its subject matter. Edward G. Robinson's investigation of Welles as a fugitive Nazi in *The Stranger* (1946) likewise predominates, although here Welles as actor allows himself a fire commensurate with the passion of the commentary he inspires. It is a unique, and undervalued, moment in Welles's acting career. *The Lady from Shanghai* (1948) also distorts Welles, this time as an unlikable, self-regarding sot and fool with an irritating brogue. The burlesque results remove any sympathy one may initially feel obliged to offer. Here Everett Sloane has the commentator's role, although it is, of course, Rita Hayworth's commentary – she is both attracted to and repelled by Welles – that is the decisive commentary. When the mirrors set up an infinite regress at film's end and then shatter, the fact that the film has all along been mostly a commentary upon its own action becomes clear. The literal dismantling of the mimetic apparatus reminds the viewer again that Welles films himself, and all actors, even Hayworth, with a directorial rather than a characterological intention. Welles's pointillism or digitalism remains the emphatic project.

The same is true many years later in *Touch of Evil* (1958). Now fat and distorted, Welles, as in *The Stranger*, uses a biographical mimesis to make cinema not less but more expansive because of it. Biography for Welles is context, not explanation. Pointillism is the rule, the search for the separation of foreground from field. The film is, as it always is, an excuse for its own filming. Though presumably interesting and filled with secrets, Welles, the sheriff of the Mexican town – a reversal of his heroic role in *Journey into Fear* (1942) – is actually uninteresting, and almost as unintelligent as his silences suggest. What croaking voice there is suggests little in the way of character. Welles's comings and goings in deep focus reflect, not his character's shadiness, nor even its shiftiness, but its elusiveness *as* character. Welles is once again, in the film's story, of interest only as something for the camera to follow. Charlton Heston, a Mexican investigator on Welles's trail to expose his corruption, is, unlike Robinson in *The Stranger*, also rendered a Wellesian being, mute and tasteless. He is not Welles's interpreter, as is Robinson, or Cotten, but his double. Heston's acting throughout his own baffling career is an awkward and undirected version of Wellesian character at large, which fades and emerges from background peripatetically. Like Welles as a character, Heston as a character is a pompous fool. It is an astonishing use of Heston on Welles's part, a rawly reflexive kind of filming in which the actor represents the kind of extravagant self-regard that he actually has as an actor. And, as usual, Welles dies at the film's conclusion. Welles films himself in order to die.

No wonder it is difficult to assign Welles a precursor as an actor and to set in motion a dialectic for Welles as a star. Welles as star is a chameleon, and a chameleon because the very status of the actor in Welles is not only to die but to disintegrate first. Old and stooped as Kane, unsympathetic as Harry, disgusting as the sheriff, Welles has no identity as an actor except as what an actor is – constantly changing, blending into the deep focus environment, already, as it were, dead.

Nor in Welles's case is this metamorphic quality transformative in any but a radically negative way. The drift is always to the body's proto-plasmic instability and decline. The body has the same fate as does celluloid.

As a director of himself, Jerry Lewis becomes, surprisingly enough, a Wellesian event. It joins with Welles's handling of himself the same narrative of the director's disintegration as an actor. When Lewis moves out of the shadow of other directors, especially Frank Tashlin, to film himself, the irony is considerable. He takes control in order to fall apart. There is, however, a different attitude toward the body's mortality and ruin than in Welles. There is a different tradition behind it. As an actor, Lewis is a revision of Chaplin. This is key to his wider strategy as a director of himself. As an actor, he undoes the perfection of balance that Chaplin achieves, whether in relation to objects or in relation to himself. He narrates, as does Welles, his own disintegra-tion, but superimposed against Chaplin's precision. Whether with Tashlin or with Norman Taurog, or under his own direction, the anti-Chaplinesque predominates, and predominates decisively. Describing a Jerry Lewis film inevitably sounds like the title of one: the compe-tent presentation of incompetence. This is Conrad, though with a comic intent. The titles of Lewis's films are, rhetorically, a play between noun and adjective in which the perception or evaluation of the thing and the thing itself trade qualities. Which is tenor and which is vehicle becomes painfully confused. Tashlin's *The Disorderly Orderly* (1964) is a good example. An orderly's orderliness can only be assessed through its negation and vice versa. The stability of an object depends for its coherence on the possibility of its incoherence. Whatever the ordered setting, Lewis is the spasmodic functionary. The settings Lewis chooses rely very specifically on the body as functionally whole in order for them to run smoothly, whether a hotel in his own *The Bellboy* (1960), a department store in Tashlin's *Who's Minding The Store?* (1963), or a hospital in Tashlin's *The Disorderly Orderly* (1964). Lewis's films are frightening because they narrate what Lacan calls the body-in-pieces – the dismembered, or disremembered, body – trying to function as a whole in highly bureaucratized environments. Lewis's speech even does this to the signifying chain of language. Like Lear's doggerel in the late scenes of Shakespeare's play, it bespeaks the breakdown of, or, in Lewis's case, the simple failure to achieve, the ability to master self-expression. The systematic machine of hotel, hospital, and department store stands in stark contrast to this poor soul's incompetence. Lewis's is not only a physical and psychological incompetence, but also a neurological one. If Welles narrates his own death, Lewis narrates his own death-in-life.

Eastwood's career as both an actor and director is also a series of dialectical escapes from precursor authority. Don Siegel's *Escape from Alcatraz* (1979) is paradigmatic. The island prison, like Siegel's direction, is the consummate symbol of authority. Films like Eastwood's own *True Crime* (1999) expand the paradigm by narrowing Eastwood's freedom even more, even if he is not under lock and key. Here Eastwood portrays himself, not under the thumb, but as a witness to the murder of a woman by the President of the United States. As a burglar, however, he cannot present himself as a witness. His high functioning as an outlaw vitiates any function he may have as a citizen. This, of course, is why his films are about outlaws, policemen, and soldiers. Each treads the digital line between context and profile, anonymity and self-revelation. Each bureaucratic *mise en scène*, like those of Lewis or of Welles, is a reflexive instance of the conditions of the pointillistic filmmaking. That Eastwood stars for others in the early phases of his acting career – first, for Sergio Leone, and then, principally, for Siegel – is also an instance of emerging from digital context, as does a Welles character. It is both a response to Welles and a response to his own Oedipal relation to his prior directors. Each phase with an earlier director works through relationships preoccupied with authority, each one more reflexive than the one before. Siegel revises Leone by giving the nameless vistas of Eastwood's no-name hero in the spaghetti westerns the names of real cities and streets, and by giving Eastwood the name of Harry Callahan. The moniker of Dirty Harry, however, prevails, erasing his proper name, which is used only by his police superiors to hail him. The freedom of directing himself leads to disappearing into the background all over again. But now it is Eastwood's signature project. He has gained control over his lack of control.

Eastwood is aided in this directorial project by his dialectic with the history of acting. As an actor, Eastwood is a revision of John Wayne. He shoulders the burden of thought that Wayne typically casts aside. Eastwood brings the melancholy shadow of film noir to bear on Wayne's thoughtless and daytime conscientiousness. As cowboy, cop, and especially as soldier, Eastwood's dutiful hero thinks through what are for Wayne, in the same roles, assumptions about duty that require no thought at all. For Eastwood, they do. Wayne is a good technical actor, but few scenes show him in thoughtful repose. Chief among them are his widower visits to Maureen O'Hara's grave in *She Wore a Yellow Ribbon* (1949), the middle film in Ford's cavalry trilogy. These scenes are Eastwood's enabling sources as an actor; by imitating them, he can turn an uncharacteristic Wayne against the characteristic one. Wayne looks at the grave, as does the viewer, although what the viewer sees, unlike Wayne, is Wayne himself looking. He looks as we do, but also not as we do. We see the watcher watching. Here Ford, unlike Hitchcock, does not position the spectator in the position of receiving the male gaze. This notion of Hitchcock and other male directors is, of course, now traditional (Mulvey, 1975, 1981; Penley, 1988). It is also the Hitchcock beyond whom Ford goes in this astonishing and largely unique moment in his films. This is a singular moment in Wayne's career, his weakest as a symbol of patriarchy and also his most powerful as an actor because of it. Ford does not position the spectator in the position of receiving the male gaze, but of seeing the male gaze position itself, or be positioned, in relation to its object. The scene's pathos derives, to be sure, from the viewer's identification with Wayne's own sadness at the death of his beloved. But it also derives from the pathos of seeing how reduced the great male hero is when confronted by the loss of the object who returns his gaze. Without it, his empowerment as a man – if I may pun – wanes. He loses his own subjectivity. Like Welles, or Lewis, he fades into the background. All that is left is his military rank, which leaves him whole but hollow. It is this Wayne – the secret Wayne on the edge of his authority as a man – whom Eastwood intercepts, and whom he takes as dialectical precursor. Eastwood's desire is not sometimes foreclosed, as is Wayne's. It is always foreclosed. This is his triumph over Wayne. He gives up desire

127

itself. He carries out his professional duties without mixing them with questions of subjectivity. Wayne, by contrast, is always on the side of desire, which is pathetic rather than tragic. As a director, Eastwood finds a new gradation in tragic emotion itself. There is an ethics beyond pathos to which the hero may aspire. It converts tragedy to Epicureanism, the original and highest form of stoicism. Eastwood has, like film itself, moved beyond the pleasure principle. It is the only way to stay alive in a world in which one is already dead. He resolves the dialectic that Welles begins. Being "high" – breathing, or above ground – is also, in Bazin's sense, being "low," or buried alive.

6

The Blues Misreading of Gospel: A History of Rock and Roll

A Scandal in Bohemia

The reception of jazz and its musical heirs, rhythm and blues and rock and roll, has always been the product of a deep ambivalence in the American grain. It is an ambivalence about "high" and "low" in a racial key. In the 1930s, the first professional jazz critics were very clear about it. They celebrated jazz for its redemptive primitivism. In the process, they had to slander the achievement that they praised. For Carl Van Vechten, the more brutal the poverty of black life, the more authentic was the music to which it gave birth. The Yale-educated John Hammond, who drove his car through the South and Midwest on the trail of legendary performers, valued musicians who could not read music more than those who did. Their illiteracy testified to the natural urgency of their expression. Beat completed this tradition. In the 1950s, Jack Kerouac and Norman Mailer also honored jazz for its atavism. For Kerouac, the spontaneity of jazz improvisation was proof of its mindless honesty. For Mailer, the power of black music lay in the presumably savage power of the black people who had invented it.

What is troubling about the modern reception of jazz is what is also historically familiar about it. Behind it looms an earlier mode of reception that it recapitulates even as it overturns: The history of American minstrelsy, the practice by which "blackface" white performers, beginning in the North in the 1830s, parodied black American music even as it deigned to exalt it. Minstrelsy, as I showed in Part I, has a central place in the history of both phrenology and of "high" and "low."

129

It also has a central place in the history of modern bohemia. Like it or not, the Beats were the direct heirs of minstrel thinking.

Mailer's *The White Negro* (1957) shares with Kerouac's "spontaneous bop prosody" (1958) the assumption that blacks in general and jazz in particular are a wellspring of natural urgency, far removed from the reach of culture. Or so it seems. *The White Negro* is the watershed hipster text, the jazz version of Rahv's "Paleface and Redskin" and Warshow's "Gangster as Tragic Hero." There is, however, a difference. Mailer did not write for *Partisan Review*; in 1955, he co-founded *The Village Voice*. He makes the dialectical leap that *Partisan Review* did not. He rereads phrenology, unlike *Partisan Review*, and he does so by reassessing jazz. This is also where he distinguishes himself from Kerouac. He covers himself on both flanks. The difference between Mailer and Kerouac on jazz reflects their difference from each other as writers. Mailer has surpassing technique; Kerouac, none at all. Mailer sees jazz as the portal to a renovated view of technique as a whole; Kerouac views technique with diffidence and even alarm. Mailer's many distinctions between black and white may disturb a contemporary reader, but his real impetus is to do away with them. Mailer views the differences, not as "polarities," to use Rahv's word, but as parts of a shift in how one views both culture and the self. Here is the American ambivalence about jazz together with its dialectical resolution:

> The Negro, not being privileged to gratify his self-esteem with the heady satisfactions of categorical condemnation, chose to move instead in that other direction where all situations are equally valid, and in the worst of perversion, promiscuity, pimpery, drug addiction, rape, razor-slash, bottle-break, what-have-you, the Negro discovered and elaborated a morality of the bottom, an ethical differentiation between the good and the bad in every human activity from the go-getter pimp (as opposed to the lazy one) to the relatively dependable pusher or prostitute. (1957, 321–2)

"Perversion," "bottom," "bad" – these are the terms of sexology and phrenology and, of course, the terms of "high" and "low." Mailer, however, transforms these "polarities" into something else: into a dynamic view of both self and artist in which polarities mix and contaminate. Things are "loosed," to use Pater's word; they are "dynamic," to use Eisenstein's. Here is Mailer's dialectical transformation of the phreno-logical assumptions with which he begins:

> Add ... the profound sensitivity of the Negro jazzman who was the cultural mentor of a people, and it is not too difficult to believe that the language of Hip which evolved was an artful language, tested and shaped by an intense experience and therefore different in kind from white slang. (322)

The "language of Hip" is a new "language," and the foundation of a new "existential state." It is in the service of something new regarding high and low, cultured and pop, black and white. The "addition" of the reconceived "jazzman" makes the real dialectical difference. High and low are both learned. No longer, as in Kerouac, is the jazzman a noble savage, or an autodidact. He is a "prophet." The difference is a simple but decisive one:

> It takes the immediate experiences of any passing man and magnifies the dynamic of his movements ... so that he is seen more as a vector in a network of forces than as a static character in a crystallized field. (Which latter is the practical view of the snob.) (322)

The "snob," or highbrow, is "static." He exists in a frozen or "crystal-lized field." The hipster is dynamic, "a vector in a network of forces." As with Welles's cinema, the world and the subject materially and psychologically are freewheeling, in constant play.

Rock and roll criticism follows most of all from Mailer's critical energies. It used the pages of *The Village Voice* to do so. As an academy-in-exile or School of Mailer, *The Voice*, unlike *Rolling Stone*, developed Mailer's double-barreled vision into a measured notion of what Mailer had sought – a sense, and a state, of cultural "hybridity," as post-colonial theory now calls it. If, as Robert Christgau avers, Richard Goldstein invented rock criticism, it was Christgau who systematized it and institutionalized it, using New Journalist techniques to describe its tensions firsthand. In addition to the birthing of New Journalism, the influence of *The Voice* included that sea change in cultural assumption represented by rock criticism as an enterprise. The very stance of rock criticism obliterates any presumable difference between high and low. It approaches the "low" with the tools of the "high," looking for a mirror of its own technique in its subject, not a foil. In this sense, its stringent aestheticism proved its politics more certainly than did any of its passing polemics about race or even class. For Christgau, all human activity was, to use Kenneth Burke's phrase, "symbolic action" – discourses with dialectical histories. Describing the polyphony of the rock text in the ironic format of the self-invented "consumer guide" (e.g., 1981) to evaluate recordings over the years allowed Christgau to "superimpose" two notions of the same cultural product, one fluid, one fixed, one upon the other. No wonder the demise of the conservative approach to culture had to come from "pop" music criticism, from its origins in jazz criticism to its apotheosis in rock. Its object gave it the best chance to do so. As "A History of High and Low" (Chapter 1) has shown, "high" culture itself created the problem of "mediocrity" by making the artist's struggle against past forms the center of Romanticism. Rock criticism, unlike other traditions of criticism, is delighted to discover the artist's relation to past forms, not, like literary criticism, exasperated by the work involved. Because Keats initiates this tradition, he is rock and roll's original poet, the first Buddy Holly or Brian Jones. The continuity between high and pop is often exact to a fault.

Goldstein's undertaking was more dramatic. Like Christgau, he identified the conflicts under which rock criticism labored, but he solved them through the use, not of a scholarly persona, but of an unrelenting autobiographical conceit. When Goldstein began to be disillusioned by the "stylization," as he called it, of late-1960s rock and roll, he turned to an ethic of authenticity that his earlier writing had viewed as dubious (for an oral history, see Powers, 2008). Goldstein's earliest memorable piece, "Gear" (1966), showed that he was a baroque postmodernist, a writer of pastiche rather than what he appeared to be, a confessional writer. The secret of his own original style was stylization. So was his view of cultural production. The flirtation with authenticity was Goldstein's intellectual prod, not the source of his thought. It was the resistance he needed to rediscover his best and earliest energies. Punk revived them in the early 1970s. As with Christgau, Goldstein's embrace of punk gave stylization a new and acceptable place in rock criticism as a whole.

Rock criticism, however, remains a peripatetic enterprise. One recalls R. Meltzer's *The Aesthetics of Rock* (1970). Despite subsequent histories organized by sound or genre (Guralnick, 1986; Gracyk, 1996), or by the development of electric guitar (Palmer, 1992; Waksman, 1999), rock criticism has no direction home. The first histories of rock and roll remain the best ones – Charles Keil's *Urban Blues* (1966), Charlie Gillett's *The Sound of the City* (1970), Robert Palmer's *Deep Blues* (1981). LeRoi Jones's *Blues People* (1963) remains the best overall introduction to American music. Some biographical traditions, particularly Dylan's, are critically rich, although idiosyncratic; some star autobiographies, particularly those of Miles Davis (1989) and Berry Gordy (1994), are superb.

Despite rock criticism's very intellectual labor, it provides no dialectical model with which to organize either rock and roll history or its relation to its chief source, jazz. One has to turn to jazz criticism, not rock criticism, to find such a model. Ralph Ellison is the best guide. Here is Ellison in 1959:

> Although since the twenties, many jazzmen have had conservatory training and were well grounded in formal theory and instrumental technique, when we approach jazz we are entering quite a different sphere of training. Here it is more meaningful to speak, not of courses of study, of grades and degrees, but of apprenticeship, ordeals, initiation ceremonies, of rebirth. For after the jazzman has learned the fundamentals of jazz – the intonations, the mute work, manipulation of timbre, the body of traditional style – he must then "find himself," must be reborn, must find, as it were, his soul. (1959, 208–9)

Jazz has a structure and a history, rooted not in the soil or in blind instinct, but in the self-conscious artistry of the musicians who play it. Jazz is a learned tradition. Like the history of any aesthetic form, it is defined by a complex interplay of convention and revolt. It is defined, that is, by dialectic. After 1950, the dialectic thickens. Reactions within jazz to bebop go on to produce a whole new epoch whose apotheosis is rock and roll.

Jazz Myth, Jazz Reality

The history of American music after 1950 falls into a three-part sequence: the emergence of bebop as a response to swing, and bop's eventual decline after Charlie Parker's death in 1955; the emergence of rhythm and blues after 1955 as a response to bop, and r & b's reinvention of swing's easy danceability in a newer key; and the emergence of rock and roll as both a resolution of this prior history and the suppression of some of its key elements, particularly its African American foundations. To tell the story by focusing on representative or canonical figures will also provide another familiar lesson about the precise mechanism of pop dialectic.

Swing music dominated New Deal America and kept spirits high in the canteens of World War II. But it had a history and its future had a horizon. If combo Dixieland had given way to the small-orchestra "jazz" of the 1920s and the Jazz Age ideology that appropriated it, then "jazz" had given way to the expansive vision of swing in the big-band sounds of Duke Ellington and Count Basie. By the end of World War II, however, swing's infrastructure began to crack economically. The mood of American culture had likewise become brooding and alienated in the shadow of the Bomb. Bebop was the music of the Beats, and Beat emphasized the solitary and the existential. The reflective bop soloist was its ideal emblem.

Parker's battle with the influence of Lester Young is the key site of musical struggle in the shift from swing to bebop, despite the attempt by some historians to blame it all on Dizzy Gillespie and his milder revision of swing trumpet. Muting the horn and graveling its tone (Gillespie also bent the bell of his instrument by accident one afternoon, leaving it that way because it looked cool). Gillespie was good for publicity. By contrast, Parker drastically alters the tone, attack, and harmonic choices of saxophone forever. He expunges the most saccharine of swing-horn mannerisms, vibrato, and introduces a tonal amplitude to saxophone that never capitulates to Young's breathiness. Parker also combines a technical appetite unmatched in jazz before or since with a depth of blues feeling second to none except for that of Louis Armstrong.

Although Parker's influence within jazz proper remains decisive well beyond his death in 1955 – not until John Coltrane does a musician of peer power emerge to change the nature of saxophone again – by the late 1940s a new player appears on the jazz stage to challenge bebop's dominance and take its place in popularity with the black listening public: rhythm and blues. Louis Jordan and his Tympani Five are the founding group, appearing at Minton's in Harlem for the first time in 1938. Jordan himself sang in a swing style over the horn section's jump riffs and played an early version of rock and roll saxophone. The latter's real father, however, is saxist Earl Bostic. If Parker invented bop out of swing, then Bostic, with his raucous transformation of swing vibrato into rock and roll flatulence, invented r & b out of swing.

Rhythm and blues eventually crossed with bop to produce "hard bop": a fusion of bop phrasing and harmonics with r & b rhythms, particularly the funky beat that becomes the *via media* for a music enduringly beset by the burdens of Parker's precedent. Bop had often used Afro-Cuban instrumentation; the presence of conga and timbales added an extra layer of density to its experimentation with rhythms and time. But the reasons for hard bop's emergence are more than circumstantial. They are dialectical. Jones (1963) and Arnold Shaw (1978) both regard hard bop as an umbrella of protection from Parker musically and from bop ideologically. Shaw even suggests that hard bop was a way lesser musicians, especially sax players, had of swerving from the demands of bop technique. The same could be said of a black public that, as Nelson George has shown (1988), had grown exhausted listening to Parker and Gillespie, and wanted easier, groovier music that it could simply relax to.

The absence of a canonical center for hard bop – one could choose among any number of group leaders, chief among them Horace Silver and Art Blakey – is a perfect example of its sensibility. Hard bop seeks the erasure of personality in the very act of securing it through deliberately generic, even formulaic means. Whether it is Cannonball Adderley, who played with Miles Davis, or whether it is King Curtis, who played with both Lionel Hampton and the Coasters, all of jazz goes on to feed on the synthesis of hard bop. As a common point of origin, hard bop joins the sound of the roadhouses of the 1950s with the revolutionary music of Ornette Coleman, Eric Dolphy, Archie Shepp, and John Coltrane in the 1960s, all of whom began as r & b horn players. Miles Davis's inspired (and still criticized) brand of "fusion" jazz beginning in the early 1970s – a mix of jazz and rock – is hard bop's greatest legacy, and the basis of virtually all later developments in jazz and rock alike. So significant is Davis's jazz-rock fusion that his earlier role in the history of bop proper is almost overshadowed by it. If Parker changes saxophone, it is Davis, not Gillespie, who changes trumpet. Not only does he take on the single most powerful influence in all of jazz, that of Armstrong, and modulate its enthusiasm into wariness. He also takes on the influence of Parker, for whom he served as trumpet sideman in the late 1940s and early 1950s. Davis's invention of "cool" jazz after 1955 – a calm, selective mode of solo improvisation – is his resolved response to Armstrong and Parker alike.

Hard bop is a superb metaphor for the many tensions that American music and culture hold in suspension in the years that follow World War II. It is a grand dialectical moment in jazz history. That is why it is a long-lasting style. The consummate jazz trope for any resolving or miscegenating style, hard bop is the stance of any number of familiar American mythologies: the fusion of cowboy and dandy in the roughneck spirit of gangster heroes from Jay Gatsby to Michael Corleone; the fusion of country and city in the churchy urbanity of African American writers from W.E.B. DuBois to Alice Walker; the fusion of low-life slang and the learned vocabulary of British Romanticism in Raymond Chandler. Philip Marlowe is not only a hard-boiled detective; with his combination of suavity, grit, and mischief, he is also a hard bop detective.

John Coltrane, who served as Davis's tenor sideman in the late 1950s, is the last of jazz's major figures. Dead in 1967, Coltrane was the influence that replaced Parker. His style remains the dominant one in jazz soloing even today. Like his contemporaries, Coltrane grew up in a climate that featured the consensus of hard bop; it also offered up hard bop's resources for sale if you wanted to be original. Coltrane was always a dialectical musician. The biting cascades of sound represent both his debt to Parker and his flight from him; the replacement of finger-snapping by the graver blues tone-poem is his surest difference from the bop approach to phrasing, even as it is scarred by the desire to escape it. How does Coltrane win his originality and overcome Parker's influence? By returning, not to Young, but to Bostic. Here he finds a means of inspiration in Bostic's earliest of models for r & b phrasing, when it is still attached to the rigors of swing. As a youngster, Coltrane had actually recorded with Bostic at a date in Cincinnati in 1952, when he was also touring with the altoist Eddie "Cleanhead" Vinson and hard bop organist Jimmy Smith.

Coltrane's revisionist propensities run so deep that they also required him to follow one album with a response in the next, especially in his last phase. The squealing, growling *Ascension* (1965), which became a kind of holy text for the "out" jazz movement of the late 1960s, is greeted, with almost preternatural haste, by *Meditations* (1965), a fearsomely shy and hesitant work. The epochal *A Love Supreme* (1964) is the most fiercely self-conscious effort in the history of jazz recording: Each of the album's movements comments upon and alters the phrasing of the movement before. Here Coltrane breaks free of jazz history as no saxist has done before or since, although he does so, inevitably, by negotiating with the very history he transforms.

Soul Synthesis

If jazz made some measure of peace with itself with hard bop, a wider form brought together rhythm and blues with the "gospel" tradition of Thomas A. Dorsey, Jr. to produce an entirely different kind of synthesis. The result is what is often known, with all its perilous history, as "soul." Soul is rhythm and blues in a post-Jordan mode. Jordan's singing, including the ensemble chorus behind it on hit tunes such as "Choo Choo Ch'Boogie" (1946), was still in the tradition of swinging jazz vocalists, chief among them Cab Calloway. Post-Jordan r & b is distinct from it thanks to Dorsey. It crosses the swing manner with another, and presumably opposed, sensibility: the sound of the hymn. Soul is, like hard bop, also the result of the synthesis of two apparent antinomies, in this case the secular and "dirty" stance of the blues and the stance of black religiosity derived from spirituals.

Gospel and blues, of course, are our old friends "high" and "low," now dressed in the garb of African American musical and cultural history. Gospel – the religious, the virtuous, the civic-minded – is "high," while the blues – the sexual, the despairing, the solipsistic – is "low." "Blue" notes – flatted thirds, fifths, and sevenths – are known as "dirty" notes. They are the specific agents of the blues misreading of gospel which produces the sound, first, of ad hoc, small ensemble rhythm and blues, and then of Motown, Stax, and Muscle Shoals.

Gospel enters this vortex already tainted. While always a religious man, Dorsey did not place the hymn on a pedestal, as did the earliest concert performers of the African American spiritual, the female Jubilee Singers of Fisk University in Nashville, who toured Europe in 1871. Dorsey the musician came belatedly to the invention of a religious or gospel music, having first been a blues musician who arranged for such luminaries as Bessie Smith and Ma Rainey. When Dorsey first heard the music of Charles A. Tindley at the annual meeting of the National Baptist Convention in Philadelphia in 1929, his own compositional instincts found both kinship and a foil. His dialectical instincts were aroused, not his submissive ones. Tindley, too, was blues-based, but not confined to the strict, 12-bar world of its musical grammar. Using instead the song models of Anglo-Irish spirituals, with 16-bar structures often supplemented by a bridge, Tindley's lyrics and moods were transcendent rather than circular and despondent. Dorsey joined the resources of this new discovery with the musical modalities of the blues. After 1929, he never looked back.

Thus, gospel was from the start a synthetic sound, a transformation of the traditional Anglo-Southern hymnal by means of the "classic blues" of the 1920s. Not only did this put two "polarities" into conversation; it also put gospel into a relation with jazz because of the now-common blues heritage. Dorsey is responsible. The discovery of a fresher country or rural realm by classic blues is not a surprising one in the history of blues tradition. Just as Dorsey discovers the sacred on the starboard hand of the secular, so Rainey had discovered the sound of the country blues that preceded classic blues only after she had thrived as a city musician. Nor does Dorsey himself cross only sacred and secular; he also crosses, like Rainey, country and city. Like the storefront churches that sprang up in the poor neighborhoods of Northern cities that counted more and more Southern emigrants among their populations after World War I, gospel is a theater of Southern inspiration within a Northern frame. By the time soul reaches its apex in the urbane studio sounds behind the voices of Otis Redding, Wilson Pickett, and Aretha Franklin (all gospel musicians who had graduated to the mainstream), the pattern was polished, and accounted for much of the music's broad appeal.

Dorsey's gospel sound blends with the jump sound of early r & b, however, through a mediator: the magnificent sound of the 1950s and early 1960s that we associate with doowop. While doowop's roots extend to the Ink Spots, an elegant vocal recording group of the swing era that emphasized tight harmonies, falsetto, and "tuba" bass, the sound's imitators included kids without benefit of instruments, the necessity that became a virtue. It created doowop's *a capella* sound. By the late 1940s, doowop had grown into a full-scale ghetto genre. By the middle of the 1950s, its recordings finally crossed over racial marketing lines with hits by the Cleftones, the Flamingos, the Moonglows, and Frankie Lymon and the Teenagers. The next generation of doo-woppers – the Platters, the Coasters, and the Drifters – paved the way for a number of solo artists whose names we know far better than those of their ancestors.

Now rhythm and blues hits its full stride. The major figures are master dialecticians. Sam Cooke's career is a case in point. He was the first gospel star to cross over into commercial success. In 1957, after 6 years as the lead singer of the Soul Stirrers, the country's leading gospel group, he recorded "You Send Me," a number-one hit and the moment that marks the transition from gospel proper to soul. The course of Marvin Gaye's career a few years later on is even more representative. Like Cooke, Gaye began by singing gospel music as a child, although his route to soul stardom included an explicit journey through doowop as a teenager. It also included marrying into the family of Motown founder Berry Gordy, Jr., who produced Gaye's first hits in the early 1960s.

With Motown, all the elements in the history of jazz, rhythm and blues, and gospel come together in the most fully realized sound ever achieved in American popular music. Memphis had the Stax house sound of Booker T. and the MGs; Atlantic Records had an outpost of progress at the Muscle Shoals studio in Florence, Alabama. But the crown jewel of soul production was Gordy's Motown label in Detroit. Motown was, as Smokey Robinson remarks in his autobiography, "a university" (1989, 212). Unlike "high culture" versions of urban art such as T.S. Eliot's *The Waste Land*, the sound of Motown presents the components of tradition not as fragmented and broken off from a whole, but as related in a multitude of ways. In the Motown sound, everything is a conversation. Gordy is a gleeful archaeologist of blues knowledge, using the shuffle beat of Chicago blues, the walking bass lines of hard bop jazz, and the harmonies of doowop-inspired vocal back-ups as scrim and collateral for an astonishing array of solo singers that included Gaye, Robinson, and Stevie Wonder.

After Sam Cooke, the epicenter of soul is Jackie Wilson. With Wilson, rhythm and blues singing becomes a school or strict canon. Wilson plays Milton to Cooke's Shakespeare, structuring the diction of a newly unfolding tradition. Even more than Cooke, Wilson isolates a doowop device – the devastating falsetto, with roots in the ancient history of fieldhouse blues – and remakes it into a vocal strategy central to the subsequent history of r & b singing as a whole. Wilson's 1957 hit, "Reet Petite" (also Gordy's first published song), features a voice in self-conscious dialogue with itself, jump-cutting from the falsetto that is now its dominant timbre to forays into the depths of a more guttural naturalness of expression.

In Wilson's train follow (like the Romantic poets following Milton) Robinson and Al Green, to name only two of the principal proponents of soul as it moves into the 1960s and 1970s. Smokey resolves Wilson's influence by resolving Wilson's self-dialogue between tenor and mezzo soprano into a single falsetto pitch. Green resolves it again by returning to the self-dialogue. Green agonizes, in the Greek sense of the word, over his relation to Wilson. Green's preacher father actually dismissed him from the family's gospel choir as a boy when he caught him with a Wilson record. To contain the anxiety of Wilson's influence, Green went on to use religious tradition as a soul device, taking much of his performance persona from the Passion of Christ. Indeed, in 1980, Green the soul star also became a minister of God. Nor is the history of soul without a punctuating irony to its dialectic, that of the "godfather of soul," James Brown. If r & b was a reaction to jazz, then "funk" was a reaction to r & b. Funk is both anti-jazz and anti-soul. Brown accents tempo on the downbeat instead of the upbeat, revising the history of both jazz syncopation and of the stomping swing of Motown and its satellites by reversing them both.

Plugging In

If Dorsey married the hymnal and classic blues, what kind of blues did gospel and doowop marry to produce the synthesis of soul? They crossed with the sound of urban blues, particularly the sound of Chicago blues. Here concrete history is symbolic. The emergence of Chicago blues can be dated with fair accuracy from the moment of Muddy Waters's arrival in Chicago from Mississippi in 1943. Waters had already garnered fame as a Delta bluesman. In 1944, however, he traded in his acoustic guitar for an electric one. The terms of his achievement expanded radically. Not only is his journey up Highway 61 reminiscent of the movement from country to city that defines much of the mythology of black American experience in the twentieth century. Through the electrification of his guitar, Waters adds to the journey the modernist lament of a fall into the nightmare of technology, away from the grace of nature. But this is to read him too jejunely. The most surprising thing about urban blues is that one sometimes cannot tell the difference between the singer's voice and his guitar. Waters, characteristically, muddies the waters separating the two. Here the difference between blues tradition and the white culture that surrounds it is especially clear. In a grand moment, Waters in effect deconstructs the presupposition behind the most presumably natural difference of all – the difference between nature and culture.

The Southern urban bluesmen who emerge out of T-Bone Walker in Texas are a more tailored bunch than their Northern colleagues (Walker actually precedes Waters, amplifying a swinging guitar with Charlie Christian's help in the late 1930s), but the same deconstruction of the difference between the savage and the civilized is at work. B.B. King of Memphis is exemplary. The dialogues between the voice and the guitar do not just cast the guitar (Lucille) as having a singing voice of her own; by implication, they also cast King's own sweet-as-can-be voice into an instrument *par excellence*. Coming as it does after Christian's invention of electric jazz guitar in the 1930s as a light and supple-toned instrument, Waters's brutal rhythm guitar of the 1940s is a self-conscious anachronism. It is deliberately atavistic.

Now Chuck Berry's pivotal position in the early rock and roll canon comes into focus. Recording on Chess records in the mid-to-late 1950s, Berry worked for the same Chicago label most closely associated with urban blues. But there the similarity ends. The pure singing voice right out of a boys' choir, riding high over jump riffs of a kind unique for electric guitar, presents a *prima facie* case for a major new turn in the history of American music. A master at managing overdetermination, Berry is not just a combination of gospel and urban blues. A complex mediation hides the shift that it only enables. The guitar timbre may be that of Waters, who mentored his younger Chess colleague. Something else, however, is afoot. The jump riffs on "Maybelline" (1955) or "Johnny B. Goode" (1958) come from a plain source, even though the continuity involved is surprising. There is autobiographical testimony to confirm it, and the invocation of the "other" Dorsey's name as well. It was, says Berry, Tommy Dorsey, the white swing bandleader, who most influenced him as a teenager, and it was Dorsey's hit, "Boogie Woogie," in 1938, that haunted him most of all (Berry, 1987, 25–6). In other words, Berry's signature guitar riffs are really the horn section of a swing orchestra translated into the language and technology of electric guitar. Berry's signature riffs retrieve the sound of the big bands suppressed by electric blues, but voice it in the latter's new electric guitar mode. Canceling each with the other, Berry acknowledges and deflects his two principal influences simultaneously. In the process, he also shifts the center of American music from jazz to rock and roll.

The Rolling Stones finish the job that Berry begins. Keith Richards's rhythm guitar, like John Lennon's, carries with it the whole history of the jazz horn section, although now it is reimagined in overdrive, with the help of the Chicago bluesmen. Not an ecumenical band like the Beatles, the Stones were less interested in doowop back-up effects than in taking on the entire history of jazz as amplification revised and refigured it. The distance from America made the British climate richer in invention, and a less inhibited climate in which to work. The most influential solo guitarists in rock history, Eric Clapton and the American expatriate Jimi Hendrix, also found an imaginative home in England in these same years.

The School of Chuck Berry was by now paying staggering dividends. Hendrix was Berry's most original disciple, hiding his dependence on the master with the groaning, shuddering swerves that define the sound of his guitar. "Purple Haze" (1967) is an overt revision of "Maybelline." Listen to the two songs back to back, or, better yet, "sample" them – play them at the same time and look out for the uncanny combination of repetition and difference that the relation between them produces. But the school had more than a valedictorian in Hendrix. It also featured guitarists such as the Yardbirds' Jimmy Page, who, with the formation of Led Zeppelin in 1968, completed Berry's transformation of swing horns into electric guitar by helping to invent the sound of heavy metal. The fashion of the ear-splitting trash guitar band is no fashion. It is the central fact in musical history that joins the big-band sound of the last era of popular jazz, swing, with the sound of rock.

Buddy Holly and the British Invasion

If American pop proceeds from anxieties about the British canon, then the British Invasion rounds this history off by wholly reversing it for the first time. It is, with great irony, a non-American rock and roll – the music of the British bands of the early 1960s – that catapults rock and roll into the transatlantic popularity that has defined it ever since. Like Hollywood and American fiction, the British Invasion allowed American music to address its "popularity" at its source – not at its African American origin, but, as with any American cultural enterprise, at its British origin. Being equal to the English by virtue of being different is something at which rock and roll succeeds more readily than any other American art besides film. Singing the praises of black American music by also singing its own native gospel praises, the British Invasion granted American culture the full legitimacy it had not had before. As proof, it crested in the same year, 1964, as the Civil Rights Act, the year of the first American Beatles tour. These were two elements in a single structure of American cultural compensation. Black America was accorded full legal status on native grounds at the same moment that America's chief anxiety of influence, British culture, did the same for America from a cultural point of view. British recognition gave American life the "gaze" it had always sought. This is why the British Invasion remains rock and roll's chief moment, and the enduring source of its influence as both a music and an iconography.

The roots of the British Invasion stretch deep into the prehistory of rock and roll, particularly its roots in another descendant of gospel: country music. Gospel music not only created soul. It also created country. While country began as an amalgamation of Dixieland, banjo, and picking blues guitar in the form of hillbilly bluegrass, it also began in Texas as country swing. Country swing was an extraordinarily sophisticated music that used polka to join the horn section with a fiddle and revise in its own way the sound of the black big bands of Kansas City. The Grand Ole Opry radio broadcasts from Nashville always counted black listeners among their audience; listeners and

144

musicians both knew how thin a line separated, or failed to separate, white America from black, especially in the South.

No wonder Buddy Holly's role in rock and roll history is decisive, particularly the way he triggers the British Invasion by touring Britain in 1958, less than a year before his death (Bramwell and Kingsland, 2005; Leigh, 2009). Members of Britain's major bands attended Holly's concerts, many as teenagers. What Holly brought to rock and roll thinking was a synthetic misreading of gospel by rhythm and blues. This prefigures not only the flatted gospel changes of most British Invasion songs, whether those of the Kinks, the Yardbirds, or the Beatles. Holly also provided a harmonic grammar for recombining blue gospel chord sequences in endless realignment. This familiar jazzing of classical tradition converts, not "high" to "low," but both to pop.

Holly's principles were hard won. Like Jerry Lee Lewis and Elvis Presley, he had two streams of influence to put in relation: country, and rhythm and blues. Synthesizing them required careful choices. Born in the Texas panhandle, Holly's choices were clear. They recalled those of Lewis and Presley, though in a more scholarly fashion befitting Holly's iconography as a proto-Williamsburg nerd. It is Hank Williams's voice together with the instrumentation of bluegrass that gives Holly and other white Southern musicians the tool with which they can cross or miscegenate rhythm and blues. Both r & b and country were too close to home. The invention of rock and roll gave Holly, Lewis, and Presley the ability to render the components of both traditions uncanny – something at once familiar and strange. Holly's "Reminiscing" (1962), written by King Curtis and recorded in Clovis, New Mexico exemplifies the crossing. King Curtis's highly manicured rhythm and blues horn dresses up Holly's wailing vocals over a studio band that is missing the one instrument that serves as the model for both the singing and the saxophone: the sound of the banjo that is common to the origins of both country music and the blues.

If hard bop organizes jazz in the mid-1950s, the synthesis of country and rhythm and blues came to organize rock and roll by the mid-1960s. The Beach Boys are its richest American example. The Beatles are its richest transatlantic example. The Beatles sum up the British Invasion, and, with it, the whole history of rock and roll. The Stones read the blues through country; the Beatles read country through the blues. The later, "psychedelic" Beatles widen this strategy by appropriating even Jamaican ska – "Ob-La-Di, Ob-La-Da" on *The Beatles* (1968) is a good example – not so much to reflect the sound of the Commonwealth as to haul even ska back into the fold of the country polka from which it derives, and from which it flees, particularly as it turns into reggae in these same years. No matter one's fascination with the Beatles' "psychedelic" period, one returns as a rule to the early Beatles for the characteristic sound that both defines them and makes their achievement clearest. While George Martin's production techniques may forecast the later history of rock recording, the early, bar-band Beatles – the 1962 Hamburg recordings give us this sound at its liveliest (1977) – recall how much the Beatles begin as an elaboration of the jazz combinations that Buddy Holly brings to the superimposition of the blues on country music. The jazz logic adds a second superimposition to the first, and prompts both Holly's and the Beatles' modular compositional phrases, which reorder their relationships in the listener's mind long after a song is over. John Lennon's booming rhythm guitar – the blues horn section – is the scrim for George Harrison's stinging cowpoke lead guitar. They serve as the instrumental counterparts to Lennon and McCartney's Hollyesque dialectic of blues and country as songwriters. Even the distinction between early and late or "artistic" Beatles implicates the Beatles in the history of "high" and "low" that they deregulate. Learning from the Beatles is a lifelong affair.

The Body English

The mournful celebrations of reggae's emergence from ska are contemporary in the British Caribbean with the shift in Britain from the British Invasion to heavy metal. Technologically, each shift has the same structure – each transistorizes the horn section into rhythm guitar – and, as in Britain, the shift is located in the development of particular musicians. Reggae, too, is dialectical. It is an internal piece of r & b history, beginning in its earlier form as ska, or the crossing of

Jamaican *mento* with horns. Ska makes plain the paths of influence that connect Kingston to Detroit and Memphis on the one hand, and, because of the horns, particularly the use of solo sax in ska, to the history of jazz. Solo sax – Rolando Alphonso is the best example – is the downfall of ska. It is what requires the declension to rock steady in 1966, and then, in 1968, to reggae proper, when the use of horns is restrained, and at last expunged.

Reggae's real specificity, however, lies in the strategy it presents to negotiate, not its anxieties about British gospel, or even jazz, but its anxieties about American rhythm and blues. The misreading of gospel by the blues now gives way to a Caribbean misreading of Memphis, Detroit, and Atlanta. The shift from ska to reggae in Kingston sees the birth of this new strategy. Compare Bob Marley's ska version of "One Love" on his debut album in 1965 with his reggae version of the song in 1977. The ska album includes covers of Motown tunes.

Reggae is a revision of the American inventions of soul and funk alike. Kingston's identifications are more post-colonial than they are British. They are American, and they are black. If the British Invasion identifies with American music, reggae negates it. It is no surprise that reggae's popularity has been more international than American. Reggae is a kind of rock and roll without either the 2/4 time of Southern country polka reflected in ska, or the 4/4 backbeat that replaces it in soul and, with James Brown's revision of soul, in funk. In reggae, the rhythmic accent is on the upbeat of the third beat, not, as in funk, on the downbeat of the second and fourth. Moving the hard funk beat half a beat forward robs it of its accelerated power over soul and replaces it with an extraordinarily reflective and paradoxically stable kind of musical vertigo. By comparison, African pop still sounds like the music of the United States. The blue flatting of gospel changes may make it continuous with traditional rhythm and blues, but its displacement of both soul and funk time also allows it to reveal that it is oppressed, not by one shadow, but by two – colonized as well as colonizer, "low," as it were, as well as "high," blues as well as gospel. The roles have been realigned in a dialectic that takes the United States as the new oppressor. Peter Tosh's preacherly vocals on "Feel No Way" (1983), like the song's minor key and flatted chords, alludes to the precise gospel models of North America from which they also deviate. Reggae is the best illustration of overcoming what Paul Gilroy calls "postcolonial melancholia" (2004).

The two major trends in rock and roll in the 1970s, disco and punk, have, at least on the surface, little in common. Disco is heir to reggae. Its rhythmic upbeat removes, as reggae does, the funk downbeat. It even allows a band originally promoted as a British Invasion band – the Australian Bee Gees – to remake itself by playing, like a reggae band, the imperial and the post-colonial off against one another. The good-time party strut of disco and the engine-like thwack of punk rhythm guitar share one central thing: an overheated and overpressured beat, uptempo and built deep into high-hat, bass, and bass drum. Their common legacy is likewise plain: it is hip hop. Whether it is the Ramones and Donna Summer, or the Sex Pistols and the Village People – sampling them together is also a worthwhile exercise – the grinding overdrive of punk tempos and the syncopated oompah of disco cymbals are resolved by hip hop time and stance. Despite its seeming radicality, hip hop itself is a profoundly conservative form of music. Its radicality lies not in the diction of its lyrics, but in its revisionary relation to precedent. The customary notion that hip hop is a derivative of reggae (Chang, 2005) is true if the derivation is read as a dialectical one. Hip hop may borrow Kingston's use of DJ "toasting" and "dub" production. But hip hop is also the return of reggae's repressed – the funk downbeat that reggae has erased reignites. In its origins from Run-DMC to 2 Live Crew, hip hop emphasizes a back beat as a heavy metal rock group would. But it includes a new dialectic as well – in a reminiscence of reggae's reversal of the customary roles of bass and guitar, it also resists its return to the backbeat by its conversational vocal stance, which is temporally skewed in relation to it. The two exchange places; percussion is lyrical, while vocals are percussive. Indie rock is synthetic in another way: also ironic, it combines gospel and blues, high and low, by combining folk and r & b, aching Appalachian harmonies and pumping Memphis guitar.

To speak as on does of "classic" rock – the Beatles, the Stones, the Beach Boys – is to gloss rock's achievement from the point of view of the wider history of "high" and "low." Keats's invention of mediocrity, as I noted in Chapter 1, finds its highest exemplification and refinement in the rock ethos, which takes mediocrity as its galling precondition. This should come as no surprise. The need to maintain generic stability – a danceable groove – always proceeds in rock and roll under conditions that do not include training. Even the rise of an affluent, post-1960s middle class that provided guitar lessons for its children was countered by punk and grunge. Rock and roll is both "high" and "low" – artistic and atavistic, learned and ignorant, skilled and unskilled. It peregrinates along this precipice. Its inner history is the dialectic between the extremes that define it. To speak of "classic" rock is both hilarious and entirely plausible. To call any phase of its history "classic" is to suggest that it is "high." All its other phases are therefore "low." Whether they are preparations for its "classic" phase or fallings away from it leaves so much to the critical imagination, however, that the real effect of saying "classic" rock is not to organize rock history more clearly, but to sow its elements in the wind.

7

Dylan and the Critics

Falling

Many years ago, in a review of Bob Dylan's *Tarantula* in *The New York Times Book Review*, Robert Christgau (1971) wisely cautioned that the book not be taken as a book of poems. To do so, he argued, would be to mistake the nature of Dylan's art, which is, book or song, pose or performance, something profoundly hybrid. For Christgau, Dylan's hybridity derives from rock and roll's enormous plasticity as a medium. Rock and roll includes everything – the history of world music, the history of world speech, the history of world movement and dress. It even includes Dylan. Dylanologists who concentrate on one thing instead of another – Dylan's words or Dylan's music – miss the full effect.

Describing this full effect has been less of a problem than defining it. No one knows where to start. The tradition of descriptive Dylan criticism is for this reason the most distinguished; it requires no choices and a surfeit of splendid adjectives. Dylan's earliest observers – Paul Williams's collected early journals are probably the best example (1990, 1992) – combined exquisite observation with an interest in fact. All of the biographies – there are five – are reasonably good because their aims are limited to portraiture and storytelling. None presents a case for much of anything, including those by gifted critics like Robert Shelton (1986) and Bob Spitz (1989). Interpretative books about Dylan are no match for them. Whether they come from the academy or the academy-in-exile of rock criticism, they are reductive to a fault.

Even a brief survey is dispiriting. For Dylan's political observers, everything is social allegory. Mike Marqusee's *Chimes of Freedom* (2003) turns Dylan's work into a quest for the "unconventional"; David Hajdu's social history of Dylan in Greenwich Village, *Positively Fourth Street* (2001), turns it into a conversation among friends. For Dylan's formalist observers, things are taken in hand no more effectively. Betsy Bowden's *Performed Literature* (1982), originally a doctoral dissertation in the Berkeley English Department, regards Dylan as a performance artist; Bowden does not wish to be reductive. Bowden's notion of performance, however, casts Dylan as a performing poet whose words come first despite their rock and roll frame. The English composer Wilfrid Mellers's *A Darker Shade of Pale* (1984) remains singularly provocative for a good reason. It is holistic, half musicology and half poetic analysis; Mellers the composer read English as a Cambridge undergraduate. But this division of Dylan in two undoes the sense of unity that Mellers wishes to create; he can find no dialectic in Dylan's double enterprise. More recently, Dylan has become a mirror for the critic rather than an object. Neil Corcoran's effusive anthology of essays, *Bob Dylan with the Poets and Professors* (2002), is self-congratulatory. Kevin J.H. Dettmar's *Cambridge Companion to Bob Dylan* (2009) is less concerned with self-congratulation than with foregrounding its baroque and burlesque complexity, a shift in the movement of Dylan studies more in accord with the shift in Dylan's own career.

Perhaps one way to read Dylan, then, is not directly – not at first, anyway – but through his critics, particularly through their lapses. Reception histories are often unexpectedly revealing. More basic to Dylan's reception than the superiority of the descriptive to the analytic is that there is much agreement about Dylan's coherence as a majestic musical figure in his high or classic phase. Everyone knows Dylan's early musical history. In his documentary *No Direction Home* (2005), even the contentious Martin Scorsese suggests that the consensus about the shape and texture of Dylan's career runs deep and true. We can feel the roots that clutch. A high-school rocker, Dylan became an impishly self-conscious folkie when he landed in Greenwich Village in 1961, exchanging Woody Guthrie for Muddy Waters and

Dave Van Ronk for Bobby Vee. When he shocked the world with an electric band at the Newport Folk Festival in 1965, Dylan was only returning to the wider theater of rock and roll, which the folk mode had allowed him to reimagine as more porous musically and more amenable to lyrical prodding.

Half of the fans booed. For them, plugging in was a fall from grace. The music had nothing to do with it. Neither did the lyrics. So central is this moment in the history of rock and roll that it is easy to overlook its real significance: Dylan was being read typologically. The idea of the Christian Dylan was already in place at Newport in 1965, well before Dylan's actual conversion to Christianity in 1979. Typology is a pervasive mode of thinking, introduced by Tertullian's Christian reading of the Hebrew Bible and trickling down into popular assumption as the Church Fathers, beginning with Augustine, made it the best way to find hope and solace in life when faced with its difficulties. A form of allegory called *figura*, typology comes from *typos,* or "prefiguration." As a doctrine of interpretation, it regards events of the Hebrew Bible as prophesying or prefiguring their repetition and completion in other spheres of action in the Christian Bible. "The persons and events of the Old Testament," wrote Erich Auerbach in 1944, "were prefigurations of the New Testament and its history of salvation" (1944, 30). The Fall of Man from the Garden is its most familiar example; Christ's suffering both repeats and redeems it. Conversion narratives bring home the truth of typology for everyman. Augustine's great conversion scene comes, in a fine literary flourish, in a Roman garden. The pagan garden is fallen, but just as Augustine is redeemed by grace, so is the garden. Formally speaking, Augustine's conversion redeems his narrative's *mise en scène* and his soul in the same typological gesture. Later events, in other words, in Scripture or in life, gain their meaning by being repetitions and fulfillments of earlier ones. Rhetorical rather than theological in its classical origins, and variable even in its later Christian schools of practice, *figura* nonetheless came to obey its typological shape. Auerbach's rugged history of the use of *figura* in late antiquity and the early Middle Ages shows just how deeply typological thinking informs the foundations of Western judgment, giving to newly converted peoples such as the

155

Goths and the Celts, for example, "a basic conception of history" (53), as Auerbach puts it, superadded to and following from their new religious beliefs.

Typology, or *figura*, structures both Dylan's popular reception and his critical interpretation. Its key trope emerges again and again: the trope of the Fall, which Dylan follows, or seems to follow, with exceeding regularity, like a Christian soldier marching, inevitably, to the earlier Jewish drum. The fall from acoustic to electric at Newport in 1965 repeated the Biblical fall from innocence to sin. Whether or not Dylan could redeem himself from it became the paradigm for thinking about him, for lining up with the devil's party, or against it. It not only set a standard of judgment with which to follow Dylan's career; it gained additional weight from Dylan's American context. Typology's familiar American pattern is, to use Leo Marx's phrase, the fall from the garden to the machine, a form of both progress and lament every bit as double-edged as the one Augustine secured. Its readily secular terms describe Dylan's own presumable fall – plugging in – but in doing so they reveal once again their religious roots. Countercultural thinking reflects this doubly sedimented history in American popular assumption with particular vividness, setting nature against culture at the level of value no matter the idiosyncratic experience of individual listeners. Even hippie categories were typological. Morris Dickstein's *Gates of Eden* (1977) is about nothing else.

Nor, after Newport, was there long to wait for an encore. The following summer Dylan fell off his motorcycle near Woodstock and cracked a bone in his spine. The die was cast: Dylan was always falling. Scorsese's film concludes here, not because he wishes to serve this religious paradigm – he never does – but because he wants to describe its tenacity. In his view, *John Wesley Harding* (1968) is Dylan's last great recording. One of its great characters is Augustine, "alive," sings Dylan, "as you or me." Afterward come the Dylan Wars, wars of religion that have continued for almost 40 years, pitting progress against decline, Dylan the mortal god against Dylan the mortal man. Forty years should be enough, at least according to the paradigm.

Is there any help for the Dylanologist amid these typological ruins? The myth of Dylan – the typological one – requires Dylan to fall in order to continue being a myth. This is an apparatus, obviously, not an assessment. Marqusee is a typologist, even though he approves of Newport; his paradise is the freedom that Dylan leaves behind when he becomes a Christian. Bowden is a typologist; her paradise is Dylan's expressiveness. Mellers is a typologist; his paradise is a Europe with blue notes in its own folk music.

The Limits of Typology

There are alternatives to the lapsarian account of a fall from grace. The first Dylanologist, A.J. Weberman, scoured Dylan's garbage on MacDougal Street for clues to the meaning of Dylan's work. Weberman was a phenomenologist, not a typologist. Dylan chased him away nonetheless, objecting to Weberman's assumptions about intent. They did not take the unconscious into account. But Weberman came back, again and again, sometimes with demonstrators, sometimes with coffee. Michael Gray, Weberman's upscale counterpart, an academic-in-exile living in the English countryside, also prefers information to revelation, although of a tidier kind. Gray's encyclopedic *Song & Dance Man III* (2000) is superficially thorough, cataloguing Dylan's various sources as they flow through his songs, and anatomizing both lyrics and music against this historical scrim. Weberman may have been tough, but Gray is a disciple of F.R. Leavis. Gray, like Leavis before him – and like Matthew Arnold before Leavis – believes that a careful reading of great poets will ensure the health of culture. For Leavis, it was T.S. Eliot; for Gray, it is Dylan. Almost typological, but not quite. For Weberman and Gray alike, a figure like Dylan is worthy of studious devotion not because of his pieties but because of his excess.

If typology is reductive, however, excess is intractable. Gray has no argument to make; Weberman had arguments only on the street. All is lost – to be typological about it. What is the pilgrim to do? Is there another trend in Dylan's reception besides typology and excess? Two figures are left standing. They predominate as readers of Dylan because they are the only ones with unified critical programs and sustained critical approaches. Dylan's best reception is the imaginary conversation

157

between them. One is an academic; one is an academic-in-exile. One is a close reader; one is a cultural critic. One is interested in the lyrics; one more engaged with the music. But they share a diligence and a penchant for systematic thinking that makes their ostensibly different approaches to Dylan two parts of a larger, single perspective.

The academic-in-exile is Greil Marcus, a critic for whom all emanations of American culture are the same. That is why they are American. *Mystery Train* (1975) established this critical terrain long before Marcus embarked on his study of Elvis (1991), and on his first study of Dylan (1997). In *Mystery Train*, Robert Johnson and Jonathan Edwards resemble one another because both share a preoccupation with solitary reflection. So, one inevitably observes, does everybody else in American culture, from Thomas Jefferson to Madonna. One appreciates the permission to be self-evident, but too little regard for context obscures the fact that such similarities arise from different historical circumstances. In *Mystery Train*, Marcus's ease of purpose allows him to range widely over the cultural terrain without being specific. Marcus's cultural criticism shares the goals but not the procedures of the academic New Historicism with which it is contemporary, and alongside of which it develops in the 1970s, just up the hillside from the Berkeley English Department. Rock criticism recapitulates literary criticism's modes of reading, and for a simple reason: Many jazz and rock critics studied in major departments of English at defining moments in the history of critical method. Jazz critic Martin Williams learned New Critical close reading at Penn; rock critic Christgau learned close reading decades later at Dartmouth. Marcus himself may have fled graduate school at Berkeley, but the damage was already done when he was there as an undergraduate. He got a sip of early New Historicism.

It is only the New Critical approach to Dylan, however, that has an overtly academic affiliation. Its avatar is Christopher Ricks. Although Ricks has lectured on Dylan for many years, his book on Dylan, *Dylan's Visions of Sin*, appeared only in 2003. Ricks is most concerned with the extraordinary perfection of Dylan's work when it is viewed simply as verse. Ricks ought to know. Unlike the many rock critics who eschew an affiliation with the academy, Ricks is an ex-Cambridge don and former Professor of Poetry at Oxford – the chair Matthew Arnold once held – who has taught at Boston University since 1986. Knighted in 2009, Ricks is a fine critic of English and American poetry, particularly of Milton, and one whose work has remained useful over the years despite historical changes in critical method. The resonances of Marcus – and the grander tones of Dylan himself – stand out best if Ricks introduces them.

Dylan as Poet

Ricks's attraction to Dylan is idiosyncratic, an outgrowth of his love for poetry, not for rock and roll. One really shouldn't call him a rock critic. But despite his obsequious charm and disingenuous avuncularity – he must appeal to the rock critic as best he can – Ricks has a good deal to say. He makes no apologies for not talking very much about Dylan's music. Odd as it may seem, he does not regard it as his job. Ricks reads Dylan as poet, and in enormous technical detail, even if his exegeses – more so than those of Milton, Keats, and Tennyson in his earlier books – are often tiresome and unnecessarily digressive. He does, however, what has to be done. Somebody had to do it. He shows how richly structured Dylan's verse, considered as verse, really is. Dylan is not only a genuine English poet, argues Ricks, but as major a poet as Shakespeare or Milton.

Although it is grandiose, Ricks's claim is also less implausible than it may appear to be. Ricks never explains why he believes Dylan to be comparable to Shakespeare or Milton – he thinks that showing the often astonishing patterns in Dylan's writing is proof enough – but the reasons for the comparison reside in a simple assumption. It is an assumption to which Ricks himself may or may not adhere because it takes one well beyond the study of poetry itself, and makes any claim for Dylan as poet alone inexact in conception. However stunning his verse may be, Dylan's own highly organized materials come from a quantitatively larger and denser database than that of literature alone. They include musical and literary tradition as well as the iconography of the singer/star, a very different and expanded kind of achievement compared to that of the traditional poet, playwright, actor, or musician. With the exception of Freud, who mixes literature with science and philosophy rather than with music and iconography, Dylan's only technical counterpart in this quantitative respect is Shakespeare, who recombines more received knowledge than any writer before Freud. That Dylan combines musical and literary achievements might lead a critic less modest than Ricks to even more grandiose conclusions.

Ricks's belief that apology is unnecessary serves him well. It allows him to work unimpeded by anxiety or by critical polemic, and to begin where we all begin with Dylan: with our impressions. We all have our favorite Dylan tunes, our own sense of what a Dylan band sounds like, or what Bob sounds like bent over his guitar, alone. There is no "white-hot center" to Dylan, to use Paul Nelson's words (1976, 210), but a specific, and different, "world of Dylan" that each of us has in our minds. No wonder it is folly to give pride of place to one phase of Dylan's career over another. No moment in Dylan's itinerary is any more or less Dylanesque than any other. A heuristic device, the Christian conceit in Ricks's title has no reductive impetus; its only job is to get Ricks going. Ricks is not a typologist; he is a dogged reader. No matter its vicissitudes, Dylan's imagination, he shows, is highly organized, and works on the same principles, early and late. They proceed from a formal predilection in Dylan's way of writing songs, especially Dylan's use of rhyme. The play of masculine and feminine rhymes, for example, throws a stutter into Dylan's language that is unusual for a poet, but compelling for a rocker. Masculine rhymes land on the downbeat. But feminine rhymes – participles, for example, or rhymes using the copula "is" – fall a syllable short of a line's last poetic foot. This allows, of all things, a syncopated upbeat – a rock and roll beat – to emerge in the silence so created.

Rhyme, however, has another pattern that serves Dylan's purposes even more. Rhyme has a curious way of creating repetition and difference in sound simultaneously. Ricks calls these moments "imperfect alignments" (2003, 207), and argues that they represent Dylan's formal strategy as a poet. Dylan's songs, says Ricks, are "founded on … deviations, where a pattern is created and respected but then finds itself modified" (282). Dylan's songs modify their patterns "by waiving," says Ricks, the "antithetical predictability" (282) that they set up. On "Lay, Lady, Lay," from *Nashville Skyline* (1969), "a perfect continuity is intimated" (154) by "lay" and "lay"; it foreshadows a presumable union between the poet-singer and his beloved. But then a singular pair of non-rhymes breaks up this expectation in the third stanza. "Day of the Locusts," from *New Morning* (1970), where Dylan pronounces "singing" as "sanging," is a denser example. Here the same word does different things at the same time: Dialect ("sanging") exudes the raw timelessness of folk tradition, while usage ("sing" and "sang" are different tenses) distinguishes very clearly between past and present.

Ricks can also resurrect songs from the later period of Dylan's career to show Dylan's continuity of purpose. Such songs are not falls, but more instances of characteristic Dylan. "Disease of Conceit," on *Oh Mercy* (1989), can serve Ricks as a Dylan template, too. The song asks an instructive question, says Ricks: "How do you vary the unrelenting?" (90). This is not a self-help question, he argues; it is a technical question that reveals what is interesting about rhyming, particularly Dylanesque rhyming. The song's anaphoric repetitions – "down the highway," "down the line," "down for the count" – carry "differences of weight" (214), shifting their presumable equivalence in meaning on the very ground of their similarity in sound. "Do Right to Me Baby," on *Slow Train Running* (1979), illustrates what else Ricks has discovered: The pairings "touch/touched" and "judge/judged" are not, as semantic items, identical either (282). "Judging" and "touching" are dissimilar.

The repetitions of which rhyme is composed, in other words, are never exact. Rhyme is a good example of what Ricks calls, simplifying Wordsworth, "similitude and dissimilitude" (32). The difference between "similitude" and "dissimilitude" is the "fraction" (289), as Ricks puts it, that guides Dylan's poetic project. But it guides more than that. Beneath Ricks's trilling lurks an argument of very considerable power. A gaudier drama beckons, the one we might have hoped for from a Milton scholar as well as a Dylanologist. What an extraordinary picture of Dylan emerges behind Ricks's modesty! Dylan's rhymes and the verbal arabesques to which they give rise are a miniature version of the wider patterns that organize Dylan's work as a whole. These do not include theme, of course – Ricks remains a consistent formalist – but they do include the last thing one expects Ricks to explain: the relation of the music to the lyrics. In Dylan's songs, the music searches for the poem even as the poem searches for its music (38–9).

The perception of "similitude and dissimilitude" is the key to this relationship. "Dylan is always," claims Ricks, "playing his timing against his rhyming" (19). "Dylan's vocal punctuation," he reminds us, "is dramatically other than that of his page" (347). As a rule, Dylan's voice is, says Ricks, "thrillingly disagreeing with itself" (116). This disagreement creates an effect that Eliot called, in relation to Swinburne's poetry, "diffuseness" (103). Ricks acknowledges that in Dylan's songs, as in Hardy's poems, this "diffuseness" has a technical spur (303). Obliquity or directness of pronunciation are both open to – are functions of – vocal performance, even in the reader's mind. Dylan's songs likewise juxtapose voice and page, warble and diphthong, yaw and pentameter.

Part III

The World of Bob Dylan

8

Words and Music

Fractions

Ricks is no typologist; Dylan's juxtapositions do not set nature against culture. Dylan weaves the elements of song – text and voice, poetry and music – into endlessly "imperfect alignments" in order to generate a hum of multiple relationships among them. "Melisma" is the technical name for the "fraction" or difference between performance and the page that sets it all in motion – "something in the timing," as Ricks puts it, "that cannot be rendered by placing and space" (2003, 459). Of course not. It is the difference between text and performance that is important, the blowing in the wind. This is Betsy Bowden's entire subject in *Performed Literature* – much of performance theory focuses on the difference between performance and text – but melisma plays no part in her assessment. She believes that the text is somehow "realized," as though it were a stable object subject to transmutation. For Ricks, by contrast, stable textuality is always the function of indirectness or "diffuseness." "Otherness" – a "dissimilitude" – is the perpetual shadow against which "similitude" comes into the light.

Melisma offers a way to understand the reciprocal relation between Dylan's words and music, between sound and sense. Melisma, or "sliding" (343), widens the gap between sound and sense, and raises questions about the relationship between them. Only context determines it. Sound constitutes sense, and sense constitutes sound. Their relation is differential, not motivated or expressive. Brent Edwards has shown (2002) that even when there is no presumable text, as in scat, the requirements of signification as a practice still put a signified in place. It need not be a linguistic or harmonic signified; in scat, the signified is purely structural, a reflex of the wish that the singing continue.

Dylan's voice, then, is not simply an expressive medium for his page, nor is his page simply a dirigible excuse for him to sing. Rather, text and voice are functions of the difference they make between them. "Love Minus Zero" on *Bringing It All Back Home* (1965) is a good example: "My love, she's like some raven / At my window with a broken wing." The grammar of the sentence is unclear until the last word of the second line. Everything depends on the position each term in the sentence has in relation to the others. Will "broken" modify "window," leading us to expect "pane" at the end of the line instead of "wing"? Grammatical relationships among words are suspended, as in Latin, until the sentence is finished. One is most familiar with this kind of problem phonetically alone in a poet like Hardy. Thematically, we are most familiar with it in Whitman, who dissolves the very self he sings as the best way to celebrate it. Dylan, in the spirit of Whitman, does the same, dissolving signifier and self alike into the weave of language that gives each their moorings. Here, too, is the secret connection of aestheticism to historicism: The dissolving aesthetic self dissolves as a rule into the components that make up its specificity as a historical subject.

Dylan's Latinate syntax recalls Milton's, but this does not prompt Ricks to link his study of Dylan with his first, and best, book, his study of Milton, *Milton's Grand Style*, published in 1963. Dylan and Milton are up to the same thing. Ricks's Milton book successfully countered a tradition of Milton criticism that acknowledged Milton's power while denying his exactitude. Ricks showed that Milton's language in *Paradise Lost* is, like the language of Dylan's songs, deeply, and delicately, systematic. Both poetic systems are based on exposing how easily language can shift its sense. Both topple the pretenses of the typologies that try to repress this linguistic play, or "sliding." For Milton, this "sliding," or slippage of the signifier, is the basic consequence of the Fall; for Dylan, it suggests that there never was an Eden in the first place. Like Dylan, who, as an artist, says Ricks, takes "the path of most resistance" (333), Milton, said Ricks in 1963, "writes at his very best only when something prevents him from writing with total directness" (1963, 147–8). This "something" is "sliding," which shows very clearly how "directness," like Wordworth's "similitude," is a function of indirectness or "dissimilitude." Milton's "greatest effects," like Dylan's own, "are produced," says Ricks, "when he is compelled to be oblique as well as direct" (148). Milton, whose father was a composer, does within poetry what Dylan goes on to accomplish in the relation between poetry and music.

Like Dylan, Milton has plugged in. He is of the devil's party for a simple reason: His poetic practice deconstructs the typology it means to serve. So does Dylan's. This is not a mere effect of either's work, but the decided focus of each one. In Milton's case, it proceeds from his antithetical relation to the history of Christian doctrine. Language, not just poetic language, is necessarily fallen. What are the terms of its use when seeking justice, or the nature of the divine? In Dylan's case, this focus proceeds from his antithetical relation to the history of rock and roll. How can you chant freedom on the shoulders of muses like Woody Guthrie or Muddy Waters? The problem is one of influence, and, like Milton, Dylan can find freedom only in tradition.

"Slippin' and Slidin'"

Musically, melisma is the particular, and anxious, source of Dylan's great debt to gospel, soul, and early rock and roll. It is its technical root. For Little Richard, bending the signifier – "slippin' and slidin'," as he calls it – applies equally to both sense and tonality. Rock and roll is not a semiotics of drama, in which performance interprets the text. Here the point is to sunder altogether the link between signifier and signified, although only – inevitably – to rejoin them. The arbitrariness of their relationship goes hand-in-hand with its social determination. This form of irony is particularly African American, especially raw in a majestic figure like Otis Redding. The minstrel myth of the "natural" black man is both sustained and exposed by the easy rupture of sound from sense. How do you pronounce "dock of the bay"? How many syllables does each word contain? What phonetic requirements are necessary for them to emerge as phonemes? Changing sound while retaining sense – Redding's song paints a memorable scene – is both outrageous and precise. The social norms of language are the only norms it has; all the rest is silence.

Melisma – this unmooring of sound from a meaning that is left in place – brings us not only to the heart of Dylan's technique. It also raises difficult issues surrounding Dylan and his cultural status. Dylan may be "diffuse," as Ricks says he is, but he is also, in this sense, well, dirty. Not just his voice, but his clothes, his hair, his manners. He is one of Whitman's "roughs." His "diffuseness" muddies all the waters whose streams make him up. But even these offenses to civility hold in prudent reserve a more recalcitrant one buried deep in the American grain. While it may be a critical commonplace to assign the cause of racism to sexuality, racism is more primarily a question of cleanliness, and of the establishment of proper borders. Anthropologists like Mary Douglas have shown that it is the fear of otherness that prompts cultures to indulge in rituals of purification (1966). The segregated water fountains of the American South made this link abundantly clear. Psychologically, such practices create a common identity or sense of sameness by stamping someone or something else as dirty or unclean. Jacques Derrida likes to pun on the word "*propre*" – what is clean is also what is one's own. Dylan's own academic scholarship is good; he names a recent album *Love and Theft* (2001), after the title of Lott's deconstructive history of minstrelsy. After 1830, blackness had to be invented as an "other" – as a "dissimilitude" – in order to produce the "sameness" or "similitude" of whiteness. This hidden dynamic is the abiding irritant in American life and the one that Dylan, chief among rockers, has addressed by making miscegenation or hybridity the technical precondition of his sound. In the process, he collapses all the differences that structure the history of "high" and "low," from phrenology to philology and sexology.

Dylan and Deferred Action

If melisma – the difference between performance and page – raises questions about signification, it also raises questions about the status of the singing self, or, rather, about the self that sings. What is it? This is the bailiwick of cultural criticism and the subject of Marcus's most recent study of Dylan, *Like a Rolling Stone* (2005). It is a fine companion volume to Ricks's. It serves as its ideal supplement by rounding out one's sense of Dylan's dialectical achievement. *Invisible Republic* (1997), Marcus's study of Dylan's *Basement Tapes*, began the trend in Marcus's career that crystallizes in *Like a Rolling Stone*: the focus on a single text. Here the text is Dylan's 1965 hit single. Marcus's strategy creates a singular critical effect. It is Marcus's new theory of Dylan. However uneven its gait, it is a far more systematic one than any Marcus has presented before. Because *Invisible Republic* involved Dylan's recuperation from his motorcycle accident, it flirted with typology. But *Like a Rolling Stone* is not typological at all. This is because of its greater sensitivity to form. Its descriptive terminology has a precise analytic strength. Like Ricks, Marcus is interested in Dylan's "diffuseness," although from a musical rather than a poetic perspective.

Marcus's book evokes the musty recording session at which "Like a Rolling Stone" was made. Key to Marcus's description of the song is that it is "unstable" (2005, 185). In the context of its later history, the song is always being revised when it is it heard again, read, inevitably, against a fugitive original hearing. This is why the song is "unstable." Marcus's book, in other words, reconsiders something that is itself always being reconsidered. This is a superb mode of critical plotting. In order to produce the effect that will vouchsafe his contention, Marcus reduplicates in his own text what happens to Dylan's song over time. What is particularly illuminating about the approach is that it begins with a typological assumption – "Like a Rolling Stone" is "the greatest record ever made" (3) – that it goes on to disrupt, again and again. The superlative is what most superlatives tend to be: a type, as it were, of the typological, a very particular kind of rhetorical assessment and critical valuation. Unlike comparatives, superlatives posit an origin from which anything else is a fall, judged historically. The "greatest" is, as a trope, the baseline of history, not history itself, its defining rather than differential measure. For Marcus, "Like a Rolling Stone" is Dylan at his purest or most exactly original. Marcus's feudal metaphorology in this trend of his argument is unsurprising: The song is central because it is "the secret" of Dylan's "kingdom" (113).

But the mechanism of listening that Marcus identifies – the way in which the later hearings redact earlier ones in order for both past and present listenings to take their proper, and unstable, places – makes such claims inappropriate. "Like a Rolling Stone" is significant not because it is Dylan when he is most himself. It is significant because it most capaciously exhibits the spectrum of Dylan's influences and the range of his purposes. It is just this capaciousness that puts in question the song's centrality. It is perpetually unstable. The song's porousness overwhelms and renders tentative any singularity it may be said to have. No wonder Marcus describes the many changes to which the song is subject, both on repeated hearings of the recording and when it is performed live. Such repetitions of the song are "utterly displacing" (78), making the song the same and not the same. These changes are Marcus's real subject, not simply the song and the session at which it was made. Whatever these displacements do, they never allow the song to "play" simply "as a memory" (79). Something else always happens.

Marcus recalls that this double effect is what Freud means by "the uncanny" (18), something at once familiar and strange. Adept at descriptive criticism, Marcus goes on to show what mechanism in Dylan determines this effect or feeling. It is also identical with Dylan's theme and technique. It is Wordsworth's "similitude in dissimilitude." The Freudian name for this mechanism is deferred action. Later events and impressions revise earlier ones, making memory a remastering, not a recording. In Freud, the primal scene the Wolf Man observed as a child becomes sexual only after he has gained a knowledge of sex and is able to revise the memory accordingly. His dream of the frosty white wolves in the tree outside his window as a 4-year-old – the childhood dream around which the analysis centers – is the deferred and disguised memory of the primal scene that he experienced, or could have experienced, at the age of 1½, that of witnessing his parents in the act of copulation. But because a child of 1½ does not yet possess the knowledge of sex required to interpret, or even to register, such a scene, it cannot properly be said to exist for him at the moment of its "real" or chronological occurrence. It is only when the dreamer gains a knowledge of sex that the memory – the primal – can emerge, retroactively.

This is typology demystified. Freud's target, like Dylan's own, is a central interpretative paradigm in Western culture that he wishes to reveal and disrupt; targeting it well reflects both the gravity and the Jewishness of Freud and Dylan alike. In Marcus's Freudian reading, Dylan's song, like the Wolf Man's primal scene, is put in place by its later hearings over the years, not, as in a Christian reading, for once and for all in a moment of determining grace. The song can remain the "greatest" only if, like the more agonistic or classical epic hero, it can be judged again and again.

This approach has its advantages. The early doesn't really predict the later; the later requires it to have occurred. It is a send-up of typology, a revelation, not of its truth, but of its mechanism. The early – as it also is in Christianity – becomes both foundational and obsolete. This insight animates Eliot's familiar description of poetic history: "When a new work of art is created ... something ... happens simultaneously to all the works of art which preceded it" (1919, 15). The endless changes that "Like a Rolling Stone" undergoes as one listens to it over time illustrate what both Freud and Eliot describe: the emergence of things against and only against a field of time. The present reinvents what precedes it. "The future," sings Dylan on *Love and Theft*, "is already a thing of the past." The famous lines on "My Back Pages" on *Another Side of Bob Dylan* (1964) describe this structure exactly: "I was so much older then, / I'm younger than that now." Any moment in Dylan is provisional rather than definitive, indicative rather than absolute.

9

Dylan Himself

The Death of the Author

Like Shakespeare's art, and like Milton's, Dylan's is not one of statement. It is an art of "instability," to use Marcus's word, or of endlessly modulated "diffuseness," to use Eliot's. Like Shakespeare's plays, Dylan's songs are subject to any number of possible readings, all of them, however plausible, also limited by their wish to foreclose further interpretation. Very recent, very readable, and very droll, Dylan's autobiographical *Chronicles* (2004) is both a description of this kind of textual behavior and a fine example of it. *Chronicles* does what Marcus cannot do in a wholly conscious way: dramatize Dylan's own labor. Of course, Dylan is not wholly conscious of himself either, but that is just the point. Dylan, like his critics, must also take himself as his own subject. He refers to other critics of his work as though he were part of their scholarly community. This is deadpan Dylan at its best, ironic and straightforward at the same time. *Chronicles* is important not because it is Dylan himself who is writing, but for the opposite reason. The man who has the seat on the stage is, like his critics, scratching his head, too. "Dylan himself" must also approach "himself" as a critic, puzzled, on the outside, looking in. Even Dylan himself wants to know who Dylan is. The lesson of *Chronicles* is plain. There is no Dylan himself. Because of the intractable excess or porousness of his work, Dylan is as non-identical with himself as the rest of us are.

Dylan's work both is and is about this dislocation within, or of, the self, especially as Dylan grows older. Dislocation is not inhibitive;

it is enabling and productive. Like the artist's work, the self is also unstable, porous. No wonder seven different actors are required to play Dylan in Todd Haynes's *I'm Not There* (2007). The film's title explains why. The self is also a text. Temporal movement or deferred action is Dylan's active principle both poetically and musically, the very nature of his labor. No wonder Dylan, Marcus, and Ricks all recur to the uncanniness of hearing old Dylan songs played in concert many years later. That experience is the most palpable example of the self-revision with which Dylan is always concerned. This apparently formalistic assessment even heightens and sharpens our sense of Dylan's central theme: the passage of time. This theme has become especially important in Dylan's later career. "It's not dark yet," he sings on *Time Out of Mind* (1997), "but it's gettin' there." Dylan's achievement is in league with time, not time's rival or enemy. As with different performances of the same songs, says Dylan himself in *Chronicles*, "circumstances never repeat themselves" (2004, 219). Neither does the self that they endless reinvent. Dylan's career is not one of progression or decline but of retrospection. This is not a Christian or typological Dylan; this is a Freudian – a Jewish, a Talmudic – Dylan.

For a text that documents how the unconscious works, *Chronicles* is supremely self-conscious. Self-revision, and the porousness that requires it for the self and the work to cohere, is Dylan's endless preoccupation. Whether he is reading himself or others, Dylan describes "diffuseness" in both music and poetry with nonchalant ease. Roy Orbison, for example, writes "songs," says Dylan, that have "songs within songs" (33). Dylan himself also writes songs that contain any number of possible relationships among their elements harmonically. As in Orbison, chord progressions inevitably stir unexpected relationships with harmonic patterns not included in the song's text. They also make new intertexual connections. "Blowin' in the Wind" (1962) is a previously unwritten bridge for "We Shall Overcome." An example of Dylan's determination by folk tradition, the song is also an example of his debt to Buddy Holly. Like Orbison, for whom he was the principal precursor, Holly writes tunes defined by their propensity to spin such additional harmonic implications. That they spill into the songs of others is another example of their unlikely labor. Poetically, Dylan's songs do the same thing, both individually and as a body of work.

This instability has its technical counterpart in Dylan's deliberate use of melisma. In *Chronicles*, Dylan recalls discovering "a new vocal technique" (156) in 1987, but this is only a clarification of how he'd been singing since way back when, including on "Like a Rolling Stone." Dylan is quick to distinguish this "new technique" from "improvisation" (162); it is similar, but also different. There are phonetic units to honor, not just phonemic ones, as in scat. The point, however, is not to worry about the link or suture with what is signified, but to let it bleed. This blues technique is, in fact, melisma – the bending of the signifier, whether in pain, delight, or some combination of the two. *Chronicles* also provides an explanation of the anxiety that arose between the young Dylan and Dave Van Ronk. It was about hijacking melisma. Van Ronk "never," observes Dylan, "phrased the same thing the same way twice" (260). The only other non-jazz singer to merit this description in *Chronicles* is Woody Guthrie, who "would," says Dylan, "throw in the sound of the last letter of a word whenever he felt like it" (244). Here the canonical precursor Guthrie masks the more burdensome, and accidental, precursor Van Ronk, who happened to be a contemporary.

The Grand Tour and the Middle Passage

Dylan resolves a grander problem of influence in a similar way. It is once again because of the advantage that retrospection and self-revision provide. When he arrived in New York in 1961, he traded in his electric guitar for an acoustic one. This was not the bland decision of a folk enthusiast, but a fiercely dialectical act. It reversed Muddy Waters's founding gesture in blues tradition when Waters moved to Chicago from Mississippi and in 1944 exchanged his acoustic guitar for an electric guitar. This was not a fall, but a liberation from a pernicious myth, half sentimental, half oppressive, about how natural black life is in the South. Dylan, to be dialectical about it, turns Waters on his head.

Dylan's acoustic guitar also symbolizes something else. It symbolizes a musical history with which Waters himself is unconcerned, and one that allows Dylan to reimagine nature through the lens of a different kind of folk stance: the tradition of Guthrie and Van Ronk that stretches back to English and Celtic hymn and jig. These regionalist and religious traditions count also among Shakespeare's sources. This history, including the history of poetry in English to which it is adjacent and which it informs, is the supplement that Dylan carries with him triumphantly when he goes on to negate his negation of Waters with a screaming blues band of his own at Newport in 1965. Rhythm and blues had already synthesized blues, jig, and hymn into one music, as had country swing, but without Dylan's literary perspicacity. Bluesman and Anglophile, Dylan brings rock and roll into its classic phase by becoming wholly transatlantic – by becoming literary as well as musical, "high," as it were, as well as "low." At Newport, the dialectic is complete. Dylan crosses the Atlantic of the Middle Passage with the Atlantic of the Grand Tour.

Who, then, is Dylan himself? The one who sings or the one who writes? The electric Dylan or Dylan unplugged? Is the real Dylan the one at Newport in 1965, or the Dylan on Scorsese's screen in 2005? The real Dylan is both at once, especially when we see him at Newport in Scorsese's film. Such a question is disastrous for the coherence of normative criticism as a whole. If Marcus deconstructs Dylan by showing him to be a weave of past and present, Ricks deconstructs Dylan by showing neither Dylan's words nor Dylan's music to exist except in their interrelationship. The endless rearticulation of these relationships is Dylan's chief activity. The later Dylan is beneficiary to the clearings felled by Dylan early.

Hortatory

Dylan's iconography and his way of talking share the strategies of his songs. Dylan's motley and his jive do not mean anything. They are designed to elicit a response, to generate a reception. In the case of the conversion, Dylan parodies his fans by being exactly what they always wanted him to be – typological. It is another example of the same dialogical strategy. The conversion was not a pose but a performance, another way, like his body, or like the electric band at Newport, of provoking a reply, of making what is unconscious in our thinking conscious, and of weaning us from the reflexes of conventional response by engaging us to react. The conversion was not expressive but pedagogical, a way of testing reactions, including, for Dylan himself, one's own reactions. Even disapproving of the conversion validates it; disapproval means that Dylan has once again fallen. We are, historically and materially, the function of our reactions to – our misreadings of – Dylan himself. He is the sum total of his effects. This history goes unknown because it is, as a reception history, also the history of its own repression. To render the avant-garde normal is a particularly American mania because American normality is itself a kind of mania. Dylan's response to American orthodoxy comes in its selfsame terms – two maniacs, as it were, staring each other down.

Most Dylanesque of all, however, is Dylan's poetical use of Biblical language in a hortatory way. It is not Christian. It turns the word against itself. It is concerned not with transcendence but with time. Its target is the belief that time can be beaten, whether in life or in death. Dylan's wrath against such narcissism is what organizes all his work thematically, early and late. It is a historical wrath. The Renaissance sonneteers, Shakespeare among them, invented a self caught between Christian faith and the free imagination. American mythology imported and inflated it. Typology and excess became dialectical bedfellows. For Dylan, the self is neither fixed nor free; it is an endless revision of its own circumstances. It is active; it shapes its surroundings. No doctrine suits it; it makes doctrine, too.

Dylan's challenge to his audience comes in this historical spirit. It sweeps together modernity from the Renaissance to the present under the pressure of this ethical assault. It is also an aesthetic assault upon typological recontainment. The two are no different. This is why Shakespeare is Dylan's best companion. Compare James Shapiro's portrait of the young Shakespeare in the bookstores of

London (2005) with Dylan's own account of his early reading practices in *Chronicles*:

> London's bookshops were by necessity Shakespeare's working libraries and he must have spent a good many hours browsing there, moving from one seller's wares to the next (since, unlike today, each bookseller had a distinctive stock), either jotting down ideas in a commonplace book or storing them away in his prodigious actor's memory. (Shapiro, 2005, 191)

> I switched on the lamps. The place had an overpowering presence of literature and you couldn't help but lose your passion for dumbness.... There were all types of things in here, books on typography, epigraphy, philosophy, political ideologies. The stuff that could make you bug-eyed.... Thucydides writes about how words in his time have changed from their ordinary meaning, how actions and opinions can be altered in the blink of an eye. It's like nothing has changed from his time to mine. There were novels by Gogol and Balzac, Maupassant, Hugo, Dickens. I usually opened up some book to the middle, read a few pages and if I liked it went back to the beginning.... I was looking for the part of my education that I never got. (Dylan, 2005, 35–6)

10

The Three Icons: Sinatra, Presley, Dylan

Iconography and Gender

The history of Dylan's iconographic sources is also a dialectical one. It is a stream of influence that overlaps his musical influences, but that also exceeds them. This is the history of Dylan's revision of the great icons who are his precursors, Frank Sinatra and Elvis Presley. Like both Sinatra and Presley, Dylan uses his body and his dress, not expressively, but to prompt a reaction. Unlike Sinatra and Presley, however, Dylan converses with his audience, not to protect its presuppositions, like Sinatra, or to reverse them, like Presley, but to mock and unravel them, particularly with regard to gender.

Dylan does not simply resolve the dialectic of poetry and music. He also resolves a gender dialectic in which the fate of male identity hangs in the balance. If Dylan erases the difference between "high" and "low," he also erases the difference between the sexes. Two become many; sex becomes gender. Dylan's instrument, like those of his great precursors, is iconography. This dialectic is not biographical; it is a dialectic of form. Here sex is the stake, just as race is the stake in Dylan's music, and British culture the stake in Dylan's lyrics. All are transformed. The three icons, with Dylan as the resolution of the prior two, tell the story of the change in male identity in the second half of the twentieth century. Sinatra, the idealized patriarchal man, is challenged by Elvis, a beautiful, feminized man. The conflict or clash between them is resolved by Dylan, who is androgynous. Indeed, Dylan provides the iconographic basis, not only for the transformation of male identity beginning in the 1960s, but, perhaps even more decisively, for the transformation of female identity. Pop's proper bed-fellow is gender; its own best myth is androgyny.

Androgyny, using iconography as its materials, is no more an ideal trope in Dylan than it is in Woolf's *Orlando* (1928). It is a fable of iden-tity, a fiction designed to reassess anatomy rather than correspond to it. What such a "correspondence" between gender and anatomy would be is always difficult to say, unless it is the symbolic privilege of the sword in feudalism, or the privilege, if it can be called that, of the fedora in late modernity – iconic rather than iconographic, metonymic rather than metaphorical. Androgyny is a synthesis based, not on a corre-spondence to ideal type, in which the sexes, which are two, somehow mix. Rather, androgyny is a synthesis based on a difference, or series of differences. Gender is more than two. Androgyny based on differ-ence is a dialectic rather than an ideal. To be one thing, one must always be at least two, or more. This memorial structure is, of course, key to the structure of any dialectic, as I have shown throughout these pages. In Dylan's case, androgyny, like his songs or his singing, or like jazz or film, is old and new simultaneously, one sex shadowing the other in prudent and endless reserve.

Gender's empirical dependence on iconography becomes clear if gender is recognized as a cluster of social signifiers, particularly the movement of the body and the body's articulation by dress. Iconography is the material of Freud's notion of gender, which Freud views as the "psychical consequences of the anatomical distinction between the sexes" (1925, 19: 248). These "psychical consequences" are no more ideal than anything else. They are constituted by – indeed, they are – imagistic differences from the start. Their origins in the self's infantile prehistory derive from a combination of identification and object-choice among the personages of the family romance. Mother and father each present themselves as an *imago* to the child. "In the indi-vidual's mental life," says Freud in *Group Psychology and the Analysis of the Ego*, "someone else is invariably involved, as a model, as an object, as a helper, as an opponent; and so from the very first individual psy-chology ... is at the same time social psychology as well" (1921, 18: 69). Even identity is dialectical. It requires a difference from someone

·else in order to be oneself. Like the self's relation to the environment, difference and sameness emerge as functions of one another. This is the theoretical basis of Dylan's very material gender performativity.

The Fedora as Phallus

Sinatra, certainly early in his career, is a surprisingly quirky figure to be the kind of decisive male icon that he becomes. This alone makes Sinatra's career the narration of a difference from itself. It is part of his legend, although one does not customarily explain it in the terms of the uncanny. As a 17-year-old singing with the Tommy Dorsey Orchestra, he was skinny and modest (Kelley, 1986). Only the extraordinary transition in vocal technique that his voice gave to jazz singing seemed to justify the appeal, particularly the sexual appeal, that he generated. But the shyness had another function. It served as a first chapter to the novel of Sinatra's career, building a foundation of theatrical understatement against which his confidence could grow.

Musically, hesitation was already built into Sinatra's voice. He was a jazz singer, and sang in syncopated measure. Jazz hesitation, or syncopation, opens a realm of self-doubt – a performative one – in the heart and soul of the jazzman. It is the central tool of the trade, a formal self-doubt that both jazz and rock singers employ for technical reasons and exploit for technical purposes. Sinatra's jazz revolution as a singer is alone legendary. It is also dialectical. Although its value is as a rule assigned to the hesitations of his phrasing, its dialectical nature should be emphasized. Sinatra, whose ease belies it, opens up the harmonic potential of melody lines with the same expansive force as do Parker and Miles Davis. Sinatra finds unexpected scales available to the soloing singer in standard pop songs, not simply measure to measure, or phrase to phrase, as the song is written, but, like the boppers, beat to beat. This strategy in jazz phrasing goes back to Armstrong. The blues scale "superimposes" itself, to use Eisenstein's word, upon the classical scale. This is a fine picture of jazz dialectic as a whole. Two musical systems co-exist in jazz. Sinatra and Armstrong both are, as soloists, like Buddy Holly as a songwriter. The labor is designed to get the maximum harmonic potential from presumably simple chord progressions. In Sinatra's case, it is, as it will be for Coltrane, to expand the scale as much as possible. In Holly's case, it is, as it will be for the Beatles, to expand the potential recombination of chords, setting off chains of combination without end.

The difference between a musical achievement that remains the same and an iconographic one that has a plot is the structure of Sinatra's very particular self-division, and the engine of his power as a star. Musically, Sinatra grew more refined rather than more developed. In his iconography, the self-divided state of mind becomes instead the familiar and endearing narrative that made him a greater and greater star. The shy boy from Hoboken became the confident man of Hollywood and Las Vegas, and the Chairman of the Board of the Rat Pack.

Elvis as Bobbysoxer

Like John F. Kennedy, Elvis Presley took off the fedora. He let the male brow shine, not because it was high or low, but because, unlike Sinatra's, it was, in Milton and Pope's sense, a beautiful brow, or face. Like Kennedy's, the sleek and assertive body also contrasted with the young Sinatra's slumped shoulders and bowed head. There was no self-division in the persona between masterful singing and self-deprecating frame. There was no tension, and no narrative of that tension's resolution into single-minded Hollywood confidence. There was only shock and alarm, from the beginning. Presley reverses the kind of male icon that Sinatra is. He turns Sinatra into a girl – into one of Sinatra's own fans from the early 1940s, the bobbysoxers. The bobbysoxers were the first twisting teeny boppers in history. Much as he will revise Sinatra's music, Elvis revises in his iconography the reaction of Sinatra's fans to his singing. He internalizes Sinatra's reception, and reprojects it. His gyrations are far more girlish than they are racial, as it is customary to believe. They are the gyrations of Sinatra's followers. The early Elvis was a bobbysoxer.

Musically, Elvis's hiccup is Sinatra's hesitation. It takes the hesitation to an extreme. It also raises a Dylanesque question: How can hesitation be extreme? Elvis hiccups to speak where Sinatra does not. He appropriates Sinatra's jazz silences, and, like James Brown, throws the hiccup's *basso* on the downbeat, where no jazzman will go. He gets his breath on the upbeat, when Sinatra, like all jazzmen, sings. He rests while they work; he plays while they slumber.

If Sinatra had achieved, like Armstrong, a state of musical constancy at the beginning, Elvis, by contrast, was on a musical arc. Apart from iconography, this difference distinguishes Presley and Sinatra most of all. Unlike Sinatra's, Elvis's later period, documented on recordings such as *From Elvis in Memphis* (1969), *Elvis Country* (1971), and *Promised Land* (1975), shows an Elvis still on the dialectical march. Musically, especially in performance, the use of large horn sections with country rock electric musicians brought the ghost of country swing face-to-face with the living sound of Memphis soul. It is folk rock in a royal, amplified key; it is Dylan, in overdrive. Iconographically, Elvis also changes, but, unlike Sinatra's iconographic change, not in contrast to a musical constancy, but in step with musical expansion. Elvis makes no bones about being the king; he comes out with it. He does not metaphorize it with the businessman's fedora and the capitalist mask of the Chairman of the Board. He is the medieval monarch in modern times, and, like Elizabeth I, a girl to boot. In Vegas, he trades in the jeans for capes and diamonds, satin and furs. He gives George Clinton the rich precedent to which Clinton responds dialectically. He does the same for Dylan in a different way.

"My Darling Young One"

Dylan counts chief among Presley's influences. As a teenager, Dylan stood up at the piano with his high school band; he did the same with Bobby Vee in 1959. Dylan's musical roots come from the same white-boy roadhouse tradition as do Presley's, Dylan's simply a thousand miles up the Mississippi from where Elvis began. For the gospel voice, he substitutes a blues voice. Iconographically, the dialectical revision is even more radical. Presley had become a girl because he had internal-ized the response to Sinatra. Dylan becomes an androgyne because he

180

internalizes Sinatra and Elvis together. The sexual role-reversal results in the fragmentation of sex, which is two, into gender, which is many. Cate Blanchett's casting as the young Dylan in *I'm Not There* well reflects this net effect. Dylan is, unlike Sinatra or Presley, both a source of identification and object-choice. He collapses this difference, too.

It is a sound way out for an ugly Jewish boy confronting English beauty and Italian finesse. Two years before Barbra Streisand appeared on Broadway in a starring role in *Funny Girl* in 1964, Dylan was already a folk legend. Streisand's own earliest appearances had also been at clubs in Greenwich Village – gay clubs. Both Streisand and Dylan cause the same shift in sexual iconography, and for the same reason. Unattractiveness becomes attractive. This happens when the icon becomes thoughtful or poetic. In both cases, a "high" purpose redeems a "low" profile. Dylan and Streisand turn Nordau on his head. Though both transform sex into gender, Streisand implicates midtown in a cultural conspiracy presumably confined to the Village below. Uptown and downtown, "high" and "low," were up to the same thing.

As an icon, Dylan is an ugly girl dancing to a rock and roll beat. He is a punker geek, a nerd, a rocker wonk, a tomboy. As with Streisand's self-absorption, this is iconography, not expressiveness. Dylan is an author who, by definition, always exceeds himself. His biographical identity is in perpetual dialogue with his iconographic identity, both of which shift, and shift in relation to each other. Dylan's music is both its motive and its result. Sinatra seeks constancy; Elvis, whose hunger is pitiless, can consume only himself. Change is Dylan's very condition. Dylan is all dialectic. Time is its costly guarantee.

Works Cited

Bibliography

Ackroyd, Peter. 1996. *Milton in America*. Rpt. London: Vintage, 1997.

Adorno, Theodor. 1932. "Kitsch." In *Essays on Music*. Ed. Richard Leppert. Trans. Susan H. Gillespie. Berkeley and Los Angeles: University of California Press, 2002, 501–5.

Adorno, Theodor. 1933. "Farewell to Jazz." In *Essays on Music*. Ed. Richard Leppert. Trans. Susan H. Gillespie. Berkeley and Los Angeles: University of California Press, 2002, 496–500.

Adorno, Theodor. 1936. "On Jazz." In *Essays on Music*. Ed. Richard Leppert. Trans. Susan H. Gillespie. Berkeley and Los Angeles: University of California Press, 2002, 470–95.

Adorno, Theodor. 1941. "On Popular Music." In *Essays on Music*. Ed. Richard Leppert. Trans. Susan H. Gillespie. Berkeley and Los Angeles: University of California Press, 2002, 437–69.

Adorno, Theodor. 1942. "Jazz." *Encyclopedia of the Arts*. Ed. Dagobert D. Runes and Harry G. Schrickel. New York: Philosophical Library, 1946, 511–13.

Adorno, Theodor. 1953. "Perennial Fashion – Jazz." In *Prisms*. Trans. Samuel and Shierry Weber. London: Neville Spearman, 1967, 119–32.

Adorno, Theodor. 1962. *Introduction to the Sociology of Music*. Trans. E.B. Ashton. New York: Continuum, 1988.

Adorno, Theodor. 1966. *Negative Dialectics*. Trans. E.B. Ashton. New York: Continuum, 1999.

Althusser, Louis. 1964. "Ideology and Ideological State Apparatuses." In *Lenin and Philosophy and Other Essays*. Trans. Ben Brewster. New York: Monthly Review Press, 1971, 127–86.

182

Arnold, Matthew. 1869. *Culture and Anarchy*. In *Poetry and Criticism of Matthew Arnold*. Ed. A. Dwight Culler. Boston: Riverside, 1961, 406–75.

Auerbach, Erich. 1944. "'*Figura*.'" Trans. Ralph Mannheim. In *Scenes from the Drama of European Literature*. New York: Meridian Books, 1959, 11–76.

Bakhtin, M.M. 1929. *Problems of Dostoyevsky's Poetics*. Trans. Caryl Emerson. Minneapolis: University of Minnesota Press, 1984.

Bakhtin, M.M. 1975. *The Dialogic Imagination: Four Essays*. Ed. Michael Holquist. Trans. Caryl Emerson and Michael Holquist. Austin: University of Texas Press, 1981.

Barthelme, Donald. 1970. "Paraguay." In *City Life* (1975). Rpt. New York: Pocket Books, 1978.

Barthes, Roland. 1964. "Rhetoric of the Image." In *Image/Music/Text*. Trans. Stephen Heath. New York: Hill and Wang, 1977, 32–51.

Bartlett, Anne Clark. 1995. *Male Authors, Female Readers: Representation and Subjectivity in Middle English Devotional Literature*. Ithaca: Cornell University Press.

Baudrillard, Jean. 1981. "Simulacra and Simulations." In *Selected Writings*. Ed. Mark Poster. Stanford: Stanford University Press, 1988, 166–84.

Bazin, André. 1945. "The Ontology of the Photographic Image." In *What is Cinema? Vol. 1*. Trans. Hugh Gray. Berkeley and Los Angeles: University of California Press, 1967, 9–16.

Bazin, André. 1958. "The Evolution of the Language of the Cinema." In *What is Cinema? Vol. 1*. Trans. Hugh Gray. Berkeley and Los Angeles: University of California Press, 1967, 23–40.

Benjamin, Walter. 1928. *The Origin of German Tragedy*. Trans. John Osborne. London: Verso, 1985.

Benjamin, Walter. 1936. "The Work of Art in the Age of Mechanical Reproduction." In *Illuminations*. Trans Harry Zohn. New York: Schocken, 1968, 217–52.

Berkeley, George. 1709. *A New Theory of Vision*. Rpt. London: J.M. Dent and Sons, 1910.

Berry, Chuck. 1987. *Chuck Berry: The Autobiography*. New York: Harmony Books.

Bersani, Leo. 1990. *The Culture of Redemption*. Cambridge: Harvard University Press.

Bloom, Harold. 1973. *The Anxiety of Influence*. New York: Oxford University Press.

Bowden, Betsy. 1982. *Performed Literature: Words and Music by Bob Dylan*. 2nd edn. Lanham, MD: University Press of America, 2001.

Bramwell, Tony and Kingsland, Rosemary. 2005. *Magical Mystery Tours: My Life with the Beatles*. New York: St. Martin's.

Brooks, Van Wyck. 1915. "Highbrow and Lowbrow." In *America's Coming-of-Age*. (1915). Rpt. Mattituck, NY: Amereon House, 1990, 1–19.

Browning, Robert. 1868–9. *The Ring and the Book*. Ed. Richard D. Altick. New Haven: Yale University Press, 1971.

Bryan, William Jennings. 1896. *"The Cross of Gold": Speech Delivered before the National Democratic Convention at Chicago, July 9, 1896*. Rpt. Lincoln and London: University of Nebraska Press, 1996.

Butler, Judith. 1990. *Gender Trouble: Feminism and the Subversion of Identity*. New York: Routledge.

Butler, Judith. 1997. *The Psychic Life of Power: Theories in Subjection*. Stanford: Stanford University Press.

Chamberlain, Houston Stewart. 1899. *Foundations of the Nineteenth Century*. Trans. John Lees. New York: Fertig, 1968.

Chandler, Raymond. 1912. "Realism and Fairyland." In *Chandler Before Marlowe: Raymond Chandler's Early Prose and Poetry, 1908–1912*. Ed. Matthew J. Bruccoli. Columbia, SC: University of South Carolina Press, 1973, 65–7.

Chandler, Raymond. 1939. *The Big Sleep*. Rpt. New York: Vintage, 1992.

Chandler, Raymond. 1940. *Farewell, My Lovely*. Rpt. New York: Vintage, 1992.

Chandler, Raymond. 1953. *The Long Goodbye*. Rpt. New York: Vintage, 1988.

Chang, Jeff. 2005. *Can't Stop, Won't Stop: A History of the Hip-Hop Generation*. New York: St. Martin's.

Chesterton, G.K. 1906. *Charles Dickens*. Rpt. London: Wordsworth Editions, 2007.

Christgau, Robert. 1971. *"Tarantula."* In *The Dylan Companion*. Ed. David Gutman and Elizabeth Thomson. New York: Delta Books, 1990, 139–43.

Christgau, Robert. 1981. *Christgau's Record Guide: Rock Albums of the Seventies*. New Haven and New York: Ticknor & Fields.

Cooper, James Fenimore. 1826. *The Last of the Mohicans*. Rpt. New York: Oxford University Press, 2009.

Cooper, James Fenimore. 1840. *The Pathfinder*. Rpt. New York: Oxford University Press, 2000.

Corcoran, Neil (ed.). 2002. *Bob Dylan with the Poets and Professors*. London: Chatto & Windus.

Cuddy-Keane, Melba. 2003. *Virginia Woolf, the Intellectual, and the Public Sphere*. Cambridge: Cambridge University Press.

Dante Alighieri. 1303–5. *De vulgari eloquentia*. Trans. Steven Botterill. Cambridge: Cambridge University Press, 1996.

Darwin, Erasmus. 1794–6. *Zoonomia*. Rpt. New York: AMS Press, 1974.

Davis, Miles, with Quincey Troupe. 1989. *Miles: The Autobiography*. New York: Simon and Schuster.

Deleuze, Gilles and Guattari, Félix. 1972. *Anti-Oedipus: Capitalism and Schizophrenia*. Trans. Robert Hurley et. al. New York: Viking, 1977.

Deleuze, Gilles and Guattari, Félix. 1980. *A Thousand Plateaus: Capitalism and Schizophrenia*. Trans. Brian Massumi. Minneapolis: University of Minnesota Press, 1987.

DeLillo, Don. 1997. *Underworld*. Rpt. New York: Scribner, 1998.

Derrida, Jacques. 1967a. "Freud and the Scene of Writing." In *Writing and Difference*. Trans. Alan Bass. Chicago: University of Chicago Press, 1978, 198–231.

Derrida, Jacques. 1967b. *Of Grammatology*. Trans. Gayatri Chakravorty Spivak. Baltimore: The John Hopkins University Press, 1976.

Dettmar, Kevin J.H. (ed.). 2009. *The Cambridge Companion to Bob Dylan*. Cambridge: Cambridge University Press.

Dickstein, Morris. 1977. *Gates of Eden: American Culture in the Sixties*. New York: Basic Books.

Douglas, Mary. 1966. *Purity and Danger: An Analysis of the Concepts of Pollution and Taboo*. Rpt. New York: Routledge, 1992.

Dryden, John. 1672. *The Conquest of Granada*. In *Dryden: The Dramatic Works*. 6 vols. Vol. 3. Ed. Montague Summers. New York: Gordian Press, 1968.

Dyer, Richard. 1979. *Stars*. London: British Film Institute.

Dyer, Richard. 1986. *Heavenly Bodies: Film Stars and Society*. London: British Film Institute.

Dylan, Bob. 2004. *Chronicles: Volume One*. New York: Simon and Schuster.

Eagleton, Terry. 2000. *The Idea of Culture*. Oxford: Blackwell.

Eby, Carl P. 1998. *Hemingway's Fetishism: Psychoanalysis and the Mirror of Manhood*. Albany: SUNY Press.

Edwards, Brent Hayes. 2002. "Louis Armstrong and the Syntax of Scat." *Critical Inquiry* 28 (Spring 2002), 618–49.

Eisenstein, Sergei. 1929. "A Dialectic Approach to Film Form." In *Film Form: Essays in Film Theory* (1944). Ed. and Trans. Jay Leyda. Cleveland and New York: Meridian, 1967, 45–63.

Eisenstein, Sergei. 1942. "Word and Image." In *The Film Sense* (1942). Ed. and Trans. Jay Leyda. New York: Harcourt, Brace & World, 1–65.

Eisenstein, Sergei. 1944. "Dickens, Griffith, and the Film Today." In *Film Form: Essays in Film Theory* (1944). Ed. and Trans. Jay Leyda. Cleveland and New York: Meridian, 1967, 195–255.

Eliot, T.S. 1919. "Tradition and the Individual Talent." Rpt. in *Selected Essays*. London: Faber, 1969, 13–22.

Eliot, T.S. 1921. "The Metaphysical Poets." Rpt. in *Selected Essays*. London: Faber, 1969, 281–91.

Eliot, T.S. 1922. *The Waste Land*. In *Collected Poems* (1963). Rpt. New York: Harcourt, Brace & World, 1970.

Elliott, Dyan. 2004. *Proving Women: Female Spirituality and Inquisitional Culture in the Later Middle Ages*. Princeton: Princeton University Press.

Ellison, Ralph. 1959. "The Golden Age, Time Past." In *Shadow and Act* (1964). Rpt. New York: Vintage, 1972.

Fanon, Frantz. 1952. *Black Skin, White Masks*. Trans. Charles Lam Markmann. New York: Grove Press, 1967.

Fender, Stephen. 1981. *Plotting the American West: American Literature and the Rhetoric of the California Trail*. Cambridge: Cambridge University Press.

Fiedler, Leslie. 1948. "Come Back to the Raft Ag'in, Huck Honey!" In *An End to Innocence: Essays on Culture and Politics* (1955). Rpt. Boston: Beacon, 1966.

Foucault, Michel. 1969. "What is an Author?" In *Language, Counter-Memory, Practice: Selected Essays and Interviews*. Ed. Donald F. Bouchard. Ithaca: Cornell University Press, 1977, 113–38.

Freedman, Jonathan. 2000. *The Temple of Culture: Assimilation and Anti-Semitism in Literary Anglo-America*. New York: Oxford University Press.

Freud, Sigmund. 1895. *Project for a Scientific Psychology*. In *The Standard Edition of the Complete Psychological Works of Sigmund Freud*. 24 vols. Ed. James Strachey. London: The Hogarth Press and the Institute of Psycho-Analysis, 1953–74. 1: 28–397.

Freud, Sigmund. 1915. "Instincts and Their Vicissitudes." *SE* 14: 109–45.

Freud, Sigmund. 1918. "From the History of an Infantile Neurosis." *SE* 17: 1–123.

Freud, Sigmund. 1920. *Beyond the Pleasure Principle*. *SE* 18: 3–64.

Freud, Sigmund. 1921. *Group Psychology and the Analysis of the Ego*. *SE* 18: 65–143.

Freud, Sigmund. 1925. "Some Psychical Consequences of the Anatomical Distinction Between the Sexes." *SE* 19: 241–58.

Gates, Lewis E. 1898. "Preface." *Selections from the Prose Writings of Matthew Arnold*. Rpt. Rahway, NJ: Mershon, n.d.

Works Cited

Gautier, Théophile. 1834–5. "Preface." *Mademoiselle du Maupin*. Rpt. New York: Modern Library, n.d.

George, Nelson. 1985. *Where Did Our Love Go? The Rise and Fall of the Motown Sound*. New York: St. Martin's.

George, Nelson. 1988. *The Death of Rhythm & Blues*. New York: Pantheon.

Gillett, Charlie. 1970. *The Sound of the City: The Rise of Rock and Roll*. Rev. edn. 1983. New York: Pantheon.

Gilman, Richard. 1969. *The Confusion of Realms*. New York: Random House.

Gilroy, Paul. 1993. *The Black Atlantic: Modernity and Double Consciousness*. Cambridge: Harvard University Press.

Gilroy, Paul. 2004. *After Empire: Multiculture or Postcolonial Melancholia*. London: Routledge.

Goldstein, Richard. 1966. "Gear." In *Goldstein's Greatest Hits*. Englewood Cliffs, NJ: Prentice-Hall, 3–7.

Gordy, Berry. 1994. *To Be Loved: The Music, the Magic, the Memories of Motown. An Autobiography*. New York: Warner Books.

Gracyk, Theodore. 1996. *Rhythm and Noise: An Aesthetics of Rock*. Durham: Duke University Press.

Gray, Michael. 2000. *Song & Dance Man III: The Art of Bob Dylan*. London and New York: Cassell.

Greenberg, Clement. 1939. "Avant-Garde and Kitsch." In *Art and Culture: Critical Essays*. Boston: Beacon, 1961, 3–21.

Guralnick, Peter. 1986. *Sweet Soul Music: Rhythm and Blues and the Southern Dream of Freedom*. New York: Harper and Row.

Hajdu, David. 2001. *Positively Fourth Street: The Lives and Times of Bob Dylan, Mimi Farina, and Richard Farina*. New York: Farrar Straus & Giroux.

Hall, Stuart and Whannel, Paddy. 1964. *The Popular Arts: A Critical Guide to the Mass Media*. Boston: Beacon Press.

Hall, Stuart. 1980. "Cultural Studies: Two Paradigms." *Media, Culture, and Society* 2 (1980), 57–72.

Hardy, Thomas. 1867. "Neutral Tones." *Collected Poems*. London: Macmillan, 1968.

Hartley, David. 1749. *Observations on Man*. 2 vols. Rpt. London: J. Johnson, 1791.

Hassan, Ihab. 1987. *The Postmodern Turn: Essays in Postmodern Theory and Culture*. Columbus: Ohio State University Press.

Haverkamp, Anselm. 2006. "The Ghost of History: *Hamlet* and the Politics of Paternity." *Law and Literature* 18: 2 (2006), 171–98.

187

Haverkamp, Anselm. 2008. "Art Awaits its Explanation." In *Adorno at the Crossroads*. Eds. Arne DeWinde, Bart Philipsen, and Pieter Vermeulen. *Phrasis* 1 (2008), 9–29.

Hemingway, Ernest. 1926. *The Sun Also Rises*. Rpt. New York: Scribner's, 1954.

Hemingway, Ernest. 1929. *A Farewell to Arms*. Rpt. New York: Scribner's, 1957.

Iser, Wolfgang. 1974. *The Implied Reader: Patterns of Communication in Prose Fiction from Bunyan to Beckett*. Baltimore: The Johns Hopkins University Press.

James, Henry. 1876. *Roderick Hudson*. Rpt. New York: Penguin, 1986.

James, Henry. 1877. *The American*. Rpt. New York: Holt, 1967.

James, Henry. 1878. "Daisy Miller." Rpt. in *"The Turn of the Screw" and Other Short Novels*. New York: New American Library, 1995, 93–152.

James, Henry. 1881. *Washington Square*. Rpt. New York: Penguin, 2007.

James, Henry. 1902. *The Wings of the Dove*. Rpt. New York: Penguin, 2008.

James, Henry. 1903a. *The Ambassadors*. Rpt. Boston: Riverside, 1960.

James, Henry. 1903b. "The Beast in the Jungle." Rpt. in *"The Turn of the Screw" and Other Short Novels*. New York: New American Library, 1995, 404–51.

James, Henry. 1904. *The Golden Bowl*. Rpt. New York: Meridian, 1972.

Jameson, Fredric. 1970. "On Raymond Chandler." *Southern Review* 6 (July, 1970): 624–50.

Jameson, Fredric. 1981. *The Political Unconscious*. Ithaca: Cornell University Press.

Jameson, Fredric. 1982. "Allegorizing Hitchcock." In *Signatures of the Visible*. New York and London: Routledge, 1992, 99–127.

Jameson, Fredric. 1991. *Postmodernism, or, the Cultural Logic of Late Capitalism*. Durham: Duke University Press.

Johnson, Samuel. 1750. "Modern Fiction." *The Rambler*, No. 4. In *Samuel Johnson*. Ed. Donald Greene. New York: Oxford University Press, 1984, 175–9.

Johnson, Samuel. 1755. "Preface." *A Dictionary of the English Language*. In *Samuel Johnson*. Ed. Donald Greene. New York: Oxford University Press, 1984, 307–28.

Jones, LeRoi. 1963. *Blues People: Negro Music in White America*. New York: Morrow.

Keats, John. 1818–19/1820. *Hyperion: A Fragment*. In *Selected Poems and Letters*. Ed. Douglas Bush. Boston: Riverside, 1959.

Keats, John. 1819/1856. *The Fall of Hyperion: A Dream*. In *Selected Poems and Letters*. Ed. Douglas Bush. Boston: Riverside, 1959.

Keats, John. 1819–20/1898. "Lines Written in the MS. of *The Cap and Bells*." In *Selected Poems and Letters*. Ed. Douglas Bush. Boston: Riverside, 1959.

Keil, Charles. 1966. *Urban Blues*. Chicago: University of Chicago Press.

Kelley, Kitty 1986. *His Way: The Unauthorized Biography of Frank Sinatra*. New York: Bantam.

Kendrick, Walter. 1991. *The Thrill of Fear: 250 Years of Scary Entertainment*. New York: Grove Weidenfeld.

Kerouac, Jack. 1958. "The Essentials of Spontaneous Prose." *Evergreen Review* 2: 5 (Summer 1958), 72–3.

Kushner, Tony. 1993. *Angels in America: The Millennium Approaches*. New York: Theatre Communications Group.

Kushner, Tony. 1994. *Angels in America: Perestroika*. New York: Theatre Communications Group.

Lacan, Jacques. 1932. *De la psychose paranoiaque dans ses rapports avec la personnalité*. Rpt. Paris: Seuil, 1975.

Lee, Hermione. 1989. *Willa Cather: Double Lives*. Rpt. New York: Vintage, 1991.

Legman, G. 1963. *Love and Death: A Study in Censorship*. New York: Hacker Art Books.

Leigh, Spencer. 2009. *Everyday: Getting Closer to Buddy Holly*. London: SAF.

Levine, Lawrence. 1988. *Highbrow/Lowbrow: The Emergence of Cultural Hierarchy in America*. Rpt. Cambridge: Harvard University Press, 1990.

Lewis, David Levering. 1993. *W.E.B. Du Bois: Biography of a Race, 1868–1919*. New York: Holt.

Limerick, Patricia Nelson. 1987. *The Legacy of Conquest: The Unbroken Past of the American West*. New York: Norton.

Lombroso, Cesare. 1876. *Criminal Man*. Trans. Mary Gibson, Nicole Hahn, with the assistance of Mark Seymour. Durham: Duke University Press, 2006.

Lotman, Jurij. 1973. *Semiotics of Cinema*. Trans. Mark E. Suino. Ann Arbor: University of Michigan Press, 1976.

Lott, Eric. 1993. *Love and Theft*. New York: Oxford University Press.

Lukăcs, Georg. 1920. *The Theory of the Novel*. Trans. Anna Bostock. Cambridge: MIT Press, 1971.

Lyotard, Jean-François. 1979. *The Postmodern Condition: A Report on Knowledge*. Trans. Geoff Bennington and Brian Massumi. Minneapolis: Minnesota Press, 1984.

Mailer, Norman. 1957. *The White Negro*. In *Advertisements for Myself* (1959). New York: G.P. Putnam's Sons. Rpt. New York: Berkley Medallion, 1966, 311–31.

Marcus, Greil. 1975. *Mystery Train: Images of America in Rock 'n' Roll Music.* New York: Dutton.

Marcus, Greil. 1991. *Dead Elvis: A Chronicle of a Cultural Obsession.* New York: Doubleday.

Marcus, Greil. 1997. *Invisible Republic: Bob Dylan's Basement Tapes.* New York: Holt.

Marcus, Greil. 2005. *Like A Rolling Stone: Bob Dylan at the Crossroads.* New York: Public Affairs.

Marqusee, Mike. 2003. *Chimes of Freedom: The Politics of Bob Dylan's Art.* New York: The New Press.

Mason, Michael. 1978. "Chandler, Men and Women." In *The World of Raymond Chandler*. Ed. Miriam Gross. New York: A & W Publishers.

Marx, Leo. 1964. *The Machine in the Garden: Technology and the Pastoral Ideal in America.* New York: Oxford University Press.

Matthiessen, F.O. 1941. *American Renaissance: Art and Expression in the Age of Emerson and Whitman.* New York: Oxford University Press.

McBride, Joseph. 1982. *Hawks on Hawks.* Berkeley and Los Angeles: University of California Press.

McGann, Jerome. 1983. *The Romantic Ideology: A Critical Investigation.* Chicago: University of Chicago Press.

Meisel, Perry. 1987. *The Myth of the Modern: A Study in British Literature after 1850.* New Haven: Yale University Press.

Meisel, Perry. 1999. *The Cowboy and the Dandy: Crossing Over from Romanticism to Rock and Roll.* New York: Oxford University Press.

Meisel, Perry. 2007. *The Literary Freud.* New York: Routledge.

Mellers, Wilfrid. 1984. *A Darker Shade of Pale.* London: Faber.

Meltzer, R. 1970. *The Aesthetics of Rock.* New York: Something Else Press.

Melville, Herman. 1851. *Moby-Dick.* Rpt. Boston: Riverside, 1956.

Melville, Herman. 1852. *Pierre; or, the Ambiguities.* Rpt. New York: New American Library, 1964.

Melville, Herman. 1853. "Bartleby the Scrivener." In *The Piazza Tales* (1856). Rpt. Evanston, IL: Northwestern University Press, 1996, 13–45.

Melville, Herman. 1855. "Benito Cereno." In *The Piazza Tales* (1856). Rpt. Evanston, IL: Northwestern University Press, 1996, 46–117.

Mencken, H.L. 1919. *The American Language: An Inquiry into the Development of English in the United States.* 4th edn (1936). Rpt. New York: Knopf, 1990.

Works Cited

Metz, Christian. 1968. *Film Language: A Semiotics of the Cinema*. Trans. Michael Taylor. Chicago: University of Chicago Press, 1991.

Metz, Christian. 1976. *The Imaginary Signifier: Psychoanalysis and the Cinema.* Trans. Celia Britton, Annwyl Williams, Ben Brewster, and Alfred Guzzeti. Bloomington: Indiana University Press, 1982.

Michaels, Walter Benn. 1987. *The Gold Standard and the Logic of Naturalism.* Berkeley and Los Angeles: University of California Press.

Miklitsch, Robert. 2006. *Roll Over Adorno: Critical Theory, Popular Culture, Audiovisual Media.* Albany: SUNY Press.

Milton, John. 1674. *Paradise Lost.* In *Complete Poems and Major Prose.* Ed. Merritt Y. Hughes. New York: Odyssey Press, 1957.

Mitchell, Juliet. 1974. *Psychoanalysis and Feminism.* New York: Random House.

Mulvey, Laura. 1975. "Visual Pleasure and Narrative Cinema." In *Feminism and Film Theory.* Ed. Constance Penley. New York: Routledge, 1988, 57–68.

Mulvey, Laura. 1981. "Afterthoughts on 'Visual Pleasure and Narrative Cinema' inspired by *Duel in the Sun*." In *Feminism and Film Theory.* Ed. Constance Penley. New York: Routledge, 1988, 69–79.

Nelson, Paul. 1976. "Bob Dylan." In *The Rolling Stone Illustrated History of Rock & Roll.* Ed. Jim Miller. New York: Rolling Stone/Random House, 206–23. In 1st edn. only.

Nordau, Max. 1892. *Degeneration.* Rpt. Lincoln, NE: University of Nebraska Press, 1993.

Palmer, Robert. 1981. *Deep Blues.* New York: Viking.

Palmer, Robert. 1992. "The Church of the Sonic Guitar." In *Present Tense: Rock & Roll Culture.* Ed. Anthony DeCurtis. Durham: Duke University Press.

Pater, Walter. 1873. "Conclusion." *The Renaissance.* New Library Edition. 10 vols. London: Macmillan, 1910.

Penley, Constance. 1988. "The Lady Doesn't Vanish: Feminism and Film Theory." In *Feminism and Film Theory.* Ed. Constance Penley. New York: Routledge, 1–24.

Pope, Alexander. 1742. *The Dunciad.* In *The Poems of Alexander Pope.* Ed. John Butt. New Haven: Yale University Press, 1968.

Powers, Devon. 2008. *Rock Criticism and Intellectual History at "The Village Voice," 1955–1972.* New York University Dissertation.

Pynchon, Thomas. 1963. *V.* Rpt. New York: Harper and Row, 1986.

Pynchon, Thomas. 1966. *The Crying of Lot 49.* Rpt. New York: Bantam, 1967.

Pynchon, Thomas. 1973. *Gravity's Rainbow.* Rpt. New York: Penguin, 1987.

Pynchon, Thomas. 1990. *Vineland.* Boston: Little, Brown.

Pynchon, Thomas. 1997. *Mason & Dixon*. New York: Holt.

Rahv, Philip. 1939. "Paleface and Redskin." In *Image and Idea: Fourteen Essays on Literary Themes*. Norfolk, CT: New Directions, 1949, 1–5.

Ricks, Christopher. 1963. *Milton's Grand Style*. Oxford: The Clarendon Press.

Ricks, Christopher. 1974. *Keats and Embarrassment*. Oxford: The Clarendon Press.

Ricks, Christopher. 2003. *Dylan's Visions of Sin*. New York: Viking, 2004.

Robinson, Smokey, with David Ritz. 1989. *Smokey: Inside My Life*. New York: McGraw-Hill.

Ross, Andrew. 1989. *No Respect: Intellectuals and Popular Culture*. New York: Routledge.

Roth, Philip. 1973. "On *The Great American Novel*." In *Reading Myself and Others*. New York: Farrar Straus and Giroux, 1975, 75–92.

Rubin, Joan Shelley. 1992. *The Making of Middlebrow Culture*. Chapel Hill: University of North Carolina Press.

Sante, Luc. 1991. *Low Life: Lures and Snares of Old New York*. New York: Farrar Straus and Giroux.

Sarris, Andrew. 1968. *The American Cinema: Directors and Directions, 1929–1968*. Rpt. New York: Da Capo Press, 1996.

Sartre, Jean-Paul. 1966. "Jean Paul Sartre répond." *L'Arc* 30: 87–96.

Shapiro, James. 2005. *1599: A Year in the Life of William Shakespeare*. New York: HarperCollins.

Shaw, Arnold. 1978. *Honkers and Shouters: The Golden Years of Rhythm and Blues*. New York: Macmillan.

Shelley, Percy Bysshe. 1820. "Ode to the West Wind." In *Selected Poetry*. Ed. Neville Rogers. Boston: Riverside, 1968.

Shelton, Robert. 1986. *No Direction Home: The Life and Music of Bob Dylan*. Rpt. New York: DaCapo Press, 1987.

Shklovsky, Victor. 1917. "Art as Device." In *Theory of Prose*. Trans. Benjamin Sher. Normal, IL: Dalkey Archive, 1991.

Skenazy, Paul. 1982. *The New Wild West: The Urban Mysteries of Dashiell Hammett and Raymond Chandler*. Boise, ID: Boise State University Press.

Sklar, Robert. 1992. *City Boys: Cagney, Bogart, Garfield*. Princeton: Princeton University Press.

Slotkin, Richard. 1973. *Regeneration through Violence: The Mythology of the American Frontier*. Middletown, CT: Wesleyan University Press.

Smith, Henry Nash. 1950. *Virgin Land: The American West as Symbol and Myth*. Cambridge: Harvard University Press.

Sontag, Susan. 1964. "Notes on 'Camp.'" In *Against Interpretation* (1966). Rpt. New York: Delta, n.d., 274–92.

Soyinka, Wole. 1976. *Myth, Literature, and the African World*. Cambridge: Cambridge University Press.

Spitz, Bob. 1989. *Bob Dylan: A Biography*. New York: McGraw-Hill.

Stevens, Paul and Simmons, Patricia (eds). 2008. *Milton in America. University of Toronto Quarterly* 77: 3 (Summer, 2008), 789–960.

Strachey, James. 1966. "General Preface." *The Standard Edition of the Complete Psychological Works of Sigmund Freud*. 24 vols. Ed. James Strachey. London: The Hogarth Press and the Institute of Psycho-Analysis, 1953–74. I: xiii–xxii.

Swift, Jonathan. 1726. *Gulliver's Travels and Other Writings*. Ed. M.K. Starkman. Rpt. New York: Bantam, 1981.

Swinburne, Algernon Charles. 1866. "The Garden of Proserpine." In *Selected Poems*. Manchester: Fyfield Books, 1987.

Tanner, Tony. 1965. *The Reign of Wonder: Naivety and Reality in American Literature*. Cambridge: Cambridge University Press.

Taylor, Dennis. 1993. *Hardy's Literary Language and Victorian Philology*. Oxford: The Clarendon Press.

Trilling, Lionel. 1939. *Matthew Arnold*. Rpt. New York: Harcourt Brace Jovanovich, 1979.

Trilling, Lionel. 1955. "Freud: Within and Beyond Culture." In *Beyond Culture*. Rpt. New York: Harcourt Brace Jovanovich, 1978, 77–102.

Twain, Mark. 1876. *The Adventures of Tom Sawyer*. Rpt. New York: Modern Library, n.d.

Twain, Mark. 1884. *The Adventures of Huckleberry Finn*. Rpt. New York: Oxford University Press, 1996.

von Treitschke, Heinrich. 1898. *Politics*. 3 vols. Vol. 1. Trans. Blanche Dugdale and Torben de Bille. London: Constable, 1916.

Waksman, Steve. 1999. *Instruments of Desire: The Electric Guitar and the Shaping of Musical Experience*. Cambridge: Harvard University Press.

Wallace, David Foster. 1996. *Infinite Jest*. Boston: Little, Brown.

Walpole, Horace. 1764. *The Castle of Otranto*. Rpt. New York: Oxford University Press, 1998.

Warshow, Robert. 1948. "The Gangster as Tragic Hero." In *Immediate Experience: Movies, Comics, Theatre & Other Aspects of Popular Culture*. Garden City, NY: Doubleday, 1962, 127–33.

Warshow, Robert. 1954. "Movie Chronicle: The Westerner." In *The Immediate Experience: Movies, Comics, Theatre & Other Aspects of Popular Culture*. Garden City, NY: Doubleday, 1962, 135–54.

Warshow, Robert. 1962. "Author's Preface." *The Immediate Experience: Movies, Comics, Theatre & Other Aspects of Popular Culture*. Garden City, NY: Doubleday, 1962, 23–9.

Whitman, Walt. 1891–2. "Song of Myself." In *Leaves of Grass and Other Writings*. Ed. Michael Moon. New York: Norton, 2002.

Whitman, Walt. 1891–2. "To Think of Time." In *Leaves of Grass and Other Writings*. Ed. Michael Moon. New York: Norton, 2002.

Williams, Paul. 1990. *Bob Dylan: Performing Artist, 1960–73*. Rpt. London: Omnibus Press, 1992.

Williams, Paul. 1992. *Bob Dylan: Performing Artist: The Middle Years, 1974–86*. Rpt. London: Omnibus Press, 1994.

Williams, Raymond. 1958. *Culture and Society, 1780–1950*. Rpt. New York: Harper & Row, 1966.

Williams, Raymond. 1970. "A Hundred Years of Culture and Anarchy." In *Culture and Materialism: Selected Essays*. London: Verso, 1980, 3–8.

Williams, Raymond. 1973. *Base and Superstructure in Marxist Critical Theory*. In *Culture and Materialism: Selected Essays*. London: Verso, 1980, 31–49.

Williams, Raymond. 1976. "Culture." *Keywords: A Vocabulary of Culture and Society*. Rev. edn. New York: Oxford University Press, 1985, 87–93.

Winnicott, D.W. 1965. *The Maturational Processes and the Facilitating Environment: Studies in the Theory of Emotional Development*. London: The Hogarth Press and the Institute of Psycho-Analysis.

Wolfe, Peter. 1985. *Something More than Night: The Case of Raymond Chandler*. Madison: Popular Press.

Woolf, Leonard. 1927. *Hunting the Highbrow*. London: The Hogarth Press.

Woolf, Virginia. 1927. *To the Lighthouse*. Rpt. New York: Harcourt Brace & World, 1955.

Woolf, Virginia. 1928. *Orlando*. Rpt. New York: Harcourt Brace & Co., 1956.

Woolf, Virginia. 1932. "Middlebrow." In *The Death of the Moth and Other Essays* (1942). Rpt. New York: Harcourt Brace Jovanovich, n.d., 176–86.

Wordsworth, William. 1800–2. "Preface." *Lyrical Ballads*. Ed. R.L. Brett and A.R. Jones. London: Methuen, 1971.

Wordsworth, William. 1850. *The Prelude*. In *Selected Poems and Prefaces*. Ed. Jack Stillinger. Boston: Riverside, 1965.

Discography

Beatles, The. 1968. *The Beatles.* Apple.
Beatles, The. 1977. *Live at the Star Club in Hamburg, Germany, 1962.* Atlantic.
Berry, Chuck. 1955. "Maybelline." Chess.
Berry, Chuck. 1958. "Johnny B. Goode." Chess.
Coltrane, John. 1964. *A Love Supreme.* Impulse.
Coltrane, John. 1965. *Ascension.* Impulse.
Coltrane, John. 1965. *Meditations.* Impulse.
Cooke, Sam. 1957. "You Send Me" (Charles Cooke). Keen.
Dorsey, Tommy. 1938. "Boogie Woogie." RCA Victor.
Dylan, Bob. 1962. "Blowin' in the Wind." *The Freewheelin' Bob Dylan* (1963).
    Columbia.
Dylan, Bob. 1964. *Another Side of Bob Dylan.* Columbia.
Dylan, Bob. 1965. *Bringing It All Back Home.* Columbia.
Dylan, Bob. 1965. "Like a Rolling Stone." *Highway 61 Revisited.* Columbia.
Dylan, Bob. 1968. *John Wesley Harding.* Columbia.
Dylan, Bob. 1969. *Nashville Skyline.* Columbia.
Dylan, Bob. 1970. *New Morning.* Columbia.
Dylan, Bob. 1979. *Slow Train Running.* Columbia.
Dylan, Bob. 1989. *Oh Mercy.* Columbia.
Dylan, Bob. 1997. *Time Out of Mind.* Columbia.
Dylan, Bob. 2001. *Love and Theft.* Columbia.
Hendrix, Jimi. 1967. "Purple Haze." *Are You Experienced?* Reprise.
Holly, Buddy. 1962. "Reminiscing" (Curtis Ousley). Coral.
Jordan, Louis. 1946. "Choo Choo Ch' Boogie" (Denver Darling, Vaughn
    Horton, Milt Gabler). Decca.
Marley, Bob. 1965. "One Love." *The Wailing Wailers.* Studio One.
Marley, Bob. 1977. "One Love." *Exodus.* Island/Tuff Gong.
Presley, Elvis. 1969. *From Elvis in Memphis.* RCA.
Presley, Elvis. 1971. *Elvis Country.* RCA.
Presley, Elvis. 1975. *Promised Land.* RCA.
Tosh, Peter. 1983. "Feel No Way." *Mama Africa.* EMI America.
Wilson, Jackie. 1957. "Reet Petite" (Berry Gordy, Jr., Tyran Carlo). Brunswick.

Filmography

Air Force. 1943. Warner Bros.

All About Eve. 1950. Twentieth Century Fox.

Basic Instinct. 1992. Tristar.

Basic Instinct II. 2006. MGM.

The Bellboy. 1960. Jerry Lewis/Paramount.

The Big Shot. 1942. Warner Bros.

Burn! 1969. Produzioni Europee Associati.

Bus Stop. 1956. Twentieth Century Fox.

Casablanca. 1942. Warner Bros.

Casino. 1995. Universal.

Citizen Kane. 1941. RKO.

Contempt. 1963. Rome Paris Films.

Dead End. 1937. The Samuel Goldwyn Company.

Deadline U.S.A. 1952. Twentieth Century Fox.

Dinner at Eight. 1933. MGM.

The Disorderly Orderly. 1964. Paramount/York.

Don't Bother to Knock. 1952. Twentieth Century Fox.

Double Indemnity. 1944. Paramount.

El Dorado. 1966. Paramount.

Escape from Alcatraz. 1979. Paramount.

Gentlemen Prefer Blondes. 1953. Twentieth Century Fox.

The Godfather. 1972. Paramount.

Goodfellas. 1990. Warner Bros.

Hatari! 1962. Malabar/Paramount.

High Sierra. 1941. Warner Bros.

His Girl Friday. 1940. Columbia.

I'm Not There. 2007. Killer Films et al.

In a Lonely Place. 1950. Columbia.

Journey into Fear. 1942. RKO.

The King of Comedy. 1982. Embassy International/Twentieth Century Fox.

The Lady from Shanghai. 1948. Columbia.

The Magnificent Ambersons. 1942. RKO.

No Direction Home. 2005. BBC/WNET New York.

Only Angels Have Wings. 1939. Columbia.

Platinum Blonde. 1931. Columbia.

The Postman Always Rings Twice. 1946. Loew's/MGM.

Prizzi's Honor. 1985. ABC.
Red Line-7000. 1965. Laurel/Paramount.
Rio Bravo. 1959. Armada/Warner Bros.
Saratoga. 1937. MGM.
Shaft. 1971. MGM.
Shaft's Big Score! 1972. MGM.
Shaft in Africa. 1973. MGM.
She Wore a Yellow Ribbon. 1949. Argosy/RKO.
Some Came Running. 1959. MGM.
The Stranger. 1946. RKO.
Sunset Boulevard. 1950. Paramount.
Taxi Driver. 1976. Columbia.
Touch of Evil. 1958. Universal International.
True Crime. 1999. Malpaso/The Zanuck Company/Warner Bros.
The War of the Worlds. 1953. Paramount.
Who's Minding the Store? 1963. Paramount/York/Jerry Lewis.
The Wild One. 1954. Stanley Kramer/Columbia.
The Young Lions. 1958. Twentieth Century Fox.

Index

198

Index

199

Printed and bound by CPI Group (UK) Ltd, Croydon, CR0 4YY

28/02/2023

03195522-0001